Suddenness and the Composition of Poetic Thought

Performance Philosophy

Series Editors: Laura Cull Ó Maoilearca, DAS Graduate School, Academy of Theatre and Dance, Amsterdam University of the Arts, Will Daddario, Independent Researcher, Asheville, NC, USA, and Alice Lagaay, Professor of Cultural Philosophy and Aesthetics, Design Department, Hamburg University of Applied Sciences, Germany

Performance Philosophy is an emerging interdisciplinary field of thought, creative practice and scholarship. The Performance Philosophy book series comprises monographs and essay collections addressing the relationship between performance and philosophy within a broad range of philosophical traditions and performance practices operating across multiple art forms and everyday life, including dance, choreography, movement and somatic practices; music, sound and silence; drama and theatre; performance art; sport; meditation and spiritual practices. It also includes studies of the performative aspects of life and, indeed, philosophy itself. As such, the series addresses the philosophy of performance as well as performance-as-philosophy and philosophy-as-performance.

Books in the series both contribute to and critique the philosophy of music, dance, theatre and performance – raising important questions about the hierarchy of the relationship between philosophy and the arts; and advancing debates on philosophical method by examining performance as both object and medium of philosophical enquiry.

Comprising texts written by philosophers, researchers from multiple disciplines, and international arts practitioners, the series offers both academic and non-academic audiences the opportunity to engage with questions of how performance thinks and how thought is performed, from the ancient to the contemporary. The series supports diversely situated authors who consider ideas and practices coming from various geographical and cultural contexts, particularly in solidarity with wider projects to address the Eurocentrism of Philosophy and the decolonization of knowledge-practices more generally.

Titles in the Series
Rancière and Performance, edited by Colette Conroy and Nic Fryer
Experiments in Listening, by Rajni Shah
Art Disarming Philosophy: Non-philosophy and Aesthetics, edited by Steven Shakespeare, Niamh Malone, and Gary Anderson
The Critical Introduction to Salomo Friedlaender-Mnyona: 20th Century Performance Philosopher (forthcoming), edited by Detlef Thiel and Alice Lagaay – By Salomo Friedlaender/Mynona
Performance in the Age of Ecological Crisis (forthcoming), by Tuija Kokkonen
Suddenness and the Composition of Poetic Thought, by Paul Magee

Suddenness and the Composition of Poetic Thought

Paul Magee

ROWMAN & LITTLEFIELD
Lanham • Boulder • New York • London

Published by Rowman & Littlefield
An imprint of The Rowman & Littlefield Publishing Group, Inc.
4501 Forbes Boulevard, Suite 200, Lanham, Maryland 20706
www.rowman.com

6 Tinworth Street, London SE11 5AL, United Kingdom

Copyright © 2022 by Paul Magee

All rights reserved. No part of this book may be reproduced in any form or by any electronic or mechanical means, including information storage and retrieval systems, without written permission from the publisher, except by a reviewer who may quote passages in a review.

British Library Cataloguing in Publication Information Available

Library of Congress Cataloging-in-Publication Data

Names: Magee, Paul, 1970- author.
Title: Suddenness and the composition of poetic thought / Paul Magee.
Description: Lanham : Rowman & Littlefield Publishers, [2022] | Series: Performance philosophy | Includes bibliographical references and index. | Summary: "Employing an extensive archive of interview materials with major Anglophone poets, this book uncovers how they think in the moments of composition, providing a lucid account of the links between poetic composition and live performative thinking"—Provided by publisher.
Identifiers: LCCN 2022000037 (print) | LCCN 2022000038 (ebook) | ISBN 9781538153529 (cloth) | ISBN 9781538153543 (paperback) | ISBN 9781538153536 (epub)
Subjects: LCSH: Poetics. | Poetry—Authorship. | Performance poetry.
Classification: LCC PN1042 .M23 2022 (print) | LCC PN1042 (ebook) | DDC 808.1—dc23/eng/20220110
LC record available at https://lccn.loc.gov/2022000037
LC ebook record available at https://lccn.loc.gov/2022000038

you Tiresias
if you know
know damn well
or
else you
don't.

Ezra Pound, note in pencil on the carbon typescript of *The Waste Land*.

Contents

Acknowledgements	ix
Introduction: On the Gradual Production of Thoughts whilst Speaking	1
PART I: REVISING TOWARDS SPONTANEITY	**13**
1 We Do Not Know What We Are Going to Say Until We Have Said It	15
2 'That's the Illusion You're Supposed to Get'	31
3 Scepticisms	43
PART II: TWO HISTORIES OF SUDDEN VERSE	**47**
4 Romantic Revision and Its Others	49
5 *The Iliad* and *The Odyssey* Were Rapidly Composed	67
6 The Desk as Stage	87
7 Oral Verse in Performance	109
PART III: WRITING IS SPEAKING	**131**
8 Not-Quite Speech	133
9 Writing as 'Oral Dictated'	145
10 Consciousness as a Window of Three Seconds	165
11 Song	185

PART IV: SUDDENNESS AND ART — 193

12 The Split in the Archive — 195

13 'Great Goblets of Magnolialight' — 201

References — 229

Index — 245

About the Author — 253

Acknowledgements

Ilona, Nina, Rupert and Trudy, what beautiful names. Thanks for sharing home with me.

Paul Collis, Adam Dickerson, Nick Gartrell, Lena Isayev, John F. Leonard, Susy Macqueen, Lucy Neave, Andrew Sartori, Russell Smith, Lillian Smyth and Denise Thwaites have been particularly generous interlocutors. Thank you for the ideas you have helped me think.

The Faculty of Arts and Design at the University of Canberra has allowed me the freedom to teach, research and wander. To my colleagues, for interpreting the work of writing in such open ways.

At the Australian National University, the School of Literature, Language, and Linguistics has provided numerous, welcoming forums for me to try out chapters of this work. The idea came about as the result of the responses to a paper Elizabeth Minchin invited me to give in the Centre for Classical Studies' biennial *Homer Seminar*. The seminar has been a mainstay of this writing in the years since then. Will Christie hosted me for a semester in the university's Humanities Research Centre in 2017, a year the HRC dedicated to the theme of "The Stranger." The value of the questions raised and the leads offered there delayed this book by at least three years. Thanks to all the strangers.

Andrew Sartori, Amy Lehrner and Izzy Sartori looked after me for weeks on end in New York, making the interview research in this book possible, sharing their lives. Lena Isayev hosted me in London and Exeter, introducing me to whole other worlds, including new ideas for what collaboration and writing can do. Thanks to Edith Southwell for letting me stay in a home dedicated to beautiful things. In Shanghai, Yao Yunfan was a consummate host.

To the poets whose voices are captured here, and the three scholars. For the generosity of your words, on and off the page.

Numerous anonymous reviewers. For your commitment to a whole other economy of thought.

Most of all, I would like to thank my mother, Anne Connellan, for her tireless scouring of the manuscript, her encouragement in the literal sense of the word, and her love of poetry.

PERMISSIONS

The author and publisher gratefully acknowledge permission to reproduce extracts from the following:

Annotation excerpts from *The Waste Land: A Facsimile and Transcript of the Original Drafts Including the Annotations of Ezra Pound.* Copyright © 1971 by Ezra Pound. Reprinted by permission of Mariner Books, an imprint of HarperCollins Publishers. All rights reserved.

Corrections, additions and marginal comments on "The Waste Land." By Ezra Pound, from New Directions Pub. acting as agent, copyright © 1971 by Ezra Pound. Reprinted by permission of New Directions Publishing Corp.

Book 1, l.346-52 from *The Odyssey of Homer by Richmond Lattimore.* Copyright © 1965, 1967 by Richmond Lattimore; © Renewed 1995 by Alice B. Lattimore. Used by permission of HarperCollins Publishers.

Transcript materials from Deborah Tannen, *Talking Voices: Repetition, Dialogue, and Imagery in Conversational Discourse.* 2nd ed. Cambridge: Cambridge University Press, 2007, reproduced with permission of The Licensor through PLSclear.

Neither Here nor There: Travels in Europe by Bill Bryson published by Transworld. Copyright © 1991, Bill Bryson. Reprinted by permission of The Random House Group Limited.

Neither Here nor There: Travels in Europe by Bill Bryson. Copyright © 1992. Used by permission of HarperCollins Publishers.

Introduction
On the Gradual Production of Thoughts whilst Speaking

'If there is something you wish to know', Heinrich von Kleist addresses an old army friend, 'and by meditation you cannot find it . . . speak about it with the first acquaintance you encounter.' Yet the point is not to benefit from that other person's opinion. 'On the contrary, you yourself should tell him at once what it is you wish to know'.[1] Kleist's essay continues in this faux dialogic vein: 'I see the astonishment in your face. I hear you reply that when you were young you were advised only to speak of things you already understood'. But that is not the only approach to learning. There have been numerous occasions when Kleist has tried to understand a difficult point of law, or a problem in algebra, only to find that if he turns to the nearest interlocutor and simply speaks about the matter, 'I learn more than I should have arrived at by perhaps hours of brooding'.[2] He might have profited by the other's skilful questioning. But,

> because I do have some dim conception at the outset, one distantly related to what I am looking for, if I boldly make a start with that, my mind, even as my speech proceeds, under the necessity of finding an end for that beginning, will shape my first confused idea into complete clarity so that, to my amazement, understanding is arrived at as the sentence ends.[3]

Kleist describes the various hesitation phenomena that discovering one's ideas in the act of uttering them is likely to involve. He might 'dwell lengthily on the conjunctions.' He might 'put in a few unarticulated sounds'. Or he might 'make use of apposition where it is not necessary', all of which strategies will serve to 'spin out' his speech, and so help him 'gain time for the fabrication of my idea in the workshop of my mind'.[4] Yet the temporal gains from such acts are minimal. The 'Gradual Production' (*allmähliche*

Verfertigung) Kleist has in mind, in titling this 1806 essay fragment 'On the Gradual Production of Thoughts whilst Speaking' (*Über die allmähliche Verfertigung der Gedanken beim Reden*), is only *allmähliche* 'gradual' in the sense of 'arrived at piece by piece'. Kleist is writing about what happens in the space of a few seconds.

He pushes on. This is not just a personal whim. 'I believe many a great speaker to have been ignorant when he opened his mouth of what he was going to say'. So the Comte de Mirabeau, responding to the Master of Ceremonies in 1789, when that royal functionary ordered the National Constituent Assembly to disperse, said 'Yes . . . we have heard the King's command', only to repeat, 'Yes, my dear sir . . . we have heard it', buying time, Kleist points out: 'As we see, he is not yet exactly sure of what he intends. "But by what right . . ." he continues, and suddenly a colossal source of ideas is opened up to him, "do you give us orders here?"'[5] Mirabeau, too, was speaking to find out what he had to say, before an entire National Assembly. Elsewhere it might have been a problem in algebra. The 'conviction that he would be able to draw all the ideas he needed from the circumstances themselves and from the mental excitement they generate' made the revolutionary Mirabeau 'bold enough to trust to luck and make a start'.[6]

A Romantic glorification of action over thought? One can detect strains of it in Kleist's other essays, and in his letters.[7] Or a truth revealed in the pressures of that disoriented time? Kleist will shortly be arrested by the French imperial army and locked up as a suspected spy. Only three years earlier, he tried to volunteer for Napoleon's invasion of England. Yet he fought against the revolutionary army as a teenage soldier. And it is a colleague from that early campaigning against revolution whom he is now in 1806 addressing, in an essay extolling Mirabeau. Nor can one ignore the state of Kleist's mind in all this: as he wrote in a letter from Würzburg to his fiancée, Wilhelmine von Zenge, not long before breaking off their engagement, 'I walked, absorbed in my private thoughts, through the arched gateway, and back to the town. Why, I asked myself, doesn't the archway collapse, since it has no support? It stands, I replied, because all the stones are on the verge of collapsing at one and the same time'.[8] Kleist's comment on his first sight of one of Caspar David Friedrich's radically new landscapes is even more traumatised: 'since in its uniformity and boundlessness it has no foreground but the frame, the viewer feels as though his eyelids had been cut off'.[9]

Those epochal and personal extremes lead Kleist to hold fast to something we prefer to ignore. No one's thoughts are immune from the risks of the present moment: 'That a certain excitement of the intelligence is necessary even to revivify ideas we have already had is amply demonstrated whenever open-minded and knowledgeable people are being examined and without any preamble are asked such questions as: What is the state? Or: What is property?'[10]

When it comes to the articulation of what we know, however, certainly we do know it, an element of unpredictability always pertains. 'For it is not we who know things but pre-eminently a certain *condition* of ours which knows'.[11]

'On the Gradual Production of Thoughts whilst Speaking' was not published until 1878, 67 years after its author's suicide. A note beneath an allusion to Kant on its final page reads 'To be continued'.[12] Yet however incomplete the essay, Kleist's reflections offer a rare opening on the most everyday of phenomena. We are all familiar with the possibility of talking off the top of our heads and are familiar with the pejorative construction so regularly placed upon it. Kleist blithely ignores such moralisms, shattering the idealisation they are secretly founded upon, and provides in their stead a stark vision of unpremeditated speaking as a pre-eminent mode of intellectual and even political inquiry. This book argues that Kleist was right. He was right in more ways than even he could know.

COGNITIVE CONSTRAINT

Kleist was right in more ways than he could know, because he did not own a tape recorder. Widely available from the late 1950s, such devices were swiftly adopted by scholars for the unprecedented access they gave to the phenomena of real-time speech production. The corpuses of utterances that have since arisen are 'fundamental to the enterprise of theorizing language', Michael Halliday and Christian Matthiessen remark.[13] They add that prior to that point linguistics had been 'like physics before 1600: having little reliable data, and no clear sense of the relationship between observation and theory'.[14] Wallace Chafe concurs, noting, 'Technology has put us now, for the first time in human history, in a position to understand what spoken language is really like, though for various reasons we have not yet taken full advantage of this potential'.[15] These three linguists are referring to evidence like the following, which is what the tape revealed of the speech patterns of a 'confident and experienced public speaker' in the course of his PhD defence in the early 1970s. Single dashes stand for pauses of anything up to half a second, double dashes pauses between 0.5 and 0.9 seconds.

(1) And it seems
(2) to be – –
(3) if a word is fairly – – high on the frequency list –
(4) I haven't made any count –
(5) but – just – – impressionistically, – – um – – the chances are – –
(6) that you get a – compound – or – another – – phonologically deviant – – form –with ah

(7) which is already in other words
(8) which is fairly frequent – ly the same – phonological shape.¹⁶

The speaker seems to have a general idea of what he wants to say and to that extent he is distinct from Kleist's experimental speaker, advancing to see wherever the sentence he has begun will take him. But it is just as clear that this PhD candidate – I am citing from Andrew Pawley and Frances Hodgetts Syder's corpus of New Zealand and Australian speakers – is improvising the exact wording of each of these eight clauses, as he proceeds. He starts making a general claim over clauses (1)–(3), hesitantly, interrupts that claim in clause (4) on realising he should clarify what grounds he has for making it, has two attempts at that clarification in clause (5), the second of these ('the chances are – –') not quite reconcilable with the first ('but – just – – impressionistically'), returns to table the claim at clause (6), only to interrupt it again at (7) ('which is already in other words') in search of a more accurate formulation, and then interrupts that attempt in turn at clause (8). Evidently this PhD candidate did not have his 'full sentence' in mind, prior to embarking upon the step-by-step process of uttering it.

What is more, the candidate makes use of the very devices Kleist reports resorting to, in the course of his seemingly more experimental speech productions. We saw Kleist claim that when engaging in that process he will 'dwell lengthily on the conjunctions', for doing so will help him 'gain time for the fabrication of my idea in the workshop of my mind.'¹⁷ Compare how the candidate pauses after the 'but –' in clause (5) above, or after the 'or –' in clause (6). The words 'be' and 'are' at the end of clauses (2) and (5), with their attendant pauses, are clearly offering similar purchase. We also heard Kleist state that he will 'put in a few unarticulated sounds' mid-sentence, as he struggles to work out how that sentence will conclude. Kleist was referring to the *äh*, *ähm* and related sounds that German speakers use as their equivalents to the 'um' in the middle of the candidate's 5th clause, or the 'ah' that concludes clause (6). Far from wrong or thoughtless uses of 'proper' language, such filler words can be seen in context to be quite literally thoughtful: they indicate that the candidate is thinking up what they have to say, in the very process of saying it. The 'in other words' in clause (7) shows the candidate engaging in 'apposition where it is not necessary' as well. What we have here, in short, is evidence of a speaker who, like Kleist, has an as yet inexact formulation in mind, decides to 'boldly make a start with that' and, 'under the necessity of finding an end for that beginning', arrives *allmähliche*, 'piece by piece', at the detailed formulation of their thinking.¹⁸

What Kleist could not have known back in 1806 is how everyday a phenomenon this is. That so few outside the professional circles of linguists, interviewers and transcribers are aware of it today underlines this point. We have surprisingly little capacity to recall the actual language we hear: the interposition of 80 syllables is enough, according to one study, for listeners to forget the syntactic structure of a sentence they have just heard – as opposed to the ideas heard in it.[19] This is so much the case that speakers in bilingual environments have been shown regularly to have forgotten the language in which they were at any given past moment speaking, even as they retain the ideas discussed.[20] Starkest evidence of all for this forgetting of the literal is the dialogue in the books and films and television series we consume nightly, a systematic departure from the piece-by-piece, fragmentary and regularly revised way in which any of us actually speak.

Countering this pervasive, popular obliviousness as to the graduated, one might even say myopic, form our speech takes, Andrew Pawley and Frances Hodgetts Syder write, 'There is in fact a sizeable collection of evidence of several different kinds that the largest unit of novel discourse that can be fully encoded in one coding operation is a single clause of eight to ten words'.[21] The reader can stop and listen closely to themselves or those around them in conversation, to get an immediate sense of this. As Pawley and Syder remark: 'When the spontaneous speaker embarks on a stretch of novel discourse extending over several clauses, he [*sic*] does not (as a rule) know in advance exactly what he is going to say beyond the first few words. He must gamble on being able to finish what he has started'.[22] What we are ultimately dealing with here are 'biological limits on what the brain can do at speed'.[23] Eight to ten words, maximum, typically much less. The rest of our thinking on any matter is a hazy 'penumbra', just out of ken.[24]

SUDDENNESS DEFINED

Everyone knows these moments: you launch into an argument and realise mid-flight you can't recall the exact data, or the salient details or the persuasive example to back up your claims. Other times you are in the middle of telling a story and completely forget what the point you are rounding to actually was. These are lovely moments because they show that the speaker has been 'bold enough to trust to luck and make a start'.[25] To try the crazy experiment of bringing to mind every single thing you know on a topic in one and the same moment is to be reminded that these risks are central to the knowledge enterprise as well. A truer picture of knowledge will arise when we admit that scholars and scientists alike – there are no 'two cultures' in this regard – weave the public speaking that is so central to their work from a combination of memory work and trust. They launch themselves into speech, trusting in the capacity of their memories to supply the requisite words that can only ever be dimly present at the invocation of any topic, however much one might have 'mastered' it. The *sapere aude* maxim – 'Dare to know!' – that Kant advanced in his essay 'What is Enlightenment?' obviously refers to observation and method; but it can also, and in some regards even more vitally, be linked to the daring that allows these meetings of memory and language to occur, as one advances step by step into one's public discourse.[26]

The fact that happy finds at times result is surely one of the prime reasons we continue to have conferences. One might draw an analogy to painting: 'In the way I work I don't in fact know very often what the paint will do, and it does many things which are very much better than I could make it do. Is that an accident? Perhaps one could say it is not an accident because it becomes a selective process which part of this accident one chooses to preserve' (Francis Bacon).[27] It is also, of course, why we interview politicians, for all their training in staying 'on message'. They, too, fall short of total mastery over *what the words will do*.

We lack the cognitive capacity to see clearly in our mind the exact wording of what we are about to say, in advance of the two or three seconds in which we come to say it. This is what I am calling *suddenness*. It is the condition of all acts of speaking, and a key factor in the shapes our writing takes as well.

One might respond that 'the exact wording' of our speech is generally irrelevant, as evidenced by the rapidity with which we forget it: all that really count are the ideas that drive us as we speak, or that we distil from another's speech as we hear it. Yet that would be to ignore those chance finds, as for instance when we are struggling to explain a concept in a lecture and, in the course of trying to imagine things from the student's perspective, alight upon an illuminating metaphor, that puts our work in a whole new light.

Others will batten down on the conventionality of our speech, the fact that so much of our discourse amounts to mere mimicry of what we have heard, something hardly original enough to merit comparison with the creative processes of a Kleist, a Bacon or a Kant. Consider the 'irreducibly conformist, retarded, academic recursion' besetting so much scholarly commentary on Freud and Marx.[28] That was Lacan's verdict. Marx, for his part, noted, 'The tradition of all past generations weighs like an Alp (*wie ein Alp*) upon the brain of the living'.[29] 'Like an Alp' is a more accurate translation than the familiar 'like a nightmare'. It is more accurate, because more alive to the enormity of that burden. 'But although the atmosphere in which we live, weighs upon every one with a 20,000 lb. force, do you feel it?', Marx asks elsewhere.[30] Perhaps a Mirabeau does ('Yes, my dear sir . . . we have heard it'). My point is that there is no creation *ex nihilo* and the concept of suddenness is not intended to imply any. To the contrary, the topic of conventional speech is central to this book and will emerge as pivotal to the theory of 'original' poetic diction in which it culminates. That argument will hold that what we call originality is not the opposite to, but rather is implied by, conventionality; the arbitrary restrictions of the latter act for poets as a kind of index to what is not typically but might be said. As for suddenness, one's 'exact wording' may be as statistically predictable as corpus linguists are increasingly showing it to be ('Adjectives are four times more common in academic prose than in conversation'), ridden with hegemonic relations of power, and even just plain banal.[31] But it is still not specifically known from the outset, and particularly not by the subject speaking, just what exact words will rise to meet their intention to talk of a given thing, as they clause-by-clause give voice to it. However well one knows one's topic, and even however much one tries to circumscribe one's speech, an element of suddenness always pertains. This can have massive consequences.

I don't in fact know very often what the paint will do.

But we can choose our words, surely? At least sometimes. *Carefully choosing one's words* even exists as a conventional phrase for the act. Surely there is a difference, the objection would continue, between giving yourself over to whatever words come to you in speaking on an uncertain topic, and that *careful choosing* we see the PhD candidate undertaking in the transcript from Pawley and Syder above, as he tries to distinguish the exact nuances of the words he is on the point of uttering, so much so that he regularly disrupts the fluency of his speech to do so (and is fostered in this, Pawley and Syder note, by the broader academic environment, as a space 'where exactness rather than fluency is most valued').[32] Surely what we have here is a clear distinction between the *thinking by speaking* Kleist promotes, and the rather more respectable act of *thinking before speaking*? These are important distinctions, because they bring to the fore the question of technique, and the varying results it can engender. But whatever nuances we might import, suddenness cannot be relegated solely to the artist's willed openness to the new. It accompanies our in-the-moment striving to choose our words carefully as well. For what actually is the act of thinking before speaking, in the close-up sense we have been considering, as the candidate meditates the next move from clause (2) to clause (3)? Is it not that one trains one's thoughts towards some specific thing – an idea, an object, a goal, a combination of all three even – the words rise to meet that intending, and one selects (or is it, encourages?) those that seem most appropriate to utter aloud? The key point here is that however careful and even wary we might be on such occasions, the initial act of speaking, the one that occurs in our heads, cannot itself be pre-meditated. Otherwise put, we cannot plan our thoughts. We say them to ourselves, finding out what they are in the process. Thinking, inasmuch as it is verbal, is itself a kind of *thinking by speaking*. The fact that thinking can happen aloud, as Kleist insists, is simply to shift the terrain a little. Thinking is suddenness in essence. Its happy finds are dependent on the fact that we lack the cognitive capacity to know the *exact* wording of what we are about to say, in advance of the second or two in which we come to utter it. This is what I am calling *suddenness*. It is the condition of all speaking, including to ourselves.

THE QUESTION DRIVING THIS BOOK

Our thoughts do not always take verbal form. But they obviously must do so for us to write. The topic of this book is the writing of poems.

Verse might constitute the exception to that colossal forgetting noted above, a reminder, well preceding the mechanical recording devices which proved it, that our focus when speaking is far more local and intense than the prose sentence would pretend. Does verse not show us, in its line-by-line insistence, the staggering of speech into tight yet somewhat loosely connected blocks of sudden, focal attention?

Perhaps this was the point of Quintus Horatius Flaccus's celebrated contention, *ut pictura poesis*: 'poetry is like painting'. We tend to feel, even though the experience often undermines this certainty (Kant noted a wavering on the matter as the effect of beauty), that we can hold a painting in a glance.[33] Similarly, and even as the diction invites us to dwell on what keeps exceeding our immediate grasping, the bounding of speech by line-break and/ or caesura approximates the amount of words we can form, or take in, in any given focus of attention. One moves to the next line, and then the next, like a tour of a gallery.

Conversely, we might say that poetry is like painting because its surface illusion of immediacy – the patina of suddenness – is slowly, iteratively, perhaps lovingly constructed.

We come to the question driving this book: Kleist's fragmentary essay, 'On the Gradual Production of Thoughts whilst Speaking', is silent on poetic composition's relation to the suddenness its poet-author observes in speech and theorises so acutely. The essay is silent on the act of writing in general. That a writer of Kleist's calibre should fail to connect his discussion of epiphany in speaking to the artform that most either captures or evokes it is odd. Nor do we have any evidence that his proposed continuation of the fragment would have said anything about writing, or indeed art of any stamp, as Kleist scholar, Hilda Brown, points out.[34] It is just possible that Kleist thought 'the gradual production of thoughts whilst speaking' had nothing in common with the writing of poems at all. Regardless of what Kleist thought, the point is that we ourselves have no clarity on the matter. The aim of this book is to repair that omission. It investigates the relationship between the act of speaking – as one speaks at any given moment, casting around for the right words, till something comes to mind – and the composition of poems for the contemporary page. Does written poetic composition rely on the same sudden mechanisms that speaking and thinking do, when generating the language it frames in lines?

Or does the fact of writing entail some other process?

APPROACH

Investigating the relationship between the writing of poems and *suddenness*, as here defined, will illuminate the relationship between poetry and thinking, one of philosophy's oldest questions, here treated from the more or less novel perspective of production. In focussing on the very seconds in which poetic thought is composed, this book will simultaneously provide a testing-ground for the severe anti-Romanticism that has become such a bulwark of our thinking about creative production for the last half-century, with its principled repudiation of words like 'individual', 'spontaneous' and 'unpremeditated'.[35] Finally, this approach, via the concept of suddenness, will raise questions about prose writings like this very book, in relation to the stark gap between the coherent, sentence-based thinking it ideally conveys, and the massive, years-long artifice necessary to produce that appearance. What kind of 'thinking' can monographs, articles and, for that matter, works of philosophy, be said to convey, once we take seriously that thought's multiply-revised form?

The questions are significant. But they fly in the face of a philosophical tradition of some decades' standing, and it will be worth justifying that from the outset. I am referring to a kind of cultural blockage affecting attempts to operationalize distinctions between speech and writing in forums like this one. There are good reasons for it. In undermining any strict distinction between the two, on the Saussurean but also post-Saussurean grounds that both materialise in signifiers (the sound in the air, the mark on the page), the identity of which can only ever be differential, Jacques Derrida rightly undercut certain hegemonic claims as to the pre-eminence of one over the other, whether these were in the service of the European invader's purportedly civilizing mission, or in celebration of the spontaneity of the unlettered, those supposedly closer to nature. Derrida effected this by proposing a far more inclusive concept of writing, one coextensive with the signifier itself: 'we say "writing" for all that gives rise to an inscription in general, whether it is literal or not and even if what it distributes in space is alien to the order of the voice'.[36] This approach did not hinder Derrida from making supple and revealing distinctions about the workings of sound and meaning in literary texts.[37] But in the context of the global uptake of post-structuralism, the massification of Derrida's already huge metaphor of writing (in *Of Grammatology*, he suggests cinematography, choreography, sculpture, political action and even athletics might all be taken as forms of writing) had some unfortunate consequences, the most ironic of which was the failure of critical theorists to take on board the stark differences between the ways we use language when speaking and the ways we use it when writing, differences that were becoming increasingly apparent to linguists over those same decades, due to the diffusion of cheap recording devices noted above.[38] Pertinently, a commitment to an epochal indistinction between speaking and writing did not stop theorists from attending conferences. Evidently writing, in the specific sense of pen, typewriter or keyboard, does import some difference to the workings of our language and its interface with thought. But to unpack just what, we need to reopen distinctions between it and speaking – without abandoning the concept of the signifier, or post-structuralist approaches to history and discourse more generally.

This book proposes three approaches to the question of how the composition of real-time speech – with all its attendant suddenness – relates to poetry writing. The striking differences between spoken and written languages will obviously play a key role. But not for some pages. The concepts introduced to this point have an extremity to them and they need to be leavened by other voices, the better to test their reality. Also, for a book about the production of poetry, sudden or otherwise, to be at all persuasive, we need to hear from the poets themselves. Part I, the first of my three approaches, is accordingly based on an archive of research interviews my colleagues and I have recorded with Anglophone poets over the past 15 years, with focus on those poets' responses to one specific question. That question contained a quotation from W.H. Auden's 1967 lecture on 'Words and the Word'. In it, Auden implies a relation between original poetic thinking and not knowing what you have to say, until you have said it. The topic of suddenness is thus never far from the surface of these discussions. But I try to bring the poets' own analyses and terms to the fore, rather than my own. This ethnographic approach takes up much of Part I, and also threads through the book as a whole. But, just as it would be remiss not to take one's bearings on the matter of poetic composition from poets themselves, one can hardly ignore the considerable scholarly work on our topic, the most illuminating examples of which concern historical materials. The second approach involves mining that scholarship. I do so throughout the book, but devote Part II specifically to the historical arm of it, with focus on what light two particular histories might shed on the relationship between the suddenness of speaking and poetic composition now. The point is not, however, to treat those two prior cultures as cognate with our own, along the lines of whatever universalism one might choose. The past is figured over those chapters in the manner Walter Benjamin espoused in his 'Theses on the Philosophy of History': as a site for estrangements, flashpoints of similarity and difference, that lead us to reconsider key aspects of the present.[39] Parts III and IV draw these on-the-ground and historical materials into an engagement with the linguistic and cognitive research introduced above, which constitutes the book's third and final approach to the questions at hand. A theory of the composition of written verse, based on the spurt-like chunks in which we actually speak and it would seem think, emerges in Part III. Part IV culminates in a second theory, concerning what Samuel Taylor Coleridge called 'the true nature of poetic diction'.[40] It is based on the severe constraints which the narrow window of conscious attention imposes on our capacity to generate language in the moment, the formulaic phrasing we rely on as a result, and the poetic thinking this in turn makes available, by implying that vast reaches of any given language are at once sayable and intelligible but unlikely ever to be said.

Parts III and IV thus supply direct answers to the questions raised in this introduction. Some readers may want to head straight to them. Parts I and II provide vital context to those answers. The whole proceeds by way of a story, concerning the divided responses that a particular question elicited from a cohort of contemporary poets.

Ngunnawal Country, 2021

NOTES

1. Kleist, "Gradual Production of Thoughts," 405.
2. Kleist, 406.
3. Kleist, 406.
4. Kleist, 406.
5. Kleist, 406.
6. Kleist, 406.
7. Kleist, "Reflection, a Paradox."
8. Kleist, qtd in Brown, *Heinrich von Kleist*, 49.
9. Kleist, "Feelings before Friedrich's Seascape," 231.
10. Kleist, "Gradual Production of Thoughts," 408.
11. Kleist, 408.
12. Kleist, 409.
13. Halliday and Matthiessen, *Functional Grammar*, 51.
14. Halliday and Matthiessen, 51.
15. Chafe, *Discourse, Consciousness and Time*, 50.
16. Q, qtd in Pawley and Syder, "Two Puzzles," 201 (my numbering).
17. Kleist, "Gradual Production of Thoughts," 406.
18. Kleist, 406.
19. Chafe, *Thought-Based Linguistics*, 49.
20. Chafe, 49, 97.
21. Pawley and Syder, "Two Puzzles," 202.
22. Pawley and Syder, 203.

23. Pawley and Syder, "One-Clause-at-a-Time," 165.
24. James, "Stream of Thought," 46.
25. Kleist, "Gradual Production of Thoughts," 406.
26. Kant, "Answer to the Question," 11.
27. Bacon, qtd in Sylvester, *Interviews with Francis Bacon*, 16–17.
28. Lacan, *Other Side of Psychoanalysis*, 71.
29. Marx, *Der achtzehnte Brumaire*, 97 (my translation).
30. Marx, "Anniversary of the People's Paper," 427.
31. Biber and Vásquez, "Writing and Speaking," 542.
32. Pawley and Syder, "Two Puzzles," 201.
33. Kant, *Critique of Judgement*, 99–104.
34. Brown, *Heinrich von Kleist*, 81.
35. For example, Boden, "What is Creativity?", 75; McGann, "Romanticism and its Ideologies," 592; Sawyer, *Explaining Creativity*, 322.
36. Derrida, *Of Grammatology*, 9.
37. Derrida, "Two Words."
38. Derrida, *Of Grammatology*, 9.
39. Benjamin, "Theses on the Philosophy of History."
40. Coleridge, *Biographia Literaria*, 1.

Part I

REVISING TOWARDS SPONTANEITY

Chapter 1

We Do Not Know What We Are Going to Say Until We Have Said It

About halfway through each interview, I would quote Auden: 'When we genuinely speak we do not have the words ready to do our bidding, we have to find them. And we do not know exactly what we are going to say until we have said it, and we say and hear something new that has never been said or heard before'.[1] I would then ask the poet how Auden's comments on speech and spontaneity related to their experience of composing.

THE SPLIT

The majority of the 14 poets I interviewed over 2013–2015 – some two-thirds of them – were well disposed to the quotation. Maxine Chernoff said that the Auden quotation captured 'what I think about my own process: why I like to write, and how I write'. We were in her office at San Francisco State: 'For me writing is very much a discovery process, in a way a performance of questions like "What am I thinking about right now? What's there? Where am I going with this today?" I have no idea when I sit down'.[2]

Noelle Kocot, seated in her study in New Jersey, told me, 'It's like going into a dream world'. She added, 'I don't try to do anything when I write, at all. I come to it with a complete beginner's mind'.[3]

Relating Auden's words to 'my own experience of writing: that journey, that search, that coming through' on the Emory campus in Atlanta, Kevin Young reflected, 'It is very much, as he says, like we do not have words ready to do our bidding. There is a way in which, even in the poem, you are wrestling with that silence, that inability to speak, or the difficulty of doing so'.[4]

For Don Paterson, whom my colleague, Kevin Brophy, interviewed in St Andrews, Scotland, Auden's words were 'right' because they outlined the very experience one wants for one's reader: 'The goal is to shock the reader into a brief state of wakefulness. You can only do that by doing the same thing to yourself'. A poem, Paterson continued 'is almost a documentary record of an epiphany that has taken place in the course of its own making'. It cannot, as such, be planned: 'If you have your revelation a week before and then try to write it up, you are already lost. It will be a bad poem. If you have a good idea for a poem, it isn't. You have to come to the page with nothing, an urge to speak – as Auden says – without really knowing why'.[5]

One might think we are in a position to assert a direct relationship between suddenness and the composition of poetic thought, on the basis of the above comments. But at this point, we have to come to terms with the fact that close to a third of the poets I spoke to rejected Auden's words, often vehemently. 'There's nothing that we can say that hasn't been said before, and we're fooling ourselves if we believe there is', Kenneth Goldsmith told me in Manhattan. 'Auden should have known better', he added. 'That's an ignorant quote. It's a real Romantic quote. It bothers me'. In response to my further question as to whether spontaneity did not in some way feature in his practice, Goldsmith replied, 'I write emails. That's about it. That's the most spontaneous I get. "Meet me for lunch at 11:30"'.[6] The concept-based work Goldsmith produces puts him at variance with most of the poets we interviewed. For instance, his book, *The Weather*, comprises the author's own transcription of 365 days of radio weather reports from the years 2002 to 2003 (including, as Goldsmith's Manhattan source station 10–10 WINS did in their broadcast, weather conditions in Baghdad during the first two weeks of the invasion of Iraq).[7] Some deny Goldsmith the label of 'poet'.[8] All of which might seem to diminish the representativeness of his response.

But C. D. Wright had similar issues with the quotation. 'It sounds like the hubris of someone painfully young who puts outsized stock in originality', she told me in Petaluma, California, in the summer of 2013. I asked Wright whether there might not still be value in the quotation, if we put aside its reference to originality. What of the link it drew between composing poetry and that daily experience of not knowing quite what you are about to say, till you have said it? Wright replied that an unexpected compositional find was 'an ultra-sweet moment'. But she immediately added: 'For spontaneity, much preparation. You have to be there and for adults it does not show up often enough'. A little later in the interview I asked her if it was always 'a matter of going back to things multiple times to try and get the right words? Does it ever just come at one time?' Wright replied, 'Very little arrives at one time, in one breath, in one circumstance, in one place'.[9] That very reply was a case in point. Wright made numerous alterations to the 'brushed-up' text of the interview transcript I sent her in 2013, made further changes to that corrected copy, and revisited the transcript on two further occasions (once in 2014, the other time in 2015) as well. This process regularly saw her revising phrases she had already corrected, for further calibration. 'Very little arrives at one time, in one breath, in one circumstance, in one place' achieved final form around the third or fourth revision, some 18 months after we spoke. The fact that no one reading the sentence when our interview was published in December 2015 would have been any the wiser as to these discontinuities in its genesis is pertinent to the issues that lie ahead of us. In fact, all of the interview materials cited here have been revised in some such manner, a standard practice, given, as we shall see, the stark gap between spoken English and publishable prose.

As for the poets to whom we put these questions, I am referring to an archive of 75 interviews recorded with major Anglophone poets from Australia, Canada, both Irelands, New Zealand, Singapore, South Africa, the United Kingdom and the United States over the years 2013–2015. The interviews were conducted in the course of an investigation into the nature of poetic judgement funded through the Australian Research Council's Discovery Projects scheme.[10] Kevin Brophy, Jen Webb and I were the three chief investigators. Michael A.R. Biggs contributed to the conceptual design of the project, while Sandra Burr and Monica Carroll contributed to the analysis of the data. Roughly 10 of the 75 poets interviewed were as celebrated as Paterson (T.S. Eliot Prize 1997 and 2003, Geoffrey Faber Prize 1997, Whitbread Poetry Award 2003, Queen's Gold Medal for Poetry 2010, Fellow of the Royal Society of Edinburgh, 2015) and Wright (the 2004 MacArthur Fellowship, the 2009 Griffin Poetry Prize, the 2010 National Book Critics Circle Award). The other 65 were less so, to varying degrees. The important point was that all were sufficiently integrated into national and international systems of judgement (prizes, anthologies and other forms of public approbation) for their responses to offer some insight into the practices generating the sorts of poems that the systems of literature currently reward, and might select to anthologize in the future.

To note that other poems, currently uncelebrated, will surely form part of that future mix is to admit that such an approach is not without its biases. These include formal biases. The institutions of judgement to which I have just referred currently platform the work of poets who write 'for the page', as opposed to those writing 'for the stage' (performance poetry, slam, rhyming) or 'the screen' (e-poetry). Further, the poets we interviewed were often, though not exclusively, writers of experimental and/or lyric free verse. Many of these poets doubled as writers of prose poetry, or shorter metrical forms like the sonnet. Only a few wrote exclusively in the three/four or five beat metres that up till the early twentieth century more or less constituted the field. In sum, the preponderance of free verse poets in the interviews cited here is because theirs is the type of poetry such prizes and anthologies most recognise, in the present conjuncture.

It is also worth adding by way of context – this time less as an admission of limitations than an indication of the gap the inquiry sought to fill – that it is not at all common to investigate a large cohort of poets' responses to one and the same set of questions. Joel Brouwer's characterisation of C. D. Wright provides an insight as to why. In 2008, Brouwer described Wright in the *New York Times* as a poet who 'belongs to a school of exactly one'.[11] The quotation underlines our tendency to treat the poems which we value as eccentric to the field in which we nonetheless classify them. Auden's contemporary and critic, Randall Jarrell, put it this way, some 50 years prior to Brouwer: 'The good in poetry is always a white blackbird, an abnormal and unlikely excellence'.[12] The fact that critics and writers alike value the 'white blackbird' in poetry seems closely related to the paucity of systematic information on the specifics of how poets as a cohort work.

Consider the specific question raised in this book: what is the relationship between the act of speaking in any given instant – when we find ourselves casting around for the right words, drawing on the energy of the moment, and the resources of language, to drive us in that at times uncertain endeavour – and the composition of poems for the contemporary page? Is writing poetry something like our experience of everyday, conversational suddenness? It is not easy to find a comprehensive answer. One certainly finds numerous authorial statements in books, essays and interviews as to how poems are composed. One can turn, for example, to the 114 titles in Michigan's *Poets on Poetry* series, to the interviews gathered over many decades by *The Paris Review*, to anthologies of authorial statements on practice like W.N. Herbert and Matthew Hollis' *Strong Words: Modern Poets on Modern Poetry*, or to the numerous essays by poets on the composition of specific poems, from Edgar Allan Poe's beguiling essay on the composition of 'The Raven' onwards.[13] Jarrell, the poet-critic whose 'white blackbird' comment I cited above, likewise wrote on how he composed and edited one of his best-known poems, 'The Woman at the Washington Zoo'.[14] There is also a substantial amount of commentary on such poetic self-reports in biographies, monographs and journal articles, almost always focused at the level of the individual practitioner. Reference will on occasion be made to those materials here. But one is hard-pressed to find answers by way of them to questions as specific as the one posed here. The sheer heterogeneity and mass of the materials defeat the inquirer. Some will retort that that is well and good: there is no poetry, only poetries, and each will be generated in ways specific to a poet's thrownness into their particular tranche of language and experience, according to whatever means they have found so as to forge art from that. I am sure there is truth in such a position and I hope some of that diversity and inventiveness will come across here. But there also seems to be something wishful in that repudiation of commonalities.

On the other hand, poets might adopt common positions either side of a division, which could well raise a question as to why. Our Auden quotation is a case in point. To platform our exploration of the split it elicited, I will add that a nationally based pilot study I had conducted some years previously found considerable disagreement among poets as to whether their poems emerge as a kind of real-time engagement with the exigencies of the immediate moment, or not. It was clear from the 14 interviews I recorded over 2006–2007 that Australian poets were divided over anything that smacked of William Wordsworth's famous description of composition as 'spontaneous overflow'.[15] In his St Kilda, Melbourne, flat in late 2006, Mal McKimmie, for instance, responded to one of my inquiries: 'I think that the problem with that question is the danger of stereotypes about the poet being a sort of shamanic medium, who receives poetry from the other side. As in Yeats' automatic writings. I am a great sceptic of that'.[16] Contrastingly, many of the poets interviewed at that time indicated that premeditation was constitutively excluded from their compositional practice. Some weeks after I interviewed McKimmie, Claire Gaskin told me in Melbourne that reading and thinking certainly informed her poetry, but not at the point of composition. She would never enter composition with a specific topic in mind: 'It's more like, I'll write and then I'll read it and discover what it's about'.[17] What is more, a number of the poets made clear that, for them, the very core of the poem, whatever later additions might come, would be produced at that first sitting.

The aim in asking the Anglophone poets in our 2013–2015 interviews to respond to the Auden quotation was to see if a similar division would be observed outside of Australia. The fact that Auden is hard to locate in any particular aesthetic tradition (avant-garde, lyric or formalist?), politics (Christian or Marxist?) or even nationality (English or American?) made his words a particularly good vehicle for such an inquiry. The division was indeed replicated, as indicated: roughly two-thirds of those interviewed over 2013–2015 assumed favourable stances towards Auden's words; the remainder were ill-disposed. The question of poetic thought's relation to unpremeditated utterance split the field of poets yet again, this time internationally. One of the key drivers of the chapters to follow is the attempt to work out why, and in the process, to come to some sense of how poetic thinking relates to the everyday act of speaking in those moments Auden describes. We are not quite sure what to say next, we press on, and the words somehow come to mind.

NOT A FAST WRITER

As the interview progressed, the reasons for C. D. Wright's impatience with the quotation were increasingly apparent. The conversational aspect of

Auden's comments on 'genuinely speaking' said little to her practice, which is iterative and revisionary.

INTERVIEWER. Can I ask how fast you write? Does it feel like a rapid process?
WRIGHT. Not a fast writer.
INTERVIEWER. Is it line-by-line then?
WRIGHT. It's a construction, a building project, laborious, sometimes tedious. Initially, of course, terrifying. You have to talk yourself through massive doubt and be bold enough to put a whole garage of lousy words down.[18]

The need for Wright to engage in some sort of free-flow writing was clear from her responses to my question as to whether she tended to hold critical faculties at bay during the initial moments of composition. Or did she feel she was composing and critiquing at the same time? 'Both at once', she replied, adding, 'The biggest inhibition about writing is self-censoring on the front-end'. But even if this response be taken as an acknowledgement of the significance of that initial writing, it would be hard to ignore the force of Wright's next comment: 'That's the usual struggle. Just to let myself get it down. Then I can go after the art'.[19]

A further, vivid indication that for Wright the art came subsequent to a first writing, through multiple acts of revision, arose during our discussion of her 1998 work, *Deepstep Come Shining*.[20] She described producing *Deepstep* as 'a joyous writing experience' and 'The most fun I have had writing. By far'. Prompted to elaborate, Wright explained that her friend and frequent collaborator, photographer Deborah Luster, had proposed they 'take a road trip, and do something related to dreams of the blind'. Luster did not, in fact, end up developing any of her photographic images. But Wright emerged from that trip through South Carolina and Georgia with a 'frog-fat notebook' and proceeded to spend a month writing it up at the Virginia Center for Creative Arts:

Studios were in an old dairy barn. Very funky – I had a junked couch, a desk, and a chair. I was still using a typewriter then, my ultra-heavy, trusty IBM. And I had a white wall on which to mount my poem. I stared at it every day, like the painters in the Center were doing. I worked on it in an expressly visual way. It is my outsider painting, untrained, unfettered.[21]

At this point I asked Wright whether, when composing such work, it feels like 'you are actually seeing the things you are describing?' She replied a little obliquely, in terms of her field trips: 'The words for seeing things can come later. But I make the notes on the spot'. Hence that notebook, 'frog-fat'. The distance between the writing it contained and the work Wright produced at the Center is emphasised in the exchange that immediately followed:

INTERVIEWER. So the perception is not necessarily there in the initial writing?
WRIGHT. True.
INTERVIEWER. It is more that you have a description of –
WRIGHT. – a description of a description I have yet to describe.[22]

I spoke with C. K. Williams in Manhattan in 2013, a week after interviewing Wright. For Williams, a poem only really arrives at the end of the writing process. His immediate response to Auden's words was to agree: 'Certainly, he's right on, when he says you don't really know what you're going to say until you say it'. Williams added, 'He's so brilliant. His is the most brilliant mind about poetry there ever was'.[23] But Williams proceeded to query the link that the quotation seems to make between the unpremeditated way the words come to us when we are speaking and poetic originality:

WILLIAMS. I think this quote must be surrounded by some other things that would elaborate on that. Because if you're really speaking, you might end up saying something new to yourself, but it wouldn't necessarily be something novel in the world, something that the world has never heard one way or another before. It's a weird quote. It's a hard one to respond to.
INTERVIEWER. The idea of something that has never been said or heard before – do you see that as a possibility?
WILLIAMS. Every poem is something that's never been seen or heard before. That doesn't mean that the meaning of it, or the music of it, to continue our two themes, haven't been heard before. But the poem, of course, didn't exist until then, so it's new, even if it's a terrible poem. He seems to imply that it won't be a terrible poem.
INTERVIEWER. The quotation does start, 'When we genuinely speak. . . .' So it does seem to imply that.
WILLIAMS. Am I genuinely speaking to you now? I think I am. But according to that definition I'd need to say something new. I don't know if I've said anything new.
Despite my admiration for Auden, I don't find it a very fruitful quote.[24]

This response was not entirely surprising, given some of the comments Williams had made earlier in the interview, when asked about his education. 'Such as it is', he responded wryly.[25] Williams nonetheless mentioned as a high point having spent weeks in the class of the Romantics scholar, Morse Peckham, studying the first 15 lines of Keats's *Endymion*. For Williams, this training in 'very detailed, syllable-by-syllable reading was terrifically useful, and remains so'. At which point he added, 'Of course that's how you write poems: syllable-by-syllable'.[26] I responded that many of the poets I had interviewed had described experiences of writing first drafts quite rapidly, certainly too fast for them to be composing syllable-by-syllable. They would engage in lengthy revisions later. In fact, I could not imagine a poem put together by syllable and I particularly could not imagine the tensile cadences of Williams's own very long lines coming about that way. To which Williams replied,

> I would say too that at least parts of the first versions of my poems are often written fast. The first versions of the whole poem, though, are usually written quite slowly and quite jaggedly. But ultimately when the poem can be called finished, the judgment always comes down to the level of the syllable. And no matter how you get started, it's how you finish that's important. And the music ultimately lies in the syllable, doesn't it? Not to accept that would be like imagining Beethoven could write without taking all the notes into account.[27]

In both Williams's and Wright's accounts, it would seem that the inspiration comes not so much at the start but rather at the end of the compositional process, in each finishing touch.

The remainder of this chapter will provide further sketches of our interviewees' positions on the Auden quotation. The chapter will stay mainly focused on poets who work and publish in the United States, as will this book more generally. The reason for that focus is that 11 of the 14 interviews I personally conducted over 2013–2015 were with US poets. The discussion will, however, also refer to interviews that my colleagues and I conducted during those years with poets in Scotland, both the Irelands, in Australia and New Zealand. And it is worth adding, at the outset, that it does not seem that national or regional differences had much, if any, impact upon the responses we garnered to the Auden quotation. Geographical differences were certainly relevant to the way poets responded to other questions; but not here. Nor did the various schools in which poets might be grouped shed much light. I should add that I cannot see any link between poets' stances on the Auden quotation and the quality, as I estimate it, of their work. Region, style, quality – none of it seems to explain why Auden's words divided poets in such a fashion.

A 'KIND OF TIGHTROPE WALK IN THE COMPOSITION'

Having told me that the matters Auden touched upon were 'very much at the heart of my practice as a writer', G. C. Waldrep, based in rural Pennsylvania, added that he never knew, when entering 'the compositional space', just what he was about to write. Nor, while writing, would he have a sense of 'more than a line or two ahead'. He continued, 'I don't know where it's going and that's part of the fun of it, that kind of tightrope walk in the composition. That's a form of pleasure for me, to write and not know where it's going'. What is more, Waldrep was happy to allow that what emerged in that unpremeditated process might amount to something 'that has never been said or heard before'. The fact that after '5,000 years of written literature, and maybe 800 years of something recognisable as English', it is 'still possible to create something new within language' was to him both 'improbable and moving'.[28]

Waldrep did, however, have a rather different reservation about the quotation:

> I have to take into account a thing that's strange for me, but true. I know which poems I wrote in a white hot heat of inspiration and passion. I know which poems of mine were written for close friends, would-be lovers, God. But you, as my reader, don't. I also know which poems were written as exercises, the poems where I came in after trimming the hedges with the thought, 'I have two hours to kill'.[29]

Usually, Waldrep continued, the result of such time-killing exercises ('I tell myself it's not creative writing, it's creative typing') would be 'garbage'. But this would not always be the case. Occasionally, a real poem would emerge. The crucial point was that in such cases no reader would be any the wiser as to whether the poem's production was passionately felt, and so in that sense 'genuine', or not. 'I'm talking about an uncanny space, where close friends tell me which poems from my books they respond to. They're almost never the ones that I feel deeply invested in. Sometimes it happens. But often, it's a poem that I recognise intellectually as a good poem, only I wrote it not out of inspiration, not out of an emotional connection'. Waldrep had little investment in composing the poem; yet somehow a friend would think it 'just pregnant with emotion and meaning, with genuineness, authenticity'.[30]

The other reservation Waldrep had about the Auden quotation concerned revision. For although Waldrep told me that he never approaches composing with a topic in mind ('I don't sit down to write "about" anything, ever'), and that he writes all his poems 'in one sitting', he immediately qualified, 'I mean the first drafts'. The editing of those drafts might take him 'anywhere from a week to ten years'. Waldrep's poems are of the moment; but they can take many years to be so. But it is worth underlining that it was clear, all the same, that for Waldrep the essence of the poem emerged in those initial moments of composition, during that 'tightrope walk' in which one does 'not know where it's going'. This altitudinous metaphor seems related to Waldrep's description elsewhere in the interview of the way poems present themselves to us as readers: 'The poetic voice hangs in a kind of space that is, for want of a better word, silence'.[31]

THE LENGTH OF A MOMENT

Another poet positively disposed to our Auden quotation was Brook Emery. To refresh, Auden's words were: 'When we genuinely speak we do not have the words ready to do our bidding, we have to find them. And we do not know exactly what we are going to say until we have said it, and we say and hear something new that has never been said or heard before'.[32] Emery and I spoke near the Sydney sea-side, at Bondi, in 2014. 'I agree totally', he responded.[33] There were, however, some interesting nuances to Emery's position. It transpired that the suddenness he associates with poetic composition also has something quite delayed about it.

Emery proceeded to note that Auden was not the only one to say it. In his 1953 National Book League Lecture on the 'Three Voices in Poetry', T.S. Eliot states that a poet

> does not know what he has to say until he has said it; and in the effort to say it he is not concerned with making other people understand anything. He is not concerned, at this stage, with other people at all; only with finding the right words or, anyhow, the least wrong words. He is not concerned whether anybody else will ever listen to them or not, or whether anybody else will ever understand them if he does. He is oppressed by a burden which he must bring to birth in order to obtain relief. Or, to change the figure of speech, he is haunted by a demon, a demon against which he feels powerless, because in its first manifestation it has no face, no name, nothing; and the words, the poem he makes, are a kind of exorcism of this demon.[34]

Emery also cited an anecdote from one of E.M. Forster's lectures on the novel. There Forster mentions a person who repudiates logic on the grounds, 'How can I know what I think till I see what I say?'[35]

Having cited these related comments, Emery turned to discuss the matter in terms of what he most wants from poetry as a reader.

> The poems that I dislike – that is probably too strong a word – the poems that do not always work for me, are poems where I can see the superstructure, or the under-structure, of an idea. The poem feels to me like an imposed illustration of that idea. Such poems do not work, they are too pat. But with good poems, the texture of the words, the rhythm of the words and whatever images that come up, carry the thought.[36]

It was interesting to hear Emery respond to Auden's words in terms of what to the contrary disappoints him as a reader of poems. The implication was that one of the strategies for avoiding that disappointing lag between a thought and its expression might be to discover one's topic in the moment. I asked if it was important for him when composing to be 'not quite sure what you are doing in that instant?' He replied, 'Yeah, often I am not. I would rather be a bit unsure. Sometimes I am not even quite sure whether I am just making notes, or writing a poem'.[37]

This led Emery to a fascinating aside about what it is to have 'an idea for a poem'. It is worth recalling at this point Don Paterson's stance on the pre-meditation of poetic thought: 'If you have a good idea for a poem, it isn't'.[38] The way Emery describes 'having an idea for a poem' is, in fact, consonant with that ban on pre-meditation. After all, Emery does not, as we have just seen, want a poem to constitute 'an imposed illustration' of an idea any more than Paterson does. Emery put it this way: 'I might have "an idea"; but it is more like a half a line that has got me going – I am not sure where I am going, or how it is going to conclude'.[39] I found this description of what it is to have 'an idea for a poem' illuminating. It shone a light on something Waldrep had told me in Pennsylvania the year before: 'Usually for me the nub of the poem is language, a piece of language that I've either come up with, or overheard, or misread'. Waldrep had proceeded to analogise his practice of writing in this fashion to having 'a sweater with a sticky, string thread to it'; it would be a matter of 'getting a hold of that little thread of language, and then hopefully drawing it out in ways I don't expect'.[40] I also heard resonances in Emery's words with Paul Hoover's observation that 'Writing begins with an intuition and just a few words, such as the phrase I read today in Pessoa: "a good sadness"'. 'Intuition', he added, 'guides all the way to the end and the words lean this way and that'. I was struck by the aphorism Hoover then advanced: 'It's not what we know, but what we know and guess'.[41] Again, we find composition described in terms of a thought that is grappling with the contingencies of the moment, and generating the poem, or at least its first draft, from whatever the language has to offer at that point.

Key to all three of these responses – Emery states it explicitly – is that the 'idea for a poem' is really a phrase sparking more phrases, a phrase that may well itself end up in the poem. What it is *not* is a prospective synopsis of the whole. Emery's observation on what it is to have 'an idea for a poem' also resonates with something Maxine Chernoff said to me. Stating that she found journaling 'counter-productive', she explained, 'Once I have written something down in any form, it seems I cannot use it again'.[42] The explanation relates to her tendency to complete each of her poems in a single sitting, repeatedly redrafting each poem on the spot till it arrives in its finished form. But it is clear from her comments that she envisages that any such journal entry, were she to engage in the practice, would itself constitute material from the poem – not a summary statement, or even a gesture towards it, but an actual phrase from it.

As for the poem, to which the compositional act of stringing more words to an initial half-line or phrase might lead, Emery proposed a sort of a mirroring action between the circumstances of the text's production and its effect on us as we read it: 'The reader is carried in the same way that the poet was. He or she thinks, "Yes, it has to go this way, yes." But it is not predictable'. A little later Emery referred to readers 'having the same perceptions and the same physical feelings as the poet, almost'. [43]

Allow me to underline that 'almost'.

Rae Armantrout's interview is interesting to cite at this juncture. We were discussing the fact that poetry demands attention from its readers. This is in San Diego, a cactus garden just outside. When I asked if 'paying attention' was important to Armantrout's compositional practice, she responded,

> I do not want to just talk about myself on this. I think it is true of pretty much all the poetry that interests me: you can see that the writer is thinking about what he or she just said, and responding to it. When I start writing, I do not really know where I am going. I start with a general feeling, sometimes it is just curiosity or puzzlement. Sometimes I have a tone in my head. But I do not know where I am going. I get a few lines down and then I start to hear what the lines are saying, or what the lines are doing, and I start to riff off that. Sometimes I will start arguing with what I have just said. I am not always arguing. But that *is* a way of paying attention. I do think that if you are only paying attention to some kind of intent, and are not paying attention to the words you are writing as you write them, then you are going to end up doing something that is not very lively. That is how I feel.[44]

Armantrout's stress on poetry having an internally dialogic character is distinct from Emery's concern with ideas that perform their meaning in the very texture of the poem. Both seem nonetheless to locate a poem's value in the impress it bears of a thinking that has occurred in the moments of composition.

The curious thing here is that, as in Waldrep's case, those compositional moments can extend over a very long time. Armantrout proceeded to note that she frequently creates her poems by binding separately composed – and initially distinct – writings into the one piece. At other times it is a matter of waiting:

> Sometimes I write something and I know it is not finished, but I do not know what it needs. I know the sort of thing I want to go there, but the actual thing

has not made itself manifest yet. I almost have to wait to see it, or hear it. I have to just be open to it and when it arrives I will recognise it and think, 'Oh, you go there'.⁴⁵

As for Emery, he would also often find himself merging separately composed pieces, on recognising that 'the obsessions that have been building up for months in them' were more or less shared, and would speak well to each other if corralled into the one poem. He, too, might come to a standstill for a while: 'You get this far along a line and suddenly there is nothing more: "I've hit a wall here, there's nothing coming." What follows might come weeks later'.⁴⁶ This is the context in which we have to understand the 'almost' I flagged above. It transpires that Emery actually finds the manner in which a poem is thought into being and the manner in which it is read to be quite distinct. The distinction has to do with the amount of time it takes each respective party to experience the poem. The words one reads in two creative minutes of mirroring another's supple and immediate-seeming utterance, might have taken the poet ten whole months or even years to generate, over intervals.

Both Emery and Armantrout responded to the Auden quotation by characterising composition as an attentiveness to the immediacy of the moment, in ways that evoked the suddenness of real-time speech scenarios. Yet they also described composition as an act spanning multiple separate occasions, through weeks, and even months. Nor were they the only poets to do so. How are we to explain this picture of intermittent immediacy?

One way might be to think of waiting for the next compositional instalment as part of the performative intensity and openness of the writing, another way of 'paying attention' as one composes. We might thereby suggest, in terms of our quotation, that while Auden *seems* to be alluding to a writing that starts and finishes at one sitting, much as speech in conversation does, we could just as well read his assertion 'we do not have the words ready to do our bidding, we have to find them' as referring to a lengthier process. Why should that process of finding the words not stretch over some months, or even years?

How long, for that matter, is a moment? In geology, the word 'moment' can stand for 'an interval of time . . . throughout which a particular faunal or floral assemblage existed'.⁴⁷ Why not imagine a 'moment' of genuine speaking as taking a good year or more to pass, even longer in some cases? Why not understand the twenty-something years Elizabeth Bishop reported spending on 'The Moose' as similarly momentary?⁴⁸ A twenty-year-long blink.

But Auden offers little licence for reading the quotation that way. He may have appreciated the way the word 'moment' is used to cover countless lifetimes in geology. Yet when Auden's discussion of those times when 'we genuinely speak' is placed back in its context, in the initial pages of the fourth and final of the *T.S. Eliot Memorial Lectures*, which he delivered in 1967, six years out from his death, we find no reference to any kind of *moment* other than the experience of being face-to-face with your interlocutor and wondering what to say next. Nor is there any discussion of revision in 'Words and the Word', as our specific lecture is titled, an 'imposing summing up', in Edward Mendelson's description, 'of all he knew about language'.[49] In fact, there is no suggestion of any strategy for poetic composition there at all, other than the one I have just described: finding out what you have to say to the person in front of you by saying it to them there and then. Poetic thinking, Auden seems to be suggesting, comes about through the private and imaginary re-creation of the inherently unpredictable, present-tense experience of conversation. It arises as suddenly as speech itself.

NOTES

1. Auden, "Words and the Word," 105.
2. Chernoff, interview by author, November 17, 2014.
3. Kocot, interview by author, July 13, 2013.
4. Young, interview by author, July 20, 2014.
5. Paterson, interview by Kevin Brophy, July 2, 2013.
6. Goldsmith, interview by author, July 6, 2013.
7. Goldsmith, *Weather*.
8. Goldsmith, *Uncreative Writing*.
9. Wright, "An Interview."
10. *Understanding Creative Excellence: A Case Study in Poetry* (DP130100402) ran from 2013 to 2016 and generated an archive of 75 hour-long interviews with Anglophone poets. I cite 15 of them in this book, 12 of which I personally conducted. The remaining eight of the 23 interviews cited here come from two sources. *The Idea of Poetic Research* ran over the years 2007–2008. That study was funded through the University of Canberra *Early Career Researcher Grant,* and generated an archive of 14 interviews with Australian Anglophone poets, five of whose interviews are cited here. Finally, I cite three interviews with scholarly writers. These were conducted in 2018, with funding from a University of Exeter *Visiting International Academic Fellowship*.
11. Brouwer, "Counting the Dead."
12. Jarrell, "Recent Poetry," 223.
13. Herbert and Hollis, *Strong Words*; Poe, "Philosophy of Composition."
14. Jarrell, "Woman at the Washington Zoo."
15. Wordsworth and Coleridge, "Preface," 22.
16. McKimmie, interview by author, January 18, 2007.
17. Gaskin, interview by author, January 20, 2007.
18. Wright, "An Interview."
19. Wright.
20. Wright, *Deepstep Come Shining*.

21. Wright, "An Interview."
22. Wright.
23. Magee, "Interview with C. K. Williams," 98.
24. Magee, 99.
25. Magee, 89.
26. Magee, 91–92.
27. Magee, 92.
28. Waldrep, interview by author, July 9, 2013.
29. Waldrep.
30. Waldrep.
31. Waldrep.
32. Auden, "Words and the Word," 105.
33. Emery, interview by author, October 25, 2014.
34. Eliot, "Three Voices in Poetry," 98.
35. Forster, *Aspects of the* Novel, 101.
36. Emery, interview by author, October 25, 2014.
37. Emery.
38. Paterson, interview by Kevin Brophy, July 2, 2013.
39. Emery, interview by author, October 25, 2014.
40. Waldrep, interview by author, July 9, 2013.
41. Hoover, interview by author, November 14, 2014.
42. Chernoff, interview by author, November 17, 2014.
43. Emery, interview by author, October 25, 2014.
44. Armantrout, interview by author, November 11, 2014.
45. Armantrout.
46. Emery, interview by author, October 25, 2014.
47. *Oxford English Dictionary*, s.v. "Moment." https://www-oed-com.virtual.anu.edu.au/view/Entry/120997
48. Bishop, "Interview," 158.
49. Mendelson, *Later Auden*, 489.

Chapter 2

'That's the Illusion You're Supposed to Get'

Recall how Rae Armantrout responded to the Auden quotation with an observation on the poetry she favours as a reader: 'I think it is true of pretty much all the poetry that interests me: you can see that the writer is thinking about what he or she just said, and responding to it'. This was a prelude to her previously quoted comment that, 'When I start writing, I do not really know where I am going. I start with a general feeling, sometimes it is just curiosity or puzzlement. Sometimes I have a tone in my head. But I do not know where I am going. I get a few lines down and then I start to hear what the lines are saying, or what the lines are doing, and I start to riff off that'.[1] Compare Ian Wedde, interviewed by my colleague, Jen Webb, in Auckland in 2013. Contrary to Armantrout, Wedde stressed a slow, meditated approach, one that starts with 'a sense of opportunity – it's not even a subject yet'. From there Wedde would work to define 'the measure of a thinking space', whether that ends up being a certain type of line, a particular stanza-form or whatever other formal frame. 'I usually', he commented, 'spend ages messing around, trying this, trying that'. It is only once 'the shape of the thinking' has been settled upon that 'various other things start to come together'.[2]

Yet for all the difference between the immersive and in-the-moment practice Armantrout described at this point in the interview and Wedde's slow building, the fact is that the two poets were very much aligned when it came to their sense of how a poem should feel, when encountered on the page. This was apparent in a comment Wedde later made on Horace, the Latin poet whose celebrated phrase *ut pictura poesis* (poetry is like painting) I cited in my introduction. Reading him is 'like being in a really fabulous conversation with someone who's got a bit of an edge; you're never quite sure if you should react or not'.[3] Wedde, too, wants a poetry that feels immediate to the moment. To say that it has to have the freshness of those situations Auden describes ('When we genuinely speak', yet 'do not have the words ready to do our bidding') would not be far off the mark. I would go further and suggest that the vast majority of the interviews converged on this point. Auden is describing a sense of present-tense openness to possibility and real-time unfolding that our interviewees would very much like to have in the poetry they write, regardless of how they actually do write it.

C. K. Williams made an illuminating comment on this score. Its implication was that there is something in the way we read verse which might in and of itself draw poets to respond positively to a quotation equating poetic composition with the immediacy of speech.

In the previous chapter I noted my surprise when Williams insisted that poetic judgement 'always comes down to the level of the syllable'.[4] His verse had always seemed to me so palpably present, so almost in the room. It certainly never felt as minutely constructed as to be composed by syllable.

INTERVIEWER. But I can't understand how you can sustain those very long phrases, which have such a sense of genuine, living speech to them, other than through improvising them in the moment. They almost strike me as something you would have to have encountered in real time as you composed.
WILLIAMS. That's the illusion you're supposed to get.
INTERVIEWER. That's fabulous.
WILLIAMS. No, that's what the lines are supposed to sound like, spontaneous, almost improvised. But of course they're not. They're composed, as I say, syllable by syllable. When you think about it, though, isn't all art experienced as improvisation?[5]

This strikes me as an acute observation. Our conversation was about poetry. But consider other arts too. Take the films that engage us. However many times we watch them, does it not feel during our watching that the actors are speaking and emoting at that very moment, there in front of us? The lyrics of pre-recorded songs sing out in a shared present as well, however many times we have played them before. Portraits stare right into us. Even scholarship speaks to us in the present. I have in mind that 'suspension of disbelief' that fictions are famously said to elicit. We tend to think of this in terms of an audience's ability to engage emotionally with scenarios they know cannot be true. But just as pertinent, surely, is our suspension of the knowledge that the plot now unfolding, the utterance now emerging from the sentence as we read it, or the picture now 'speaking' to us from the wall, each unfolded, emerged or spoke well prior to the present moment, and will go on to do so in the future as well. Of course, we know this – but somehow banish it from our minds while immersed in a work. The fact or fiction of its content is irrelevant to this other, even more mesmerising illusion. We lull ourselves into ignoring the non-contemporaneity of the work's utterance.

Plato, or at least one of his voices (not necessarily the one who believes in presence), noted it too.[6]

And consider that other, related suspension of our knowledge of time. I am referring to the practice of ascribing a coherent personality and even ethic to the artist behind such works, as if a novel, a poem, or for that matter a philosophical text, were somehow a centralised and simultaneous set of decisions to represent the world thus, even when it is clear from the archival record that the work was composed through multiple acts of drafting, that is multiple instances of temporally distinct authorial intentionality, with all the difference in emotional and intellectual states of affairs and even selfhood which that intermittency implies.[7] The text seems to perform its content in the very moment, the author to perform his or her speaking or otherwise communicating in that very moment too. Could we more flagrantly deny time?

Auden connects poetry to the everyday, conversational fact that we 'do not know what we are about to say until we have said it'. Recall Williams's enthusiasm for this aspect of the quotation. It is just that, for Williams, that raw, everyday feeling of immediacy and creative newness is what one tries as a poet artificially to imbue, by revising and revising one's poem to the point that it might trigger that sense of real-time engagement in another. As far as Williams is concerned, suddenness is the end-product of that long labour, a property of the poem's finish, its gift to the reader of something it never actually possessed.

Might that seeming suddenness end up convincing its author as well?

There is a possible argument to make here. It is an extreme one and I will not ultimately support it, but it is important to raise. That argument would hold that the reason so many poets were favourable to the Auden quotation was that it reflected qualities of immediacy we cannot help reading into the surface of any literary text. We irresistibly read an immediate voice there, disavowing in the process our knowledge of the fact that it is only through extensive critique and rewriting, not to mention the intervention of other hands, that a literary work arrives at its final, illusorily immediate, state.[8] That argument would hold that the reason the poets differed so starkly on whether poetic thought is a product of the immediate compositional moment, or not, was that two-thirds of them were seduced by the overwhelming presentism of writing itself. They were mistaking the ambience of the product for the process of getting there – as we all do, constantly. It is important to add that Williams made no such claim about our interviewees. But might one?

And what of the other questions begging here: what is the evidentiary value of artists' self-reports on their own compositional practices? Are poets really the best spokespeople for how their own thinking proceeds?

'THE LYRIC'S COLLECTIVE VOICE'

The presentist tendencies discussed above, already immensely powerful in our encounters with painting, film, pre-recorded song and novels, are only exacerbated when it comes to poetry. The sort of poetry that trips us up through the strangeness of its speaking is a particular case in point. It can make an author feel uncannily present. I will sketch an argument to this effect now, drawing on the Dickinson scholar, Sharon Cameron, and then on Aristotle, to convey poetry's heightened capacity to elicit a sense of suddenness, regardless of how any given poem was actually composed.

Consider, as a way into the heightened immediacy poems bear for their readers, Cameron's paradoxical thesis that lyric poetry mimics speech (its 'fiction lies in the illusion that someone is really talking'), at the same time that it 'lies furthest of all the mimetic arts from the way we really talk'.[9] For Cameron, the issue is that the poems we canonise as lyric speak in impossibly multiple ways:

> Could our thoughts be pitched as the lyric's, we might in fact shatter time with the determined voice of our musings. But we speak in a single voice whose pitch the lyric always rises above or drops below. The lyric's collective voice, or more accurately the voice of its collective moments, bound together as one, is not equal to a human voice.[10]

I am citing from Cameron's book *Lyric Time*, which focusses on the work of Emily Dickinson in the belief that Dickinson's writing is symptomatic of a contradiction besetting the tradition as a whole. Take the following quatrain, from poem 576.

The Mind is smooth –
No Motion – Contented as the Eye
Opon the Forehead of a Bust –
That knows it cannot see –[11]

These lines presume to represent the thoughts of a present-tense speaker. Yet such dense, scarcely reconcilable thoughts could only, Cameron argues, visit a real, historical speaker if their genesis were spread over time – considerably more time than the 10 or so seconds it takes to utter them. Whether it is Dickinson we are reading, or some other poet of like calibre, the lyric poem 'is a sequence that conceals its progressions, or synthesises them so that it appears a completion no process could have prepared for'.[12] In the terms we have rehearsed to this point, you might say that lines of this multivalent brilliance can have little do with what anyone might generate in the spoken moment. They could not come about without their composer engaging in 'extensive revision'.

Cameron ignores Freud's thesis that slips of the tongue arise from the pressure of conflicting speakers within one and the same individual.[13] But wherever one stands on that point, the curious thing Cameron's analysis forces us to realise is the vividness with which a person named Emily Dickinson emerges from her work, all the same, for all its extraordinary polyphony. Randall Jarrell reported that he felt like 'all the absolutes and intensives and eccentricities of an absolutely intense eccentric' had passed over him 'like a train of avalanches', after consuming all three volumes of the first critically established edition of Dickinson's poems in 1955. Shouldn't he have been reeling from the impossibility of finding any temporally coherent person there at all? Why, given how impossible the lyric present apparently is, did Jarrell get such a strong sense of Dickinson from that experience, to the point that he proceeded to describe her in that same review as 'one of the most individual writers who have ever lived', adding, 'You live with the poems – or rather with the poet – in an almost intolerable intimacy'.[14]

We might, in this same, strangely animating light, turn to another comment Ian Wedde made in the interview cited at the head of this chapter. To reiterate, Wedde was discussing the conversation-like immediacy he wants from the poems he reads, or for that matter, comes to write. Yet that immediacy needs, he insisted, to bear a density of reflection, to the point where you can tell 'the person who's written the piece has actually had self-consciousness, and has thought about where they're located in this'. There is something paradoxical here. In fact, it is the very paradox Cameron describes. Complexities that we would expect one needs time to generate are in the poem presented as if occurring in the course of a real-time address. It is as if, for Wedde, the reader has to get a sense that the poet has counter-intuitively lived an extra dimension within the few seconds it takes to utter any line. And it is just this sort of scarcely possible speaker whose work will make Wedde feel like he is 'in a really fabulous conversation with someone who's got a bit of an edge; you're never quite sure if you should react or not'.[15]

For all the 'impossibility' of her diction, Emily Dickinson evokes a sense of intense authorial presence. We have just seen Wedde refer to Horace in similar terms. I will argue that the amplified immediacy of such poets' work is not in contradiction to, but rather predicated upon, the seemingly impossible elements of their diction, the very things leading Cameron to claim that lyric lies 'furthest of all the mimetic arts from the way we really talk'. For what makes such poets' work feels so lively, almost as if they were in the room with us, is the fact that we have to work so hard to construe it. Aristotle implies as much, in his theory of metaphor's role in bringing the qualities of 'activity' and 'liveliness' to a discourse.[16] Far from becoming obsolete over the millennia since Aristotle composed the lecture notes we now know as the *Rhetoric*, it is a theory that can help us to grasp how Dickinson's elliptical and jarring lines might nonetheless give readers such a strong sense of the poet's personal presence as they read her. That presence is their own.

Aristotle's discussion begins with the seeming truism that we, as orators, achieve an effect of 'liveliness' by 'making our hearers see things'. Strategies for this include personifying the things that we describe and representing those things as 'in a state of activity'.[17] Aristotle cites a line from Homer in illustration:

Curved waves, crested with white, some in front, others behind[18]

He comments that in this line, the poet 'represents everything as moving and living. And activity is movement'.[19] But it is crucial to realise that, for Aristotle, achieving the kinds of energy and vividness associated with 'making our hearers see things' is not simply a matter of constructing imagery from things in motion, or ensuring a surfeit of verb forms. Another vital resource is metaphor. 'It is from metaphor that we can best get hold of something fresh'.[20] Yet for this to be the case it is crucial that they not be entirely straightforward. 'Metaphors must be drawn ... from things that are related to the original thing, and yet not so obviously related'. A gap of this nature is called for because, 'just as in philosophy', so here, 'an acute mind will perceive resemblances even in things far apart'. The point is to involve one's audience. 'Liveliness is specially conveyed by metaphor, and by the further power of surprising the hearer; because the hearer expected something different, his acquisition of the new idea impresses him all the more'. Nor is metaphor the only means for doing so. 'The liveliness of epigrammatic remarks', Aristotle adds, 'is due to the meaning not being just what the words say'.[21] As Richard Moran puts it, in his gloss on these pages, we cannot understand what Aristotle means by 'setting things before the eyes' (Moran's preferred translation of *pro ommatōn poiein*, given above as 'making our hearers see things'), until we grasp that the 'requirement of activity' is incumbent not only on the part of the speaker, but 'on the part of the responses of the audience as well'.[22] In other words, the feelings of vividness you as reader gain from a striking metaphor or epigrammatic remark are as much as anything a function of the life you yourself put into it, in bringing its seemingly discordant or missing parts together.

Aristotle's subject is public-speaking, but we can see here one of the 'strategies' to which Peter Shillingsburg alludes, in suggesting that it takes 'experienced writers' to compensate for the stark gap between communicating in a specific speech situation, and communicating in the comparatively context-free space of writing, given, for instance, that punctuation is such a 'coarse substitute for intonation and gesture'.[23] It is a matter of tapping into the reader's pleasure in filling in gaps, something Aristotle attributes to our innate desire to learn, a desire he sees as equally manifest in the pleasure we take in the use of our senses.[24] To bring this back to Dickinson would be to claim that the extraordinary vividness of her writing is as much our own – dealing with the gaps she presents us – as hers. And to perform that imaginative, gap-filling role, however disavowed, is a genuine readerly pleasure. In other words, Aristotle's analysis of the role metaphors and epigrammatic remarks play in importing activity and liveliness (he also mentions riddles and jokes) can be applied well beyond these specific devices, into our understanding of what happens when we encounter the kinds of features which Cameron detects in Dickinson's work and sees as representative of lyric poetry, in general: 'Fragmentary lines, the refusal of syntax and diction to subordinate themselves to each other, the subsequent absence of context and progression, the resulting ambiguity and tension'.[25]

In sum, not even the polyvocal, tonally discrepant and/or temporally mind-boggling aspects of lyric utterance, provided they be wielded by writers as skilled as those we are considering, escape C. K. Williams's dictum that all art is experienced as 'spontaneous, almost improvised'. To the contrary, much of the striving in our reading of such poetry seems to be to find and perform that impossible confluence of speaking positions as we read it. Which is why it boggles us. So we go back, read and re-read, till the poem somehow seems to click into place, a place proliferating with possibility. *One might have all this in one's head.* To be sure, such a performative uptake is bounded, as Wolfgang Iser notes, by the risk of 'overstrain', in the face of texts we label 'difficult'.[26] The book might well get closed. But when Cameron writes that 'All poetry is characterised by problems', she is alluding to the fact that its readers self-select, on the grounds of their willingness to go there; to go there and find a speaking position that might give embodied coherence to the impossible, all the same.[27] All of which is to say that poets, by getting us to do so much more readerly work than other authors, by the same token feel much more intimately present to us.

The illusion that leads us to imagine that poem and poet are speaking to us in the very moments in which we read them, regardless of how multiply and slowly constructed their work in fact was, and even regardless of how long it takes us to find a way of 'getting the poem', naturally inclines to a sort of heroism. So we come to the figure of the poet as possessed of a preternatural brilliance and sensibility, the type we line up for Nobel prizes. After all, none of this ended with Byron at Missolonghi. Nietzsche refers to the *Übermensch.* Is that notion really any more than a projection of the immediacy, emotional insight and power we attribute the authors of our favourite (and in fact most gap-ridden) works, regardless of how they actually wrote them? The lively. Even when they are gone.

TELLING MORE THAN WE CAN KNOW

There are very real problems with assuming poets' self-reports will be at all accurate. The issue is not simply to do with the illusions of authorial presence which literature elicits from its readers and perhaps even its authors. There is also the fact that the interviews we are considering regularly involve a poet discussing his or her own mental processes.

The social sciences have repeatedly raised doubts about the validity of subjective introspection on mental processes, whatever the field of activity. Richard E. Nibsett and Timothy Decamp Wilson's 'Telling more than we can know: Verbal reports on mental processes' is among the most quoted papers in the social sciences, with over 15,000 citations to date. Published in *Psychological Review* in 1977, it opens by reporting on a barrage of experiments conducted by Nisbett, Wilson and others over the preceding two decades. Each experiment involved inducing cognitive processes that might escape the conscious awareness of the very subjects experiencing them. A 1970 experiment by Bibb Latané and John M. Darley, for instance, involved gathering test subjects and without warning subjecting them to what sounded like someone having an epileptic seizure in the next room. The number of other subjects with one in the room was varied for different iterations of the experiment. Not only did the experimenters in this fashion demonstrate that 'people are increasingly less likely to help others in distress as the number of witnesses or bystanders increases'.[28] They discovered that those same subjects consistently denied that their conduct related to how many others were present. In fact, the subjects in Latané and Darley's experiment persisted in their denials, even after the experiment was explained and results shown them that unambiguously demonstrated that each must on some level have been counting how many other people were present, to act as they had. Other experiments which Nisbett and Wilson report involve the swallowing of placebo pills, subjection to electric shock and exposure to persuasive speakers, all of which interventions were calculated and shown to have undetected effects on subjects' retrospective accounts of their thoughts and decisions. The cumulative effect of this literature, Nisbett and Wilson conclude, is to undermine 'traditional assumptions about the conscious, verbalisable nature' of the processes undergirding peoples' 'choices, evaluations, judgements and behaviour'.[29]

On the basis of these materials, Nisbett and Wilson hypothesise that 'when people are asked to report how a particular stimulus influenced a particular response, they do so not by consulting a memory of the mediating process, but by applying or generating causal theories about the effects of that type of stimulus on that type of response'.[30] Nisbett and Wilson's subsequent experiments show their hypothesis overwhelmingly to be the case. The pair's strategy is to perform another series of manipulation experiments on volunteer subjects. But they recruit a second set of volunteers as well, and these are *not* subjected to the various experimental stimuli the others experience, but are merely asked what they think is likely to happen to anyone experiencing such phenomena. Nisbett and Wilson find that their second group's explanations for what would be likely to happen in such circumstances overwhelmingly coincide with the actual test subjects' attributions of cause, whether those attributions be correct or not – and often they are not. This leads Nisbett and Wilson to conclude that introspective accounts of mental processes are thoroughly unreliable.

Nisbett and Wilson's demonstration of the way 'a priori causal theories' act to infiltrate and replace subjects' introspective accounts of events suggests the need to adopt a *prima facie* scepticism towards poets' attempts to recall their thought-processes during past acts of composition.[31] Those attempts might have no heuristic value at all. It is worth adding that Nisbett and Wilson cite in corroboration of their experimental data a number of passages from Brewster Ghiselin's well-known anthology of artists' and scientists' statements about creativity. They point, in particular, to the fact that the authors in the anthology regularly report having no idea where a particular work or discovery came from: 'even the fact that a process is taking place is sometimes unknown to the individual prior to the point that a solution appears in consciousness'.[32] Nisbett and Wilson ignore the irony in their taking artists' self-reports on this matter as further evidence for people's incapacity to self-report.

Nor is psychology the only discipline that would encourage us to take a sceptical attitude towards poets' reflections on their own practices. For sociologist Pierre Bourdieu, writers' capacity to grasp 'the logic of the game' they are playing is constitutively 'excluded by membership of the field which presupposes (and induces) belief in everything which depends on the existence of the field, i.e. literature, the writer etc'.[33] One might also call to mind the scepticism which Thomas Kuhn, Bruno Latour and Steve Woolgar have advised us to adopt towards scientists' representations of their work practices, contoured, as such self-reports so often are, around their field's vested ideals.[34] Why expect poets to be any freer from the cultural images that envelop them?

IN A NUTSHELL

Over the course of this chapter we have ventured into Literary Studies, Philosophy and Psychology, and have touched upon Sociology as well. Evidently, there are significant and diverse grounds for a scepticism towards the fact that a two-thirds majority of the poets interviewed were favourably disposed to a proposition linking poetic composition to finding the words in the very act of saying them. At the same time, I hope the stakes of this book have started to become apparent. It concerns questions as to how the poets in our sample compose their poems, certainly, but it implicates something much broader. It has to do with whether we are even capable of thinking poetically, outside the printed page. For if the poems that engage us so intellectually and physically do not model the precise, complex and far-reaching ideation and emotional acuity, however idiosyncratic and even insane, that we ourselves are capable of generating in as short a space of time; if the movement of words in the lines is only illusorily akin to our actual possibilities for speaking (out loud, or to ourselves); if the whole show is just one giant printed illusion – what actually is poetic thinking?

Would it not be more apt to call it *poetic rethinking*?

Philosophers and theorists of all stripes (Marxists, post-structuralists, Lacanians, diverse students of 'the material encounter') are happy to find in poetry a kind of thinking that unsettles fixed categories, that intervenes even as it speaks, and that might just, for its openness to difference, serve as a model for what the political act could become. Then there is the idea of creative thinking, that awkward accompaniment to the authoritarianism and inequity of the current division of labour. But is the idea of thinking creatively really anything more than a fiction projected back from the finished surface of works produced under vastly different circumstances? The perfect speech of some super-human being, artificially constructed to make us appear greater, more intelligent, more alive than we are. Isn't poetic thinking really just the illusion we're 'supposed to get', another of those 'ideas' – as Spinoza once wrote of political theory – 'that could only be realised in Utopia, or in the Golden Age of the poets', before adding grimly, 'where of course they were least required'?[35]

NOTES

1. Armantrout, interview by author, November 11, 2014.
2. Webb and Wedde, "Slipperiness of Being."
3. Webb and Wedde.
4. Magee, "Interview with C. K. Williams," 92.
5. Magee, 92.
6. Plato, *Phaedrus*, 80–81.
7. Bushell, "Textual Process," 100–101.
8. Stillinger, *Multiple Authorship*.
9. Cameron, *Lyric Time*, 19; 207.
10. Cameron, 208.

11. Dickinson, "576," 260.
12. Cameron, *Lyric Time*, 206.
13. Freud, *Psychopathology of Everyday Life*, 101.
14. Jarrell, "Year in Poetry," 244.
15. Webb and Wedde, "Slipperiness of Being."
16. Aristotle, *Rhetoric*, 2253.
17. Aristotle, 2252.
18. Homer, *Iliad* 12.799, qtd in Aristotle, *Rhetoric* 3.11.1412a (my translation).
19. Aristotle, *Rhetoric*, 2253.
20. Aristotle, 2250.
21. Aristotle, 2253.
22. Moran, "Artifice and Persuasion," 393; Aristotle, *Rhetoric* 3.11.1411b.
23. Shillingsburg, "Text as Matter," 61.
24. Aristotle, *Metaphysics*, 1552.
25. Cameron, *Lyric Time*, 18.
26. Iser, *Implied Reader*, 275.
27. Cameron, *Lyric Time*, 18.
28. Nisbett and Wilson, "Telling More Than We Can Know," 241.
29. Nisbett and Wilson, 238.
30. Nisbett and Wilson, 248.
31. Nisbett and Wilson, 233.
32. Nisbett and Wilson, 240.
33. Bourdieu, "Field of Cultural Production," 72.
34. Kuhn, *Structure of Scientific Revolutions*, 136–143; Latour and Woolgar, *Laboratory Life*, 15–42.
35. Spinoza, *Tractatus Politicus* 1.1 (my translation).

Chapter 3

Scepticisms

I do not find the various sceptical grounds advanced above sufficient to justify ignoring what two-thirds of the poets told us at interview about the at least occasional suddenness of their process. To the contrary, I find myself wondering just how rigorous those scepticisms are. Consider, to hone in on the psychological objections, the fact that the experiments at the heart of Nisbett and Wilson's demolition of introspective evidence are all focused on subjects' reports on what they believed to be their thought-processes during one-off laboratory encounters. In contrast, the poets whom my colleagues and I interviewed were offering introspective reports on practices they engage in again and again in the course of their life-work. To realise the ease with which Nisbett and Wilson generalise very specific laboratory experiences to stand in for all modes of introspective observation, under any conditions whatsoever, is instructive.

Anthony Jack goes on the offensive: 'Introspection bashing serves an important social function for psychology – it establishes its scientific status'.[1] Less heatedly, one might point to the fact that 'first person methods of accessing and describing conscious experience have started to make a scientific comeback'.[2] Wallace Chafe is a proponent for the value of introspective evidence, particularly when corroborated by observable phenomena. His research on the relations between speaking, writing and consciousness will feature in subsequent chapters. I will consider Russell Hurlburt's 'descriptive evidence sampling' method for eliciting introspective reports on inner speech later as well. As for Jack, he is commenting upon 'A Gap in Nibsett and Wilson's Findings? A First Person Access to our Cognitive Processes', an article by Claire Petitmengin and her colleagues, which reports on the team's use of 'elicitation interview' techniques at the self-reporting stage of experiments like the ones that Nisbett and Wilson describe. Petitmengin's team discover that when an interviewer encourages a subject to perform various acts of focussed recollection, that subject can indeed recover much of the detail of his or her decisional processes. Overall, they calculate that the detection rate increases from 33 percent to 80 percent when using this protocol, in place of the simple direct questions that Nisbett, Willson and their colleagues applied. Petitmengin, Remillieux, Cahour and Carter-Thomas conclude that while it is true that 'naïve descriptions of our decision-making processes are usually poor and unreliable', it is 'possible to access these processes by carrying out specific acts' aimed at evoking a cluster of events and then 'directing one's attention towards its different dimensions'. To accept this is to have access 'to vast and almost unexplored deposits of data'.[3]

One might point to ways to temper Bourdieu's similarly extreme stance on artists' constitutive ignorance of the 'logic of the game' they play. The artist's potential awareness of what it is that truly drives them is, as we saw Bourdieu in the previous chapter state, 'excluded by membership of the field which presupposes (and induces) belief in everything which depends on the existence of the field, i.e. literature, the writer etc'.[4] By his lights, that true driver is the accumulation of symbolic capital: 'making a name for oneself, a recognised, known name'.[5] But is the acquisition of prestige really the key motivation for the poets we interviewed? Compare what C. K. Williams, a Pulitzer Prize winning poet, had to say of the social gains his work brings him:

> What a strange phenomenon it is: this limited group of people through history who become committed to poetry, to this one odd way of using language that the rest of the people around them very rarely connect to. Yet the poets keep reproducing ourselves over the generations. I've thought that if there were the slightest blip in the continuity, poetry might just end. I mean, what does it do? Who reads it? We bemoan the fact that most of the people who read poetry are poets, but by my age you learn we shouldn't complain, we should be grateful for the readers we have, who tend to be passionately devoted. If you want more readers, you do something else.[6]

Is contemporary Anglophone poetry (as opposed to the late nineteenth-century, French context Bourdieu generalises from) really all about 'making a name for oneself, a recognised, known name'?

One has to admit that Bourdieu has a point all the same. Nisbett and Wilson likewise.

To draw the obvious methodological response to the various grounds for scepticism adduced over the previous chapter, all of which have elements of truth to them, it is clear that any archive consisting of poets' accounts of how they compose their work needs to be corroborated with findings based on other sources. If the poets' various positions on the Auden quotation are to help us come to some sense as to whether poetic thinking has anything to do with the suddenness we experience when we speak and think, those positions, and the division they betoken, will have to be explained through materials external to the interview scenario itself.

But how? We need to rule out, from the start, observing poets in the act of writing. If only one could write on cue, with the observer and/or recording device ready. But reliability does not seem to be a key feature of the skills the poets we interviewed practice, judging from their comments on the unplannable nature of the art. Nor does it seem that the deforming effect of laboratory conditions could be at all accounted for. We will have to seek corroboration elsewhere. And we will have to draw on a less clinical notion than 'corroboration' in the process. A first strategy will be to see if there is any evidence, in any other period, for anything like the unpremeditated, speech-like compositional practices to which we have seen a sizeable number of contemporary poets, lay claim.

What one realises, in seeking out such materials, is that there is ample evidence in poets' draft manuscripts for the proposition that rapid and relatively unrevised composition can produce at least stretches of poetic works of quality. I am referring to poems that have since entered the various canons. This manuscript material may not quite amount to evidence for a compositional practice based around the sudden finding that occurs when speaking, or even more pertinently thinking, in the moment, nor to explain how such an activity might pair with the act of writing the words down. But it will serve to make both Kleist's and Auden's claims about the riches that unpremeditated speaking brings seem more feasibly related to what contemporary, literary poets do. On the other hand, what the patchwork, multiply-attempted nature of poetic manuscripts in the Romantic and post-Romantic periods reveals of the intermittency of compositional fluency will help explain why so many of the poets we interviewed found Auden's words, silent on the matter, so repudiable. That will be the first, small step. The next is huge. For there is also, and even better documented, evidence of totally unrevised extraordinary poetry being composed in real-time and enjoyed in that setting, live. A fair portion of Homeric scholarship is now based on the idea. It seems clear that the pre-literate poets who sang *The Iliad* and *The Odyssey* down into the classical period, improvising those tales on the spot again and again, were effectively engaging in a rhythmic version of real-time speaking, finding the poetic words they needed in the very process of uttering them.

The four chapters to follow (chapter 4 on the Romantics, and chapters 5, 6 and 7 on the Homeric poets) will thus mine the possibility that Kleist makes available, and that Auden tables with such guile. Guile? The poets we interviewed were unlikely to realise this, but the quotation we put to them seems, in its actual context, to represent a characteristically Audenesque entrapment, designed to catch us out in our enthusiasms and then to cut us down with the stark truth, as the later Auden saw it, that nothing in art could be better than the encounter with God's great silence.[7] For the 'Words and the Word' lecture proceeds, shortly after our quotation, to pour scorn on the idea that verse could ever do more than ape Christ's true revelation, the real gift of the tongue.[8] But also characteristic of Auden is that over the remainder of that lecture he never quite retracts the 'when we genuinely speak' observation used to set us up in the first place. Paterson and others among the poets we interviewed insist upon the possibility as well. The sort of brilliant, multi-faceted, aesthetic thinking critics point to in published poems might well be generated quite quickly, in something like real-time.

The effort to explain the extraordinary phenomenon to which I have just alluded – that the Homeric poems were composed anew on the spot, each and every time they were said – will take us to cognitivist and linguistic work on the topics of real-time speech processing (Part III) and conventional phrasing (Part IV). Consideration of such materials will make clear that what Auden observes of the improvisatory tenor and happy finds of those times 'when we are genuinely speaking' is true of verbal production in general. There is actually no other way to speak, think, or come up with words, than to let the impetus of being in the moment do much of the thinking for you. And contemporary lineated poetry, contrary to all the forms of writing that try to hide that fact, brings it to the fore.

It is suffused with suddenness.

NOTES

1. Jack, "Tipping Point," 671.
2. Froese, "Interactively Guided Introspection," 672.
3. Petitmengin et al., "Gap in Nisbett," 667.
4. Bourdieu, "Field of Cultural Production," 72.
5. Bourdieu, "Production of Belief," 75.
6. Magee, "Interview with C. K. Williams," 95–96.
7. Auden, "Living Thoughts of Kierkegaard," xx.
8. Auden, "Words and the Word," 117.

Part II

TWO HISTORIES OF SUDDEN VERSE

Chapter 4

Romantic Revision and Its Others

Clarence Brown witnessed Keats write 'Ode to a Nightingale' in a few hours while the poet was sitting 'in a grass-plot under a plum-tree'.[1] Yet Keats was not just fast, he was accurate. As with all the draft manuscripts, there are occasional crossings-out and replacements in the text of the ode. But that first draft is still startlingly close to the poem as we now read it. I am referring to epistolary and photographic documentation provided by scholarly editor and textual theorist, Jack Stillinger. We are searching for evidence that Romantic poets might have written canonical lines at pace, revising only minimally prior to print, as a first step towards the possibility that suddenness might have something to do with the generation of literary verse. Stillinger provides that evidence. In Ve-Yin Tee's *Coleridge, Revision and Romanticism*, Stillinger is referred to as '*the* major textual Romanticist of the 1990s'.[2] The scholar's status and proofs are indeed persuasive.

But I have to admit that I am wary of entering these waters. Paul de Man's comments from 1967 ring just as true today: 'it could be shown that whenever romantic attitudes are implicitly or explicitly under discussion, a certain heightening of tone takes place, an increase of polemical tensions develops, as if something of immediate concern to all were at stake'.[3] The crude polemicism that can often result caused Robert Pinsky, a decade later, to voice his dismay at critics who make 'facile reference to an ''imaginative one-ness with nature'' in Keats's 'Nightingale' ode.[4] The same problem fuels Zachary Leader's more recent bid that we adopt 'Romanticist' as a more discriminating term than 'Romantic' to denote 'a bias against cognitive or controlling aspects of creation'.[5] It hasn't happened. An author noted for expressing 'Romantic notions of creativity' in the contemporary humanities is by that same phrasing disqualified.

This is curious because, as Pinsky points out, the aesthetic and epistemological issues the 'Nightingale' ode raises are inescapably contemporary – the moment its treatment of nature is approached 'not as a doctrine but a dilemma'.[6] Could not a similarly recuperative operation be performed on the Romantics' descriptions of compositional practice? What would it cost us to approach these texts not as doctrines, but rather as attempts to make sense, in the various discourses of the day, of complex experience? Are they all that far removed from how poets discourse on their practices now?

Consider, to stay with Keats, his statement in an 1818 letter to Richard Woodhouse that 'if Poetry comes not as naturally as leaves to a tree, it had better not come at all'.[7] The quotation has become a peg for all sorts of references to that familiar, now little-loved Romantic equation of poetic creativity and organic growth. But Keats's words around the topic are interesting. The account he offered to his friend, Richard Woodhouse, gives this same organic metaphor a more practical spin:

> Keats has repeatedly said in conversation that he never sits down to write unless he is full of ideas – and then thoughts come about him in troops, as though soliciting to be accepted, and he selects. One of his maxims is that if Poetry does not come naturally, it had better not come at all. The moment he feels any dearth he discontinues writing and waits for a happier moment.[8]

Discontinuation and waiting evoke something of the practices of in-the-moment composition and pause which we saw Brook Emery and Rae Armantrout, respectively, describe in Part 1. The reference to Keats selecting from a plethora of inputs while in the thick of composing finds echoes in other of our interviews as well, particularly when paired with another Keats quotation from Woodhouse's account: '"My judgement" (he says) "is as active while I am actually writing as my imagination. In fact, all my faculties are strongly excited and in their full play"'.[9] Armantrout reports that she is judging as much as creating during composition.[10] So does C. D. Wright.[11] Many of the poets we interviewed do. Why should they not, given what Stephen Berkoff, Augusto Boal and other theatre artists have written about the simultaneity of judgement and performance during live stage-acting?[12] Concert violinist, Naomi Cumming, has tracked similar issues in her own art form.[13] These artists' observations on performing live are surprisingly similar to what the poets told us at interview about how they often find themselves creating and judging in one and the same act.

'Manuscript after manuscript shows him getting *most* of the words right the first time', Stillinger notes.[14] In evidence, he provides a photographic reproduction of the first page of the 'Nightingale' draft. It contains 199 words of which 188 of them are in the very form in which we read them today, landed.

Stillinger also refers to Keats's practice of stopping mid-flow in a letter to compose a poem, prior to resuming the thread of his message. 'La Belle Dame Sans Merci' was one of these. 'Ode to Psyche' another. What is more,

> there is practically no evidence that he wrote his longer or more ambitious poems in any other way. The extant drafts of documented spontaneity – the enthusiastic responses, the entries in sonnet competitions, the drafts in letters – are no different in appearance from the extant drafts of the best odes and narratives. (The long narratives were not, of course, written at single sittings, but they can easily be viewed as aggregations of shorter units.)[15]

Keats wrote fast, and extraordinarily well. He, as Hannah Sullivan puts it in *The Work of Revision*, her 2013 historicisation of the practice, was a Romantic poet 'who, at least within certain bounds, practised what he preached'.[16]

We are looking for evidence that poems on the level of 'Ode to a Nightingale' might be generated through the very means by which speech comes to us in any given conversational or otherwise spoken moment. Can one really utter, in the same amount of time it takes to recite some lines of poetry, thoughts of that order of sophistication, acute emotion and critical power? Or is the whole thing just a fantasy, a type of thinking that writers can only ever achieve through repeated sessions of slow accretion and artifice? Not poetic thinking, but poetic rethinking. But if that is what poems really purvey, why did so many of the poets insist that Auden's comments were pertinent, during their interviews? The fact that a work as canonical as 'Ode to a Nightingale' seems to have been written in a few hours does not definitively answer such questions. It is, however, a start.

Yet it has to be added at this point that only so many of the Romantic poets do seem to have practised what they 'preached'. Take Percy Bysshe Shelley. In *A Defence of Poetry*, Shelley describes the individual poem as the 'perfect and consummate surface and bloom of all things'. In that same text, he repudiates the idea that poetry proceeds from 'labour and study'.[17] Carl Fehrman, undermining this claim in turn, points to the 'slow and gradual process' of writing and rewriting that we can deduce from Shelley's notebooks: '"Labour and study" show themselves, despite Shelley's contention, to lie behind the most famous lines of his major poems'.[18] Samuel Taylor Coleridge's 'Kubla Khan' is a classic instance, but there are numerous other poems, Duncan Wu reminds us, which Coleridge 'framed as the product of a single improvisational bout' – for all the fact that they were 'overhauled across the decades'.[19] The citation is from Wu's *30 Great Myths about the Romantics* ('Myth 6: Romantic poems were produced by spontaneous inspiration'). Wu includes in his list Coleridge's first major conversation poem, 'The Eolian Harp', describing it as a poem that 'dramatises its own composition, as if written in a single sitting, yet Mays dates it Aug-Oct 1795; also Feb? 1796'.[20] (Yet again, one might say, a desire to spot Romantic mythmaking leads to this curious outcome whereby the authors of many a first person fiction – *The Sorrows of Young Werther, The Turn of the Screw, Cat's Eye* – might stand accused of spreading lies about process as well. In fairness to Wu, he cites Stillinger on Keats's evidenced extemporising as well).[21] I alluded in chapter 1 to William Wordsworth's characterisation of composition as a form of 'spontaneous overflow'. It is, of course, one of the most famous literary-critical phrases of the era. Even so, *Peter Bell* was not published until 21 years after first completion, *The Prelude* did not go to press until 45 years after the (many think complete) 1805 version, with changes to nearly half of that earliest version's lines, while *Guilt and Sorrow* underwent a full 48 years of post-compositional changes before publication.[22] Yet dissimulation is not really the right category here either. Although 'in literary historical terms the Wordsworth remembered is the Wordsworth of "spontaneous overflow"', the poet had, as Zachary Leader reminds us, 'as much to say about "labour", "judgement", "finish", "poetical pains"'.[23] I leave analysis of this apparent contradiction to a later chapter. After all, my aim here is not to 'defend' the Romantics, but simply to cast light on whether their compositional practices might have had aspects of real-time speaking to them.

More immediately pertinent in this regard is the case of George Gordon Noel Byron, Lord Byron. Leader points to the extraordinary rapidity of Byron's work. Byron's claim that the 1272 lines of *Lara* were composed in just four weeks 'while undressing after balls and masquerades' sounds exemplary of poetic mythologising.[24] But he did write it in four weeks. We can also tell, on the basis of textual, epistolary and other evidence, that Canto I of *Don Juan*, the most revised Canto of the 17, took a mere four months. 'With later cantos', Leader comments, 'time of composition is measured in weeks or days'.[25] The 111 eight-line stanzas of Canto XIII were, for instance, written in a week.[26] Byron's comment in an 1820 letter to his publisher, John Murray, 'When I once take pen in hand – I *must* say what comes uppermost', seems to have had genuine truth in it. As for revision,

> Nobody ever succeeds in it great or small. – Tasso remade the whole of his Jerusalem but whoever reads that version? – All the world goes to the first. – Pope added to the 'Rape of the Lock' – but did not reduce it. – You must take my things as they happen to be – if they are not likely to suit – reduce their estimate *accordingly*.[27]

The variorum edition of *Don Juan* shows that the poet was not above revision, actually.[28] Both Keats and Byron do, all the same, provide examples of how poetry of great weight might be written at the sort of pace we have come to regard as mythic. This heads us at least part of the way towards the idea that such poems might be composed through the very means by which we speak in the moment, as our Auden quotation seems so tantalisingly to suggest.

That is the aim. But at this point it is worth pausing to ask why we have become so unwilling to believe that the sort of rapid composing Keats and Byron both mention in their letters could be a genuine possibility, why we have tended instead to relegate the whole issue to the categories of fabrication and Romantic myth. Hannah Sullivan's *The Work of Revision* is gripping on the topic. Much of the reason for our prejudice, she argues, is that there have been such massive changes in attitudes towards revision in the two centuries since. Sullivan charts how a 'romantic creed of antirevisionism' persisted through the nineteenth century, with impetus from the Byronic topoi cited above.[29] She mentions, as an instance, Robert Browning's 'fury on reading Tennyson's revised 1842 poems: "The alterations are insane. Whatever is touched is spoiled"'.[30] Sullivan proceeds to cite Algernon Charles Swinburne, who later in that same century wrote that to revise his works for each subsequent edition 'would be a dog's life to lead – worse than a galley slave's'.[31] But as the twentieth century opened, the tables were decisively turned. Ezra Pound emerges as a key figure here, with immediate influence not only on T.S. Eliot and Gertrude Stein, but also on Ernest Hemmingway, and so, indirectly, upon a gamut of twentieth-century literatures from avant-garde to realist.[32] Pointing to Vladimir Nabokov's quip that 'My pencils outlast their erasers' and John Irving's claim that 'The value is in how many times you can redo something',[33] Sullivan argues that Romantic literary culture offers a 'mirror image of our own'. For while many Romantics 'did more reworking than they or their publishers liked to pretend', it has in the present day become 'difficult for writers to claim they don't revise'.[34] The enthusiasm with which so many of the poets responded to the Auden quotation is surely an indice of this difficulty. 'In the post-war period, literary value has become closely correlated with "revisedness"'.[35] It requires someone of Auden's stature to buck that.

But the changes revision has undergone since the nineteenth century have not merely been in attitude. They have involved a whole new set of practices. By Sullivan's analysis, what happened was a shift from forms of revision contained at the level of phrasal substitution to those massive experiments in excisional and ampliative revision we respectively associate with Pound and, if a little less famously, with Joyce. To understand the largely substitutive nature of revision prior to then, take the fact that the 1805 and 1850 *Preludes* can be printed on facing pages, where lines like

And, on the shape of the unmoving man,
His fixèd face and sightless eyes, I looked,
as if admonished from another world.

can jostle with

And, on the shape of that unmoving man,
His steadfast face and sightless eyes, I gazed,
as if admonished from another world.[36]

As an example of the new mode of ampliative revision, consider Joyce's 1939 work, *Finnegans Wake*. David Hayman describes how Joyce 'often doubled or tripled the length of passages' when revising the *Wake*. A manuscript page will bear evidence not just of additions 'but also additions to and changes in additions; there are not only changes but changes in and additions to changes'.[37] No one wrote works like the *Wake* in the nineteenth century ('those lashbetasselled lids on the verge of closing time, whiles ouze of his sidewiseopen mouth the breath of him, evenso languishing as the princeliest treble treacle or lichee chewchow purse could buy').[38] The implication of Sullivan's argument is that this can in key regards be attributed to the fact that no one revised in Joyce's massively amplifying way either. Tripling the length – and verbal density – of a manuscript in the course of revision was new.

Nor do we find, in the nineteenth century or earlier, instances of the sort of radically excisional practice which Pound performed upon *The Waste Land*, reducing the 1,000-odd lines that Eliot brought him in Paris in January 1922 to a first edition count of 433. In what is 'widely recognised as one of the greatest acts of editorial intervention on record', Lawrence Rainey observes, Pound 'urged Eliot to remove the large tracts of narrative which furnished the beginning to Parts I, III and IV of the poem', some 226 lines, as well as a further 60 odd lines scattered throughout, not to mention another 260 lines of miscellaneous poems intended for insertion into the poem, or for co-publication in the same volume.[39] Here are some of the 70 weakly Augustan lines that still opened Part III, at the point of Eliot's passing the materials to Pound. Eliot had already, tentatively, marked up a few revisions on those pages. His pencil revisions on the typescript are represented in strike-out (for cuts) and italics (for substitutions):

Fresca was ~~baptised in~~ *born upon* a soapy sea
Of Symonds – Walter Pater – Vernon Lea.
The Scandinavians bemused her wits,
The Russians thrilled her to hysteric fits.

~~For~~ *From* such chaotic misch-masch potpourri
What are we to expect but poetry?[40]

Pound would have none of this. 'One of the gashes through the lines runs so deep that the ink has bled onto the other side of the paper'.[41]

Let me make an aside here, pertinent to our overall inquiry into the potential for poetic works to be written at pace. For Louis Martz, Pound's 'critical slashing away of all those weak and in part offensive Popeian couplets' in Part III served to make way for 'the voice of one who is so reluctant to live that April becomes the cruellest month . . . the voice of a modern Ezekiel'. Effectively, Pound changed 'the tone' of the poem 'from conversational to prophetic' by paring back the former.[42] These are acute observations. But it is worth adding that the effect of Pound's editing was not just to bring out a prophetic voice in the lines Eliot had *already* written. It also spurred new lines. Looking at the manuscript facsimiles published in 1971, six years after Eliot's death, one discovers that the mesmeric lines now opening Part III –

The river's tent is broken: the last fingers of leaf
Clutch and sink into the wet bank. The wind
Crosses the brown land, unheard. The nymphs are departed.
Sweet Thames, run softly, till I end my song.
The river bears no empty bottles, sandwich papers,
. . .[43]

– those nine lines down to 'By the waters of Leman I sat down and wept' were scrawled in pencil on the back of the first page of Fresca lines, in fact right over the top of Pound's bled-through-the-page slash mark. The lines appear there almost exactly as we have them now. And the brief crossing-out of an infelicitous phrase at the start of one of them hints at the possibility that this pencilled page is where they first came to mind. The hand is otherwise unbroken. The recoil from Pound's terrific, accurate violence seems, in other words, to have involved Eliot writing fast and stunningly.

But back to Sullivan's argument: no one, the record is clear, revised with this degree of excision in the nineteenth century, nor earlier. Some of the reasons for this were material: the high cost of paper alone meant that prior to the twentieth century, authors 'were more likely to content themselves with one draft'.[44] A related issue concerns the cost of correcting printed copy. In the nineteenth century it was rare for authors to see proofs at all; in the UK case, it generally required a trip to London.[45] The invention of linotype in 1886 made it much easier to action changes on printed copy. It was only from then that the whole sequence of galley proofs, revised proofs and page proofs became potential sites for revision.[46] We simply would not have a book like *Finnegans Wake*, with its relatively anodyne, much more storytelling first drafts (compare 'his lashful lids at closing time, and out of his sidewaysopen mouth the breath of him, as sweet as any golden syrup you could buy' to the passage cited above), were it not for these material changes.[47] In such ways, Sullivan attacks a key problem in contemporary evaluations of revision: 'Both those who advocate revision and those who denigrate it tend to assume that it works in the same way for all writers at all points of time, regardless of medium'.[48] Her work, on the other hand, points to the fact that there have been times when the composition of verbal artworks in verse has been much more akin, not just in its image but also in its practice, to the registration on the page of a form of live performance.

By the same token, she, Stillinger and Leader, respectively, demonstrate that there have been great variations in these regards between individual authors, though they be in epochal terms with each other's exact contemporaries. We see this when we compare Coleridge, Shelley and Wordsworth's compositional practices with those of Keats and Byron. A split on these matters would seem to be nothing new.

My first step towards providing some external parallels to Auden's suggestive claim that lines of poetry might be generated with the suddenness of speaking has been to show some attested instances of rapid composition. Curiously, that material has come not just from the likely suspects, Keats and Byron, but from a handwritten section of *The Waste Land* manuscripts, those lines which 'represent something much closer to first thoughts' than the ones that surround them in the version we now read.[49] The discussion has, nonetheless, indicated that poets have become even more likely to revise since the late nineteenth century, and that they now have even more means for doing so.

Sweet Thames, run softly, for I speak not loud or long.[50]

A SIXTH SENSE

But what are we to make of a contemporary poet who repudiates the value of revision altogether? Medbh McGuckian was the last poet I interviewed for this project. Our dialogue was conducted by email, Canberra to Belfast, Belfast to Canberra, in early 2015. We turned rapidly to the question of how McGuckian writes:

INTERVIEWER. Can I ask you about the play of the senses in composition? I am wondering if you feel any sensory modality is uppermost when you write: sight, sound, even touch. Do you, for instance, see in your mind's eye the things you are describing as you write them?
MCGUCKIAN. I believe what happens is what Baudelaire and the symbolists described as association of senses, where a sixth sense is aroused that contains

all the others but is a single sensation of learned experience. So they all act as one the words react against and with each other to create a cinematic reality maybe stronger than reality in that it doesn't fade with the changing time but stays crystallised in the amber of the words like the Grecian Urn.[51]

I had by this point spent much time thinking through the other interviews and had even come up with a phrase that seemed to summarise some of the poets' responses.

INTERVIEWER. The idea of a sixth sense makes sense of many of the things I have heard about composition, not to mention my experience of reading. Do you find that it often requires revision fully to achieve it? Is it a matter of revising towards spontaneity, so to speak?

MCGUCKIAN. Revision I am not good at here it is anathema to say you are a revisionist it means twisting the facts of history into suitable lies and segregation. Spontaneity can't be infused if it is not there to begin with but at present I am slogging on with dead matter in the hope the worm may turn with the spade.[52]

It was hard to know how to respond to this insistence that only an initial composition could attain the 'cinematic reality maybe stronger than reality' that McGuckian had sketched so vividly in that earlier email. McGuckian composes an exhilarating, confounding poetry that feels at once cinematic and etched on the page. How could her lines achieve such conflicting effects of immediacy and permanence, if not through repeated revision?

You, who were the spaces between words in the act of reading,
A colour sewn on to colour, break the blue.[53]

And what are we to make of that curious comment that even though spontaneity 'can't be infused if it is not there to begin with', McGuckian was at this moment 'slogging on with dead matter'? If spontaneity cannot be retrospectively infused, what point could there have been to that slogging? Was this simply a contradiction on McGuckian's part – or a pointer to something about revision that our current discussions lack the words for?

WHAT IS REVISION?

The sources pointed to above suggest that a rapid and relatively unrevised mode might generate extraordinary poetry. At least some celebrated poets have written fast, and well. The fact that we in our reading tend to treat the literary and especially the poetic text as 'speaking' to us, and even in some sense as spontaneously generated, is not in question. One might go so far as to claim that reading is itself a kind of Romanticism. But none of the facts about reception assayed in Part I invalidate the possibility that a brilliant text might be generated on the fly. The two matters are logically distinct. But what of the rather more far-reaching question with which we began, the possibility poets might compose in a manner akin to the experience we have all had of searching for the words we want to say and only finding out what we had to say in the process? Perhaps Keats did write with that sort of suddenness. Again, there would be no logical difficulty in that being true, even though we cannot help on some level being deluded into feeling that *it is true* as we take his verse in, due to the very way we tend to read. Some illusions are true, by dint of causes separate to those which produce the illusion.

The idea that Keats spoke lines into being much as you and I speak in conversation, finding out what we have to say in the process, might sound like a fantasy all the same. But if that image of speaking poetically is dubious, we will, as noted, probably have to admit that the idea of poetic thinking is itself a fantasy, an illusion achieved through a manipulation of time on the page, that makes our possibilities for speaking, thinking and even acting in the moment seem so much more endowed than they are. We might perform a debunking of philosophical 'genius' on the same grounds: Spinoza, Kant, Kierkegaard, Peirce, Heidegger, Wittgenstein et al. were all writers, people who revised and revised to create the illusion of a super-human self who thought and spoke that way straight-up. We feel we know their voices, their distinct ways of thinking. What we know are their revisions, spliced together to generate the illusion that some specific human, the philosopher, might actually have that brilliance in real time.

As it happens, Auden's disingenuous picture of poetic composition by speaking is not so much trap or fantasy as powerfully corroborated, at least in the case of oral works. Shortly, we will turn to contemporary accounts of how *The Iliad* and *The Odyssey* were most likely composed. But prior to broadening our discussion in that manner, it will be worth honing in on something about revision that has emerged from the preceding arguments. This will not answer all our questions, but it may shift the terrain a little.

The idea of revision I have worked with to this point has encompassed any changes to a work that take place after what genetic critic, Pierre-Marc De Biasi, refers to as 'basic compositional rough drafts' (an example of the latter would be the kind of document we saw Keats generate in a few hours while sitting 'in a grass-plot under a plum-tree', at the start of this chapter).[54] I will continue with this definition over the pages to come. Carl Fehrman offers a representative way of figuring the phenomenon of revision, thus defined, in his discussion of the 'labour and study' that went into

Shelley's 'Ode to the West Wind', for all the poet's representations to the contrary.

Fehrman quotes a line from the ode:

Lulled by the coil of his crystalline streams[55]

He observes that this line 'might well be thought to provide a good example of what Valéry called a *vers donné*'.[56] Valéry's idea was that a 'given' line might arrive as if from nowhere; but that the means by which it will develop into further such lines must be sought with time and care, if the sum of them is to amount – as the 'natural growth of an artificial flower' – to a full poem.[57] But in the case of Shelley's line, we only have to look into the notebooks to realise that this seemingly 'given line' had a predecessor. Shelley's first attempt was:

Lulled by the silence of his crystalline streams[58]

The gorgeous 'coil of his crystalline streams' is so apt we almost cannot help but think of it as spontaneously generated. But we can see from the evidence of the relevant notebook, Fehrman concludes, that it was really 'a *vers calculé*'.[59]

This play on Valéry's '*vers donné*' is, of course, somewhat humorous. But in the act of making this joke, Fehrman underlines our tendency to associate instances of revision with a controlling rationality. I wonder about that. Is revision necessarily *calculé*? The interviews can shed light here: Eiléan Ni Chuilleanáin offers an interesting analogy for the practice. Kevin Brophy, interviewing her in Dublin, asked whether she has to be 'in the right mood' to compose poetry. In her response, Ni Chuilleanáin stressed the need for something to react to:

I think you need a stimulus and the stimulus produces the mood or else it produces the five minutes that it takes to write down the idea which you perhaps can't return to. But I would say one has to be disciplined, one has to be professional. You don't find Anne Sofie von Otter saying, 'I'm not in the mood to play this concerto,' if the orchestra is out there waiting. You have to work at it. What I find with poetry is that if I put the work in, if I write and rewrite and rewrite and rewrite again, something does appear at the end of it. And it's not usually a question of mood, but it is a question of time.[60]

The reader will by now have noticed the frequency with which metaphors from stage or other performance work figure in the poets' discussions of composition. What is so curious here is the way a metaphor from live concert performance seems to do service for revision as well. Anne Sofie von Otter's singing in front of others night after night stands for the process whereby Ni Chuilleanáin will 'write and rewrite and rewrite and rewrite again'. Note too Ni Chuilleanáin's phrasing, in claiming that, if she puts the time in, 'something does appear at the end of it'. It is a curious way of speaking, not at all close to the decisive mood and mastering attitude one might have attributed to the rewrite. Actually, it makes the products of revision sound more like *vers donnés*. But if this is so, it would be pertinent to rethink some basic assumptions. The fact that a poem has been revised does not necessarily amount to evidence that it was produced calculatedly at all.

Other interviewees concur with Ni Chuilleanáin in this regard. Don Paterson has a wonderful metaphor for getting the line you are trying to revise right. As we saw in Part I, Paterson is very much a proponent of poetry as an in-the-moment phenomenon, one that provides its reader with an epiphanic experience by dint of its author having undergone one in real-time, composing. This puts him at a distance from Ni Chuilleanáin, who relishes the fact that composing is *not* real-time. But for all his insistence on finding the poem there and then, Paterson does, of course, report a practice of revision. I write 'of course': does not McGuckian herself report one, in saying that, although she does not revise, she is 'slogging on with dead matter in the hope the worm may turn with the spade'?[61] This suggests, as I indicated above, that there may be a form of revision that is not 'revision' in our typical sense of the term at all. Here is how Paterson puts it: 'You are listening to the line, turning things very slowly to one degree here or there, left or right, and all of a sudden you hear a click and the whole line just goes clear, it opens up and you're into the safe'.[62] Consider this picture of a poet working, in safe-cracking fashion, to break back into the time of the poem. It is a picture of feeling for the words, much more than calculating them. In fact, it involves ignoring the numbers on the lock! Say rather that the reviser's task is to listen attentively and feel their way into the give and take of the mechanism. It is something you do with your body, interfacing with the object, which is why Paterson's analogy has such strong elements of *donné* about it as well.

It is not out of the question that this is what it was like for Shelley, each and every time he revised.

You suddenly crack into the safe:

DA
DATTA. ~~we brother~~ what have we given?[63]

Could this have been what happened to Eliot?

After the torchlight red on sweaty faces
After the frosty silence in the gardens

After the agony in stony places
The shouting + the crying[64]

Pound's comment above is 'OK' in green crayon. Then 'OK from here on I think' just next to that, in ink.[65] One scans down. Favourite lines appear verbatim through the six leaves of the pencilled first draft of Part V. Other lines have landed, almost in the form we know, but with occasional additions and crossings-out (the former are again indicated in italics, the latter in strike-through):

Who is the third that walks *always* beside you
When I count, there is only you and I together
But when I look ahead up the white road
There is always another *one* walking ~~there~~ beside you
Gliding wrapt in a brown mantle, hooded
I do not know whether a man or *a* woman
– But who is that on the other side of you?[66]

Hugh Kenner refers to 'the remarkable upwelling of language to which the holograph draft of Part V is testimony'.[67]

DA
Dayadhvam. ~~friend, my friend~~ I have heard the key
Turn in the door, once and once only.[68]

It is Eliot's very topic:

My friend, my ~~friend,~~ *blood* ~~beating in~~ *shaking* ~~within~~ my heart,
The awful daring of a moment's surrender
Which an age of prudence ~~cannot~~ *never* retract –
By this, and this only, we have existed,[69]

Whether in reaction to a month away from his torturous marriage, or through the effects of intensive psychotherapy with Dr Vittoz in Lausanne where he wrote these lines, or in anticipation of his upcoming meeting with Pound in Paris on his route back to England, it seems that Eliot composed Part V in one long burst and was teeming:

DA
Damyata. ~~the wind was fair, and~~ the boat responded
Gaily, to the hand expert with sail and ~~wheel.~~ ~~rudder.~~ *oar.*[70]

Consider again that *calculé* Shelleyan line to which Fehrman draws our attention. Why *calculé*? Who is to say Shelley did not find that second version of the line in as *donné* a manner as the first? Does its coming after the first version really prove anything about calculation?

Or rather, what is this model of calculation that has nothing to do with suddenness? Compare Martin Heidegger: 'We never come to thoughts. They come to us'.[71] See too, neuroscientist Antonio Damasio, sending up the idea that rational thought works through cost–benefit analysis.[72] Note, back before either Heidegger or Damasio, William James's 1890 consideration on the fact that 'thought goes on. . . . If we could say in English "it thinks," as we say "it rains" or "it blows," we should be stating the fact most simply'.[73] These brief references leave aside the questions of intention and technique, as raised in our Introduction and explored further in the pages to follow, not to mention the matter of knowledge itself, and its relation to memory. But the point remains.

What I am taking issue with are the beliefs about poetry and rationality we seem to have packed surreptitiously into this word 'revision', to the extent that the mere fact of a poem having been revised is taken to myth-bust that poet's claim to have partaken in any sort of immersive act. The wealth of poetic manuscripts published in recent decades might, to the contrary, profit from an approach that looks in them for evidence of the sort of 'upwelling' Kenner diagnoses here, or that Sullivan identifies at the start of 'The Fire Sermon' and characterises as the section of Part III of *The Waste Land* closest to 'first thoughts'.[74] To do so would provide a welcome corrective to the gaze that automatically equates revision with a phantasmic rationality, and, at its worst, ignores the insight manuscripts can so richly provide: that most poems are a patchwork from different sittings. Surely that is what the interviewees who responded positively to our Auden quotation, and yet stressed their practice of revision, were telling us, again and again. A poem so *donné* that its draft manuscript looks like a fair copy manuscript is 'a rare specimen', Fehrman writes, adding 'but it would be unscientific to deny its existence'.[75] The case of 'Ode to a Nightingale' is there, but it is actually very rare, even though our writings, literary and non-literary alike, are almost always revised so as to appear like further instances of that kind of compositional immediacy. One of the uncanniest things about *Finnegans Wake* is Joyce's refusal to cover over – by making the syntax cohere – the everyday compositional fact that so many of its sentences were generated over multiple separate sittings. Which is why the book reads like a psychosis.

On the other hand, Fehrman warns us against the danger of assuming an 'exaggerated belief in what manuscripts can teach us'. There will always be 'intermediate links and underlying intermediate stages, about which we can know little'.[76] This is as true for 'Ode to a Nightingale' as it is for 'Lulled by the coil of his crystalline streams', or Parts III and V of *The Waste Land*. Other documentary sources can, of course, help. Kenner notes of Part V that

'Eliot more than once testified that he wrote it almost at a sitting, apparently so late in his stay in Lausanne that he did not have time to make a fair copy.... the rapid writing of the holograph bears him out'.[77] But even in such cases, gaps and questions of evidence remain. Poems are ultimately mysterious in manuscript, if not quite as mysterious as on the printed page.

Let me conclude this discussion on a personal note. My last collection of poems was eight years in the writing: 62 pages. The frustration of words not being right, and having to return to them, so often fruitlessly, not knowing if one's corrections are right or not, puts me in a horror of voicing anything that might make poetic composition sound easy. I suspect that were it put to me I would also have responded to that divisive Auden quotation in the negative. Its silence on matters so integral to, and popularly misunderstood about, the art amounts to an obfuscation one might well want to combat. It does seem, all the same, that the *work* that goes into revising poems has little to do with 'a controlling rationality', as the phrase is typically understood, and is much more about dwelling with repeated, frustrated action.

A case in point, among *The Waste Land* drafts we have been considering one finds a sheet of 20 lines in pencil, marked for insertion towards the end of the 70 Fresca lines Eliot later deleted, an amplification of those 70 doomed lines. Here we read of 'Venus Anadyomene', of 'Lady Katzegg', of Aeneas ('To Aeneas, in an unfamiliar place,/Appeared his mother, with an altered face').[78] The script is the same rapid scrawl Eliot used to write the apparently *donnés* lines cited above ('The awful daring of a moment's surrender'). I suspect all of these Venus Anadyomene lines were produced calculatedly as well, in the new sense I am trying to hammer out here: that is, by paying close attention to the moment and responding to whatever it offers. What else is there to go on? Midway through the passage one finds a swathe of even more numerous crossings-out and replacements and crossings-out of replacements. Sullivan describes the Venus Anadyomene lines as 'the most heavily revised lines that survive in the entire facsimile'.[79] They were composed in Lausanne, during the same six-week *mirabilis* period from which Part V emerged.[80] And the lines are bad, as bad as any of the preceding 70 about Fresca. I am referring to my judgement here, but also to Pound's, and that of multiple critics succeeding him. It can seem so obvious in retrospect. But the pile of crossings-out on crossings-out inspires the speculation that Eliot himself had little idea whether he was onto something as good as 'What the Thunder Said', or not.

SUDDENNESS AT LAST

The second and more powerful corroboration of those poets endorsing the Auden quotation comes from what may initially seem a strange source:

contemporary Homeric scholarship. The pathway is obscure and I invite the reader simply to sit back and allow the following story – I believe it is a compelling one – to take you where it will. But it will be worth noting at the outset that pursuing what the Homerists and other scholars of oral poetries have to say on the topic of 'rapid composing in performance' will take us right to the core of our inquiry into the possibility of real-time poetic thinking, and will bring us directly to the question of the relationship between the act of speaking and the act of writing in the process.[81] For the generations of poets we have come to know as 'Homer' did, in fact, compose those two epics on the spot, at something like the very pace at which we speak.

NOTES

1. Stillinger, "Keats's Extempore Effusions," 311–313.
2. Tee, *Coleridge, Revision and Romanticism*, 4.
3. De Man, *Romanticism and Contemporary Criticism*, 3.
4. Pinsky, *Situation of Poetry*, 55.
5. Leader, *Revision and Romantic Authorship*, ix.
6. Pinsky, *Situation of Poetry*, 49.
7. Keats, *Selected Poems and Letters*, 46.
8. Woodhouse, qtd in Stillinger, "Keats's Extempore Effusions," 311.
9. Woodhouse, qtd in Stillinger, 311.
10. Armantrout, interview by author, November 11, 2014.
11. Wright, "An Interview."
12. Berkoff, *I am Hamlet*, 37; Boal, *Games for Actors*, 35–37; Schechner, "Magnitudes of Performance," 36–37.
13. Cumming, *Sonic Self*, 30–42.
14. Stillinger, "Keats's Extempore Effusions," 309.
15. Stillinger, 311.
16. Sullivan, *Work of Revision*, 30.
17. Shelley, *Defense of Poetry*, 656.
18. Fehrman, *Poetic Creation*, 13.
19. Wu, *30 Great Myths*.
20. Wu. The reference is to Coleridge editor, J.C.C. Mays.
21. Wu.
22. Stillinger, *Multiple Authorship*, 72–74.
23. Leader, *Revision and Romantic Authorship*, 24.
24. Byron, qtd in Leader, 78.
25. Leader, 104.
26. Leader, 79.
27. Byron, qtd in Manning, "Don Juan," 210.
28. Byron, *Variorum Edition*; see too Steffan, *Making of a Masterpiece*, 100–114.
29. Sullivan, *Work of Revision*, 31.

30. Browning, qtd in Sullivan, 3.
31. Swinburne, qtd in Sullivan, 37.
32. Sullivan, 101–145.
33. Nabokov and Irving, qtd in Sullivan, 7.
34. Sullivan, 29–30.
35. Sullivan, 12.
36. Wordsworth, *Prelude: A Parallel Text*, 288–289 (7.620–622 [1805]; 7.647–649 [1850]).
37. Hayman, "Introduction," 10.
38. Joyce, *Finnegans Wake*, 474 (474: 8–10).
39. Rainey, "Introduction," 23.
40. Eliot and Eliot, *Waste Land: A Facsimile*, 26.
41. Sullivan, *Work of Revision*, 138.
42. Martz, "Form in Four Quartets," 141.
43. Eliot, *Waste Land*, 70 (3.173–177).
44. Sullivan, *Work of Revision*, 23.
45. Sullivan, 36.
46. Sullivan, 38.
47. Crispi et al., "Introduction," 12; Joyce, *First-Draft Version*, 228.
48. Sullivan, *Work of Revision*, 8.
49. Sullivan, 128.
50. Eliot, *Waste Land*, 70 (3.184).
51. McGuckian, interview by author, emails of February 19, 2015 (Magee) and February 21, 2015 (McGuckian).
52. McGuckian, emails of February 26, 2015 (Magee) and March 3, 2015 (McGuckian).
53. McGuckian, "Breaking the Blue."
54. De Biasi, "What is a Literary Draft?," 35; Stillinger, "Keats's Extempore Effusions," 311–313.
55. Shelley, qtd in Fehrman, *Poetic Creation*, 12.
56. Fehrman, 12–13.
57. Valéry, qtd in Jarrety, "Poetics of Practice and Theory," 108.
58. Shelley, qtd in Fehrman, *Poetic Creation*, 13.
59. Fehrman, 13.
60. Ni Chuilleanáin, interview by Kevin Brophy, June 17, 2013.
61. McGuckian, interview by author, email of March 3, 2015.
62. Paterson, interview by Kevin Brophy, July 2, 2013.
63. Eliot and Eliot, *Waste Land: A Facsimile*, 77.
64. Eliot and Eliot, 71.
65. Pound, qtd in Eliot and Eliot, 71.
66. Eliot and Eliot, 73.
67. Kenner, "Urban Apocalypse," 43.
68. Eliot and Eliot, *Waste Land: A Facsimile*, 79.
69. Eliot and Eliot, 77.
70. Eliot and Eliot, 79.

71. Heidegger, "Thinker as Poet," 6.
72. Damasio, *Descartes' Error*, 171.
73. James, "Stream of Thought," 22.
74. Sullivan, *Work of Revision*, 128.
75. Fehrman, *Poetic Creation*, 16.
76. Fehrman, 15.
77. Kenner, "Urban Apocalypse," 41.
78. Eliot and Eliot, *Waste Land: A Facsimile*, 29.
79. Sullivan, *Work of Revision*, 133.
80. Rainey, "Introduction," 17–24.
81. Lord, *Singer of Tales*, 17.

Chapter 5

The Iliad and The Odyssey Were Rapidly Composed

Milman Parry was born in Oakland, California, in 1902. By the mid-1920s he was squarely focussed on the issues raised by *The Iliad* and *The Odyssey's* strange, multi-dialectical and in part archaic language. The issues were complex, but also far-reaching, for they brought into question Homer's very existence. The mixture of Aeolic, Ionian and Arcado-Cyprian language in the two poems had, for instance, long raised doubts 'about the possibility of one man using dialect forms from several regions and archaisms from different periods'.[1] Also confusing were the poems' numerous small inconsistencies, the fact, for instance, that the Trojan Melanippos is killed three separate times in *The Iliad*: by Teukros in line 276 of Book 8, by Antilochos in line 576 of Book 15 and Patroklos in line 695 of Book 16. Perhaps *The Iliad* and *The Odyssey* had numerous authors, and were later compiled? And yet both feel so cogent as narratives, so tonally mastered. Might their multi-dialectical diction and small slips instead be attributable to errors in memory in the passage from Homer's reputed composing sometime in or before the ninth century BCE, down to whenever the work was inscribed? That thesis would require an otherwise accurate, centuries-long oral transmission of some 28,000 lines. Over the nineteenth century scholars argued the case by pointing to 'the "fantastic memories" so "well-attested"' among populations without writing.[2] But this, too, was only so convincing.

Parry would later write that 'many, if not most of the questions we were asking, were not the right ones to ask'.[3] For there was one specific and highly revealing fact that all these various 'unitarian' and 'analyst' positions on the Homer question had failed to take into full account. Parry attributed the omission to his predecessors' failure to conceive of authorship in any way other than the one to which they were accustomed. Scholars simply assumed, for instance, that a known poem would not be repeatedly composed anew. As for the specific and highly revealing fact they had failed to accommodate, it was this: Homeric diction is not just multi-dialectical, archaic and prone to minor error. It is also formulaic. The poems, Parry demonstrated in his 1928 doctoral thesis, comprised pre-fabricated phrases, many of which bear the poly-dialectical traits noted above. The demonstration put Parry in a position to attribute the linguistic diversity noted above to the fact that the two poems' phrasing had been inherited from diverse times and places, over the course of the centuries during which *The Iliad* and *The Odyssey* had been performed. Parry called these regularly repeated phrases *formulas* and came to believe they were there for the sake of speed. One could compose faster by relying upon them.

The most obvious of the phrases Parry had in mind were the noun-epithets and short phrases that are so striking to the contemporary reader of the poems, even in translation:[4]

polutlas dios Odusseus
much-suffering, divine Odysseus[5]

epi oinopa ponton
on the wine-dark sea[6]

podas ōkus Achilleus
swift-footed Achilleus[7]

epea pteroenta
winged words[8]

The first of these expressions occurs 33 times in *The Odyssey* and five times in *The Iliad*, always as the final phrase in the line. The second, the famous *wine-dark sea*, appears 16 times over the two poems, in three variant forms; it occupies the terminal position in the line in all but one of these 16 instances. The phrase *podas ōkus* (swift-footed) prefaces the name Achilleus 28 times in *The Iliad* (but not once in *The Odyssey*). Whereas *epea pteroenta* (winged words), the most common of these four formulaic phrases, appears 61 times in *The Iliad*, 63 in *The Odyssey*.

Phrases of this nature constitute the most obviously formulaic elements of the poem, but there are many more. For instance, both *polutlas dios Odusseus* (much-suffering, divine Odysseus) and *podas ōkus Achilleus* (swift-footed Achilleus) often appear embedded within larger formulaic structures, of which they form substitutable elements. Consider the 148th line of *The Iliad*:

ton d' ar' hupodra idōn prosephē podas ōkus Achilleus
Swift-footed Achilleus looking darkly then said to him[9]

There are actually a whole series of lines in this form (13 in *The Iliad*, seven in *The Odyssey*): the *hupodra idōn prosephē* (looking darkly then said) element remains the same in wording and position throughout, while the two surrounding phrases vary in wording, depending on the gender and number of the person or persons addressed, and which hero or god is speaking to them, respectively. Parry tabulates some of the options. To accompany his table with a rough English translation (i.e. one determined by the Greek word order) gives the selection-set in table 5.1 below.

What we have in both the left and right columns here is what Parry referred to as a 'system of formulas', which he defined as 'a group of phrases which have the same metrical value and which are enough alike in thought and words to leave no doubt that the poet who used them knew them not only as single formulas but also as formulas of a certain type'.[11] As for the template sentence overarching these two systems, in Part IV, we will see such partially fixed expressions referred to as 'constructions' (also as 'lexicalised sentence stems') and will note their pervasiveness in the English we ourselves speak.[12] The point for now is that they pervade the Homeric epics. Some of them may even be familiar from translation, which at times tries to convey their repetitiveness for poetic effect.

But the epics' formulaic nature extends well beyond these at least partially familiar and resonant phrases. One finds formulaic elements in expressions that hardly seem poetic at all. Here a comparison is in order. When a poet like C. D. Wright is referred to as belonging 'to a school of exactly one' (Brouwer), it is because her work is replete with lines as *sui generis* as

Chlorophyll world. July. Great goblets of magnolialight.[13]

or

Push his nose. He'll let you off whatever floor you want.[14]

and even

Table 5.1

ton		podas ōkus Achilleus
To him		swift-footed Achilleus
tēn		krateros Diomēdēs
To her	d' ar' hupodra idōn prosephē	mighty Diomedes
tous	looking darkly then said	nefelēgereta Zeus
To them		Zeus the cloud-gatherer
		koruthaiolos Hektōr
		Hector of the flashing helmet[10]

1 Parry, *Traditional Epithet*, 16.

I pass the tree often, at the end of a head-jammed-up-in-a-shitstorm but
   sluggish run and
hunker under the canopy to breathe.[15]

In contrast, what strikes the reader of Homer's Greek is the repetitiveness of phrases as mundane as *enth' alloi men pantes* (At this all the rest of them). It occurs 10 times across the two poems, always at the start of the line. Here are the first five instances of it in *The Odyssey*.

(1) *enth' alloi men pantes, hosoi fugon aipun olethron*
    At this all the rest of the men who had escaped sheer death[16]

(2) *enth' alloi men pantes akēn esan, oude tis etlē*
    At this all the rest of them held silence and no one dared[17]

(3) *enth' alloi men pantes akēn esan huies Achaiōn*
    At this all the rest of the Achaian sons held their silence[18]

(4) *enth' alloi men pantes apephthithen esthloi hetairoi*
    There all the rest of his brave colleagues died[19]

(5) *enth' alloi men pantes apephthithen esthloi hetairoi*
    There all the rest of his brave colleagues died[20]

My translations are intended to bring out the formulaicity a little more than literary translators tend to do. But I could not manage it in (4) and (5), which serve to show that the attempt to translate literally will itself at times obscure formulaic features, simply to convey the contextual meaning of a polysemantic word (*entha* can mean either 'at this' or 'there'). Note too how prepared the Homeric poet is to repeat a formula he has just sung: (5) comes just 23 lines after (4), and in fact repeats not just our *enth' alloi men pantes* formula, but the subsequent, also formulaic phrase, *apephthithen esthloi hetairoi* (his brave colleagues died), and thus in fact the whole line. Similarly, note how in (2) and (3) Homer follows *enth' alloi men pantes* with the equally formulaic *akēn esan* (held silence). Formulas appear alongside and embedded in other formulas, just as we saw with the *hupodra idōn prosephē* (looking darkly then said) complex above. In the context of the poems as a whole, the sense of formula-upon-formula swiftly compounds. One soon comes to realise, for instance, that the phrase *huies Achaiōn* (the Achaian sons) in (3) is also formulaic, being found at *Od.* 2.115, 2.197, 3.104, 3.139, 4.285 et seq. – always in the same, terminal position in the line. The *aipun olethron* (sheer death) in (1) crops up in many other lines through the two poems as well, maintaining the same terminal position in the line in all but two of the 25 instances in which it does so (*Od.* 1.37 and *Il.* 14.99).

The formulas keep coming.

(6) *enth' alloi men pantes apephthithen esthloi hetairoi*
    There all the rest of his brave colleagues died[21]

(7) *enth' alloi men pantes eneplēsan t' edosan te*
    At this all the rest of them filled his wallet and gave him gifts[22]

(8) *enth' alloi men pantes epeuphēmēsan Achaioi*
    At this all the rest of the Achaians shouted assent[23]

Translation will often, if not always, obscure the Homeric poet's repetitive phrasing, in the laudable attempt to get a sensitive English or other language version across. So Richmond Lattimore, closer to the flavour of the Greek than most, provides distinct translations for *enth' alloi men pantes* in each of the first three cases listed above (although his translation does reflect the fact that (4) is repeated verbatim just 23 lines later, as (5)).[24] What is thereby just as regularly lost in translation is the repetitiveness that arises from the fact that formulas will generally occupy a set place, or number of places, in the Greek line, importing a repetitiveness in rhythmic cadence as well. Hence the strange surface of the two poems, composed of a mass of repetitious phrases that are diverse in origin and yet feel curiously mastered, as if one single poet is indeed speaking to us, which seems very much to have been the case. The Homeric poet speaks through a panoply of ancient, contemporary, foreign and local set-phrases, as if in clichés. These have, however, taken on a strange poetic patina, through archaism and repeated use, an effect felt even in translation: *Poseidon the Earthshaker . . . the swift ships of the Achaians . . . Owl-eyed Goddess Athena.*

Parry was not the first to notice the formulaic quality of Homeric diction. His doctoral supervisor at the Sorbonne, Antoine Meillet, an Indo-Europeanist and former student of Ferdinand de Saussure, had remarked upon the pertinence of formulaic diction to the two epics, as had other scholars. But it was Parry's brilliance to draw from the fact of its pervasiveness the following two interlocking conclusions. The first was that Homeric diction must be part of a tradition that exceeded any putative author. As Parry argued in 1930, it 'is not possible . . . that one man by himself could work out more than the smallest part of the series of formulas'.[25] There must have been a tradition of telling the tales, during the course of which elements of current speech that were both 'good poetically' and 'useful metrically' had settled into set phrases, or set phrases with substitutable elements.[26] It was a thesis that served to explain the curious fact noted above: the existence of islands of archaic and/or regional diction in a poetic language that had otherwise kept pace with the speech of the day. Parry's second conclusion had to do with why such a pervasive set of prefabricated, metrically-apt building blocks would have emerged in the first place. He believed it was for speed.

This conclusion carried with it a corollary, an idea that is still startling to consider today, even after decades of wide-spread scholarly discussion. The poems were composed at the same speed in which they were recited. In fact, those two acts were identical. The Homeric epics were actually generated anew, each and every time they were sung. That is how they persisted down the centuries prior to writing. The idea is startling, but it also makes sense. For how else would the poems have been transmitted, given their length, the 15,693 lines of *The Iliad*, the 12,110 of *The Odyssey*, given the centuries of time involved, the vagaries of human memory? How else, if not in the form of a more or less set group of stories, told again and again, in a language laced with formulas and formula systems? These traditional elements could effectively do the remembering for the poets. And if it was not an exact poem they thus enshrined, formulaic diction could at least convey the culture's specific and repeated ways of doing poetry. To marshal it in the moment would be the poet's task, and the reason a palace performer like Phemios in Book 1 of *The Odyssey* might merit the title *theios aoidos* (the divine singer), even though he is clearly only singing a 'cover'.[27]

I will try to recreate the scene. We are in the palace on Ithaka. Penelope's unwanted suitors are gathered in the main hall. There has been a feast and Phemios is singing a poem of the Greeks' fates on their various returns from Troy. Penelope overhears, and comes down the stairs into the hall,

holding her shining veil in front of her face, to shield it,
and a devoted attendant was stationed on either side of her.
All in tears she spoke then to the divine singer (*theion aoidon*):[28]

Penelope calls on Phemios to stop singing the tale that is causing her such grief. But Odysseus's son, Telemachos, rebukes her for this. The strangeness of his rebuke has often been noted:

Why, my mother, do you begrudge this excellent singer
his pleasing himself as the thought drives him? It is not the singers
who are to blame, it must be Zeus is to blame, who gives out
to men who eat bread, to each and all, the way he wills it.
There is nothing wrong in his singing the sad return of the Danaans.
People, surely, always give more applause to that song
which is the latest to circulate among the listeners.[29]

It seems clear from the first two lines of this second excerpt that inventing the words he will sing, 'as the thought drives him', is just what a *theios aoidos* (divine singer) like Phemios would be expected to do. But the last two lines make it just as clear that Phemios is singing a pre-existing song. In fact, that song is a 'hit!' Parry's theory could explain this anomaly, showing it to be no anomaly at all. Singers improvised their poems as they sung them. But they were performing repertoire, all the same.

Actually, the phrase *theion aoidon* (the divine singer) in the first of the two excerpts is itself formulaic. Demodokos, who sings a poem about the Trojan war to Odysseus and the other guests in King Alkinoos's palace later in *The Odyssey*, is also described as *theios aoidos*. He is given the epithet five times in the course of the poem (at *Od.* 8.43, 8.47, 8.87, 8.539 and 13.27), while Phemios is described this way six times (*Od.* 1.336, 16.252, 17.359, 23.133, 23.143 and 24.439). The epithet is also bestowed upon that otherwise undistinguished *theios aoidos* who is noted in passing performing alongside two acrobats and a troupe of dancers in Menelaos's palace at *Od.* 4.17.

Consider, to add one more element to this picture of a handed-down culture of rapid, speech-like composition, the parallel between the way the veiled Penelope breaks down, in reaction to Phemios's singing of her husband's failed return from Troy in Book 1, to the way the still-anonymous Odysseus himself breaks down, pulling his veil over his face as he does so –

(9) *enth' allous men pantas elanthane dakrua leibōn*
 At this from all the rest of them he hid the tears he shed[30]

– on hearing his deeds at the sack of Troy recounted by Demodokos. *Singer interrupted by the grieving of a veiled audience member, personally implicated in the tale sung.* This would seem to be one of the 'typical scenes' that Parry began to analyse towards the end of his short life – that is, one of the 'fixed action-patterns' that recur throughout the two epics, just like the formulas.[31] Homerist and ethnographer, Albert Lord, who greatly expanded this fledgling element of Parry's analysis, referred to such set pieces as 'themes' and showed that they pervaded *The Iliad* and *The Odyssey*.[32] Lord would later point to a third category of formulaic utterance as well: the 'story pattern'.[33] This term served to name the recurrent narrative structures contouring whole poems: the return narrative, the return-rescue, the feud and so on. These would become part of 'oral formulaic theory' too, their repetitive aspect likewise explained in terms of the functional requirement that poems like *The Iliad* and *The Odyssey* be repeatedly composed anew, in real-time before an audience.

Parry's thesis seemed finally to have solved the 'Homeric question'. What is more, it seemed to explain poems from other cultures. Similar practices, Parry began to realise, had been described in ethnographic accounts of Afghan, Berber, Estonian, Finnish, Kirghiz, Russian and Serbian performance traditions. Here were oral cultures whose literatures revolved around the live extemporisation of epic poems that were at once formulaic in diction and familiar in plot.[34] The encounter with those reports in the late 1920s led Parry to the suspicion that he had stumbled upon the chief mode of poetic composition and transmission in cultures without writing, globally: the recreation of received stories, through the live 'mixing' of prefabricated units.

THE BALKAN EPICS WERE RAPIDLY COMPOSED

Although Parry had already been reading ethnographic accounts of performance in other oral cultures, it seems to have been his meeting with the Austro-Slovenian scholar, Matija Murko, in Paris in 1928, that gave him the idea of testing his philological conjectures in a contemporary setting. Murko attended Parry's defence of his doctoral dissertation ('The Traditional Epithet in Homer') at the Sorbonne, and there informed the Californian of a thriving practice of performative composition among illiterate villagers in the then Kingdom of Yugoslavia. Not long after, Parry decided to travel to the Balkans to see how oral epic was being composed in the present, staging his first field-trip there in 1933. Parry was prompted by the richness of his initial findings to return over 1934–1935, this time accompanied by Albert Bates Lord, whom he employed as his research assistant. 'In the early thirties of this century when Milman Parry began to write the book from which this one takes its name', Lord would later write, 'what was needed most in Homeric scholarship was a more exact knowledge of the way in which oral epic poets learn and compose their songs'.[35] Focussed on these questions of transmission and composition, Parry's two trips resulted in a huge amount of ethnographic data. In addition to field notes, the team brought back 3,580 12-inch phonographic recordings, and over 12,500 texts.[36]

Parry died, lamentably, in 1935. A gun went off in his suitcase when he tried to open it. He was 33 years old and had just begun his book about the Homeric practices of oral poets in the contemporary Balkans. Lord would continue the work. By 1937, he had become a Junior Fellow at Harvard. He returned to the former Yugoslavia that year, widening the collecting to include Albanian singers. He returned again over 1950–1951, and staged further trips in 1958 and 1959, which allowed him to collect comparative material in Bulgaria. It was on the basis of these researches that Lord was to compose the comparative monograph that Parry could not.

Lord's *The Singer of Tales* was published in 1960. Parry's son, Adam, also a classicist, would later contest the continuity between his father's ideas and Lord's, casting doubt on both the strength of the Balkan analogy and Parry's commitment to it.[37] Others have contested Adam Parry's criticisms, in turn.[38] What cannot be doubted, however, is *The Singer of Tales*'s impact, and power. Influential on a wide variety of fields, from classical studies and folkloristics through to anthropology, linguistics and even cognitive psychology, Lord's book remains, Gregory Nagy notes, 'the most definitive book on the subject of oral poetry'.[39] It is also the most definitive book on the subject of composing poetry by speaking in it.

The work is in two parts. The first ('The Theory') sets forth Parry's ideas on formulaic composition, while offering in-depth accounts of how South Slav epic singers trained and performed over the 25 years in which Parry, and then Lord, conducted their fieldwork. This part of the book includes descriptions of the various 'experiments' and observations the two made in their search for Homeric parallels. The extraordinary speed with which the South Slav singers produced their verse, and the fact that those recitals could proceed for hours – at times even days – emerge as key facts, as does their verse's repletion with formulas, formula systems and themes. The second part of Lord's book ('The Application') concerns the ramifications which these fieldwork confirmations of Parry's ideas have for our grasp of the two Homeric epics, and includes a hypothesis (the 'oral dictated poem') as to how those poems might have entered into writing. A concluding section offers suggestive discussion of formulaic elements in *Beowulf*, *La Chanson de Roland* and the eighth century CE Greek epic, *Digenis Akritas*. Lord argues that all three of these poems were repeatedly composed anew before live audiences, and only at some later point inscribed.

What a thumbnail sketch of *The Singer of Tales*'s contents cannot, however, capture is the way Lord transforms the philological brilliance of Parry's thought into a series of precisely honed generalisations, with compelling effect. Consider Lord's sharp observations on the poverty of his own culture's understandings of the arts in traditional societies. Noting that 'the present vogue of revival of folk singing on the concert stage and elsewhere has distorted our concept of the essence of oral composition', Lord explains that in the Homeric and South Slav cases he is considering, there is no difference between recreating the original song and creating a new one. Any traditional song you sing is, by that same token, a new one.

> In a sense each performance is 'an' original, if not 'the' original.
>
> The truth of the matter is that our concept of 'the original', of 'the song', simply make no sense in oral tradition. To us, it seems so basic, so logical, since we are brought up in a society in which writing has fixed the norm of a stable first creation in art, that we feel there must be an 'original' for everything. The first singing in oral tradition does not coincide with this concept of 'the original'. We might as well be prepared to face the fact that we are in a different world of thought, the patterns of which do not always fit our cherished terms. In oral tradition the idea of an original is illogical.

It follows, then, that we cannot correctly speak of a 'variant', since there is no 'original' to be varied![40]

Each performance is a 'multiform', an event that is both utterly singular to the given moment, and one of many like it. The singer's art is to stay true to that multiformity, ancient and new at one and the same moment: 'the picture that emerges is not really one of conflict between preserver of tradition and creative artist; it is rather one of the preservation of tradition by the constant re-creation of it'.[41] Lord's prose ripples with this sort of thetic tension, insisting we think again about our hackneyed understandings of what it is to be traditional.

The other feature that a thumbnail sketch of the contents of Lord's book cannot convey is the sheer insistence of the fieldwork data he marshals, showing in case after case the pertinence and accuracy of Parry's theories. To get a sense of this, take Lord's analysis of the phonographic recordings the team produced of repeat performances of the same song by the singer, Petar Vidić. Focussing on the divergences in phrasing and plot apparent from the transcripts of these recordings, Lord demonstrates that the illiterate Vidić was not relying on some extraordinary, verbatim memory when asked to repeat the same song in 1934 that he had sung for Parry in 1933. He was composing it anew, much as Parry had suggested the epic poets would do. What is more, Vidić was chanting that old/new poem at a more or less speaking pace, accompanying himself on a single-stringed, bowed instrument (the *gusle*) as he did so.[42] Speed was a feature of all the performances the researchers observed: their recordings provide evidence of compositional rates of between 'ten to twenty ten-syllable lines a minute'.[43] Finally, the transcripts prove that Vidić's songs were pervasively formulaic, much as Parry had found Homer's to be.[44] In fact, all the Balkan singers' poems demonstrated formulaic features. Lord could even show this quantitatively. One of his demonstrations involves sampling 15 lines from the transcript of a 1934 recording of Salih Ugljanin's performance of the 'Song of Bagdad'. Lord compares the excerpt with 12,000 other lines which the team recorded of Ugljanin's singing, over 11 songs. By searching that 12,000 line corpus for other instances of the phrases found within this 15 line sample, Lord calculates that one quarter of the 15 lines in his sample, and one half of the half lines, are formulas. As in the Homeric case, the formulaicity is pervasive. On the other hand, the fact that Ugljanin was using his formulaic diction to produce a poem on the spot at between 10 and 20 lines per minute was there to hear on the phonograph.

Significantly, Lord detected artistry in these extemporisations as well. His comments on the elaborate alliterations and assonances in a passage from this same recording are revealing.

Had Ugljanin been a literate poet who sat down with pen in hand to devise these lines with their inner balances and syncopations, he could not have done better. One can even fancy the over-literate 'interpreter of literature' innocent of Salih's ignorance of such matters, extolling the syncopation as the artful intent of the poet to indicate the zigzag search of the messenger for Alija![45]

Elsewhere Lord describes a passage which Avdo Međedovič composed on the spot for Parry as 'reminiscent of Telemachus's journey in *The Odyssey*, and not un-Homeric in quality'.[46] The importance of such aesthetic evaluations and analogies for Parry and Lord's general project will be apparent. (That said, one might note something curious in Lord's offhand assumption that literary poets achieve their effects through planning and 'artful intent', while Salih Ugljanin apparently has no idea. It is hard to see what grounds Lord would have for either of these beliefs).

Lord's book also provides compelling accounts of how these illiterate Balkan poets managed to learn new songs. It transpires that Parry, having heard a number of Balkan singers make the astounding claim that they could repeat a new song after a single hearing, decided to put the matter to the test. An opportunity soon arose. In August 1935, Mumin Vlahovljak chanted a longish, 2,294 line poem for Parry and his team. Avdo Međedovič was also present. Discovering that Međedovič had never heard the song before, Parry waited till Vlahovljak had finished and then asked Međedovič if he thought he could repeat the song from this single hearing. Međedovič 'replied that it was a good song and that Mumin had sung it well, but that he thought he might sing it better'.[47] He sang it to his one-stringed *gusle* there and then. Looking over the transcripts years later, Lord detected the formulaic elements that 'made possible what seemed to be on the surface an incredible feat'.[48] It was just as Parry's theory had predicted. For Parry had speculated, a year prior to any of the Balkan fieldwork, that when it came to learning a new song, an oral poet would most likely 'fuse' the formulaic diction and 'typical scenes' already in his possession with certain novel elements in what he had just heard.[49] As to how this theory was borne out in Avdo Međedovič's spontaneous re-performance of Mumin Vlahovljak's poem, it helped that Lord had an archive of Međedovič's recorded performances at hand. For this allowed him to see that Međedovič's rendition of the poem's opening assembly scene had much in common with the way an assembly is described in a poem Međedovič had already sung for the researchers. 'Avdo already had worked out a very similar theme before he heard Mumin'.[50] A similar consideration applied to the 'arrival of a messenger' theme. The character of the 'poor and despised hero at the foot of the assembly' was 'no stranger to Avdo' either. In short, Međedovič 'had many other models in addition to Mumin's song. He was not creating out of whole cloth'.[51] So one hears a poem for the first time and repeats it there and then.

The historical implications seemed clear to Parry's team. Far from resorting to their 'fantastic memories' of some 27,803 lines of verbatim epic, the Homeric poets must have transmitted the epics in some similarly inventive fashion. Of course one can compose *The Iliad* in real-time. 'This is, indeed, his whole art: to make a poem like the poems he has heard' (Parry).[52]

CRITIQUES AND IMPACTS

The universalist strains in Parry's work have struck many readers. Johannes Haubold has suggested an unsettling parallel between Parry's image of a practice of composition that 'lacks time' to do other than repeat the past in formulaic phrases and themes, and the 'essentially ahistorical' way Parry could analyse Homeric poetry alongside 'poetry from very different periods in history', as if all oral verse functions alike.[53] The three anthropology courses Parry took as an undergraduate at Berkeley under Ursula K. Le Guin's father, A.L. Kroeber, were imbued with a strong sense of the radical equality of all human cultures, derived in turn from Franz Boas's work, and Parry may well have drawn his sense of disparate cultures' comparability from there.[54] The comparative linguistics of Parry's Sorbonne supervisor, Antoine Meillet, may have been an influence in this regard, as well.[55] As for Haubold's critique, he attacks Parry for flattening time and space in this 'essentially ahistorical' manner, but he also acknowledges that the resultant figuring of Homeric poetry, as an artform with 'dual citizenship in the republic of letters and that of oral epic', would come 'to play a decisive role in the ongoing project of opening up the canon of 'literature'. The power of Lord's analogy between Avdo Međedović, an illiterate butcher from Bijelo Polje, and Homer, the 'father' of the European literary tradition, at the start of the decolonising 1960s should not be underestimated either. Parry and Lord's work put on the agenda 'epics that might not be considered literature at all'.[56]

There are, at any rate, clear elements of overstatement and misanalogy in Parry and Lord's claims. It has been demonstrated, for instance, that both went too far in repudiating the role of rote memorization in the cultural productions of societies without writing.[57] Anthropologist Ruth Finnegan has marshalled numerous examples of orally transmitted poetries where composition and performance are distinct, and where rote memorization bridges the gap between the two. She reports, for instance, that oral poets in Somalia work and rework their poems in private. The best of these compositions circulate under their authors' names. What is more, those Somali poets work with such rigid formal constraints that trivial alterations are at once rendered unlikely and by the same token quickly picked up by listeners.[58] Finnegan cites further cases from Eskimo, Gaelic, Gilbert Island and other traditions.[59] These cases tend to involve 'shorter, more lyrical poetry, rather than the narrative poems mainly stressed by the oral-formulaic school'.[60] Denis Tedlock's repudiation of Parry and Lord's generalisations, in relation to the four-hour long *Kyaklo* chant delivered verbatim by Zuni tribesmen, is also worth noting.[61]

One can cite counter-arguments from Homeric scholars as well, including those who work closely with Parry and Lord's ideas. I have in mind Gregory Nagy's work on 'text fixation or textualisation' in the oral transmission of the Homeric poems, 'the process whereby each composition-in-performance becomes progressively less changeable in the course of diffusion'.[62] We might imagine this 'text fixation' in terms of a shift from the type of 'rapid composing in performance' modelled by the palace bards, Phemios and Demodokos, in the *Odyssey*, towards the recital competitions that form the backdrop to Plato's dialogue *Ion*. It is clear from that dialogue that by Plato's era, a Homeric poet, or *rhapsode*, worked with a set text and took it as his task to perform that text verbatim.[63] But even in earlier, less textually fixed, times, there would seem to have been elements of rote-memory recital. Elizabeth Minchin suggests that the 265-line long 'Catalogue of the Ships' in Book 2 of *The Iliad* could be an instance of this. Drawing on ethnographic evidence of nineteenth-century Kirghiz oral epic performances, where long lists are treated as special moments of 'performance within a performance', being closely anticipated by audiences and applauded wildly if performed word for word, Minchin argues that the 'Catalogue of the Ships' was probably a passage of this order, an island of fixed text in an otherwise (much more) free-floating composition.[64] The discrepancies others have noted between the various Greek forces described in the catalogue and those who populate the battlefield in the other parts of the poem support this.[65]

Yet even taking such matters into account, that fact that Finnegan, one of Parry and Lord's most acute critics, nonetheless concludes that, since the publication of *The Singer of Tales*, it is 'no longer possible to argue that the only way to explain lengthy oral poems is in terms of memorisation by the performer' is surely pertinent.[66] Parry and Lord's work has been fruitfully applied to 'more than one hundred language areas as disparate as Chinese, African, Australian and Native American'.[67] A 2010 conference on the 50th anniversary of Lord's book featured papers on Parryan features in Irish heroic tales, in Kazakh epic, in Iranian oral traditions, the Finish Kalevala, epic improvisation in the Arabic of North Egypt, Sami Yoicks, the *Njalsaga*, Appalachian folktales and more.[68] Even taking the various critiques of Parry and Lord's Homeric/Balkan analogy into account, it seems hard to deny the central finding they advanced by means of it: much of what we call traditional oral epic is created live, at something like the pace at which we speak.[69]

The Iliad was rapidly composed for centuries.

As was *The Odyssey*.

But also *The Mahabharata. Beowulf, The Poem of The Cid, The Song of Roland.*

Sections of the Old and New Testaments.

Elements of 'Chaucer'.[70]

Even taking all the necessary nuances into account, it seems clear that what Parry alighted upon implicates 'the preponderance of the world's verbal art: those myriad and vital oral traditions that', considered over the full course of human time, 'dwarf written literature in size, content, and diversity' (John Miles Foley).[71]

RELEVANCE TO WRITTEN LITERATURE?

But how might these Parryan materials relate to the compositional practices that forms the empirical focus of this book? How, in particular, might they aid us in the task of determining the relationship, if any, between the suddenness of speaking and the act of composing verse for the contemporary page?

For Lord, the relation is one of outright opposition. We noted his sarcastic reference to that 'over-literate "interpreter of literature"' who would take the syncopation in Salih Ugljanin's rapidly composed lines as evidence of the singer's 'artful intent'.[72] That critic's mistake, for Lord, would be in treating Ugljanin's poem as if it were composed slowly and intentionally enough to be artful. But it only makes sense that Lord would see a necessary link between originality in verse and a poet's possession of sufficient 'leisure' to pre-meditate and revise.[73] After all, the whole rationale Lord offers for the formulas and formula systems, the themes and story patterns, is that speaking formulaically is *necessary*, if one is to achieve 'rapid composing in performance'.[74]

Parry was even more insistent on this point. Take his 1929 discussion of Homer's propensity for stringing phrase on prior phrase, an approach to syntax ('parataxis') whereby 'the successive ideas join on to one another in the order that they occur to the mind'.[75] Reflective of the speaker's thinking in the moment, the sort of slapdash (from a certain, in fact debateable, perspective) syntax that results is for Parry an unavoidable consequence of the verse's real-time composition. 'The Singer has not time for the nice balances and complications of unhurried thought'.[76] Parry's implication is that whatever 'balance', and 'complication' one finds in literary verse can only have been achieved through slow, meditative thought. Formulas, we read elsewhere in Parry, undergo ready alteration – provided their metrical qualities stay intact. 'But any less simple alteration in the word-group supposes thought of some length on the part of the poet'.[77] Breaking formulaic patterns takes time. The singer, Parry argues in one of his final publications, 'has no pen and ink to let him slowly work out a novel way of recounting novel actions'. Novelty requires pen, paper and time. The singer, in contrast, 'must make up his tale without pausing, in the speed of his singing'.[78] Again, Parry's implication is that the only way for anyone to compose oral verse is for them to rely on the fixed elements that are already in their possession.

all' hote tetraton ēlthen etos kai epēluthon hōrai
But as the fourth year arrived and the seasons came round again[79]

aps peritellomenou eteos kai epēluthon hōrai
But as the year unfurled and the seasons came round again[80]

all' hote tetraton ēlthen etos kai epēluthon hōrai
But as the fourth year arrived and the seasons came round again[81]

all' hote tetraton ēlthen etos kai epēluthon hōrai
But as the fourth year arrived and the seasons came round again[82]

This, for Parry, is the 'strong conservatism of the formulaic technique'.[83] Or is it a 'strong conservatism' in his model of the mind? Are we really reduced to formulas, when channelling signs at speed?

Parry and Lord's insistence on the pertinence of formulaicity to what did, after all, became known as 'oral-formulaic theory', would seem to bring my project of finding convincing parallels with contemporary practices there to a decisive halt. The Homeric case might even be taken as a definitive *disproof* that a contemporary poet could write lines at any sort of speaking pace, given the extreme demand for 'originality' such poets now labour under, and their consequent incapacity to avail themselves of the formulaic mechanisms 'rapid composing in performance' apparently requires. That would be this chapter's sorry conclusion, were it not for the following fact. Parry and Lord's work has been most criticised on this very front. The link both draw between rapid composing and mechanisation has been consistently attacked, particularly in recent decades. It transpires that current work in the field puts Homer and Avdo Međedović much closer to Medbh McGuckian and Don Paterson than either Parry's papers or Lord's *The Singer of Tales* will allow. In fact, the work of contemporary Homerists offers a picture of oral poetic composition – improvised in the moment from received elements, yet not at all mechanical – that strongly evokes Kleist's essay on 'The Gradual Production of Thoughts Whilst Speaking'. Passages in this scholarship are redolent of our Auden quotation on the creativity of real-time speaking as well. For we are, in fact, composing each time we speak, and the Homerists, more than any other scholarly professionals concerned with poetry, have had to confront that fact. They have had to learn to think of speaking as itself a form of proto-poetic composing, because it is ultimately the only way to make sense of the materials Parry brought to light.

CODA

To foreshadow some of those future discussions of originality in formulaic speaking, a theme that will run through to the end of this book, let us return to the passage in *The Singer of Tales*, where Lord describes how Avdo Međedovič listened to Mumin Vlahovljak sing 2,294 lines and immediately repeated them, in his own style. Actually, our earlier description downplayed something intriguing. It is not merely that Međedovič recreated Vlahovljak's poem in his own terms, immediately after hearing it. The transcripts reveal that in doing so Međedovič shifted the placement of the themes, changed the order in which the dramatis personae appear and introduced a plethora of new ornament, in the process more than doubling, and in fact almost tripling, the length of the song, from the 2,294 lines in Vlahovljak's performance to Međedovič's 6,313.[84]

But how then, one wants to know, did Međedovič imagine he was merely repeating Vlahovljak's song?

What is it, to be traditional? One of the most compelling passages in *The Singer of Tales* tackles this issue squarely. Lord writes there of Đemo Zogić, another singer who claimed the ability to reproduce a song upon a single hearing. Not only would he repeat that other poet's song, Zogić asserted, it would be 'the same song, word for word and line for line'.[85] Actually, Lord is in a position to check this, for he has a recording of Suleiman Makić performing a song and he has a recording of Zogić repeating that very same song on first hearing it. The transcripts of those two singings make the matter clear.

> Zogić did not learn it word for word and line for line, and yet the two songs are 'recognisable versions of the same story'. They are not close enough, however, to be considered 'exactly alike'. Was Zogić lying to us? No, because he was singing the story as he conceived it as being 'like' Makic's story, and to him 'word for word and line for line' are simply an emphatic way of saying 'like'.[86]

There are two issues here. The first is that these illiterate Balkan singers do not actually know what, in the literate culture's terms, a *reč* (word) actually is. When asked for examples, they variously point to a phrase, a line, or even a whole song.[87] This can seem strange to us, but really it just shows that *reč* has a different meaning in their speech. The literate culture will define a word as an item of vocabulary separated by spaces when printed, or in some such manner – actually, there is 'no generally accepted or completely satisfactory definition of what constitutes a word', as etymologist Philip Durkin notes.[88] As far as the singers are concerned, a word is really just 'a unit of poetic utterance, small or large'. Their usage has its own precision too, so much so that the Homerist-cum-Slavicist, John Miles Foley, will adopt the Balkan poets' use of *reč* to denote the basal blocks of oral poetry, in preference to Parry's 'formula'.[89]

But what is harder for us to assimilate is that the kind of equivalence the singers feel the need to satisfy, if they are to recite a poem 'exactly as they heard it', is quite distinct from that which we would feel compelled to satisfy, in making any such claim.[90] What matters for Zogić is that he reproduces 'the stable skeleton of narrative, which is the song in his sense'.[91] Lord stresses the singer's fidelity in such matters, underlining Zogić's 'constant emphasis' on his role as 'the conserver of the tradition'.[92] Međedovič too is 'deeply conservative' in his art, 'religiously maintaining the meaning of a song'. The singers have a strong commitment to the preservation of the story. After all, 'if the singer changes what he has heard in its essence, he falsifies the truth'.[93] It is simply that tripling the length of a song from 2,294 to 6,313 lines through adding a plethora of new phrases, descriptions and nuancings of character does nothing, as far as the South Slav poets are concerned, to stop it from being exactly the same song.

We do not share the same sense of sameness. Hence the irony of Lord's polemical claim that a singer like Međedovič is 'not a mere carrier of the tradition but a creative artist making the tradition'.[94] For though this is true, it is clear that the sort of three-fold expansion Međedovič performs on Vlahovljak's song is far less radically creative (or even extemporised!) in Međedovič's own mind, than it is for us. Lord underlines this point: oral poetic culture is 'essentially conservative in traditional lore, all outward appearances to the contrary'.[95] Wittgenstein argues that the idea of exactness is ultimately ethical ('"Inexact" is really a reproach, and "exact" is praise'), in the course of his ferocious attack upon the alibi that the scientific era finds in quantitative reasoning.[96] There is something of that power here, in Lord's quiet demonstration that our canons of sameness are just as culturally given as any other categories, and could well appear illogical – and what is more, repeatedly improvised – to future or foreign eyes.

NOTES

1. Lord, 8.
2. Lord, 10.
3. Parry, "Oral Verse-Making I," 268.

4. Unless traditional, or otherwise noted, the translations accompanying the Greek texts in this section are my own. I have followed Richmond Lattimore's practice of transliterating proper names from the Greek, rather than Latinising them.
5. Homer, *Od.* 5.171, 5.354, 5.486, 6.1, 6.249 et seq.
6. Homer, *Od.* 1.183, 2.421, 3.286, 4.474, 5.132 et seq.
7. Homer, *Il.* 1.58, 1.84, 1.149, 1.215, 1.364 et seq.
8. Homer, *Il.* 1.201, 2.6 et seq. ; *Od.* 1.122, 2.269, 2.362 et seq.
9. Homer, *Il.* 1.148.
10. Parry, *Traditional Epithet*, 16.
11. Parry, "Oral Verse-Making I," 276; 275.
12. Croft, *Ten Lectures,* 2020, 1–32; Pawley and Syder, "Two Puzzles," 208.
13. Wright, *Deepstep Come Shining*, 193.
14. Wright, 223.
15. Wright, "Tree of Obscurity."
16. Homer, *Od.* 1.11.
17. Homer, 2.82.
18. Homer, 4.285.
19. Homer, 5.110.
20. Homer, 5.133.
21. Homer, 7.251.
22. Homer, 17.503.
23. Homer, *Il.* 1.22.
24. Lattimore, *The Odyssey of Homer*, 27, 41, 72, 91.
25. Parry, "Oral Verse-Making I," 314.
26. Parry, "Oral Verse-Making II," 330.
27. Homer, *Od.,* 1.336.
28. Lattimore, *The Odyssey of Homer*, 35 (*Od.*, 1.334–336).
29. Lattimore, 35–36 (*Od.* 1.346–352).
30. Homer, *Od.* 8.94.
31. Parry, "Typical Scenes," 406.
32. Lord, *Singer of Tales*, 68–98.
33. Lord, *Singer Resumes the Tale*, 11–13.
34. Parry, "Oral Verse-Making II," 329–338.
35. Lord, *Singer of Tales*, 3.
36. Lord, "Homer, Parry and Huso," 473.
37. Parry (Adam), "Introduction," xxxviii–xliii; xlviii, liii–lvii.
38. Mitchell and Nagy, "Introduction," xvi–xvii.
39. Nagy, "Albert Lord," 487–488.
40. Lord, *Singer of Tales*, 101.
41. Lord, 101.
42. Lord, 113–115.
43. Lord, 17.
44. Lord, 235–241.
45. Lord, 57.
46. Lord, 107.

47. Lord, 78.
48. Lord, 81.
49. Parry, "Oral Verse-Making II," 333–337.
50. Lord, *Singer of Tales*, 80.
51. Lord, 81.
52. Parry, "Oral Verse-Making II," 334.
53. Haubold, "Homer after Parry," 34–35.
54. García, "Milman Parry and A.L. Kroeber."
55. Mitchell and Nagy, "Introduction," xvi-xviii.
56. Haubold, "Homer after Parry," 44.
57. For example, Parry, "Oral Verse-Making I," 330; Lord, *Singer of Tales*, 280 fn.9.
58. Finnegan, *Oral Poetry*, 74–75.
59. Finnegan, 73–76.
60. Finnegan, 80.
61. Tedlock, "The Spoken Word," 235, fn.5.
62. Nagy, *Homeric Questions*, 40.
63. Lord, *The Singer of Tales*, 17. Plato, *Ion*.
64. Minchin, *Resources of Memory*, 92.
65. Bowra, *Homer*, 89–92.
66. Finnegan, *Oral Poetry*, 69.
67. Foley, *Oral Tradition and the Internet*, 151.
68. "Singers and Tales—Schedule," The Center for Hellenic Studies, Harvard University, Updated November 2, 2020, https://chs.harvard.edu/singers-and-tales-schedule/
69. Foley, *Homer's Traditional Art*, 37–111.
70. For references on the oral-traditional character of these texts, see Foley, *Oral Tradition and the Internet*, 137–138.
71. Foley, 153.
72. Lord, *Singer of Tales*, 57.
73. Lord, 22.
74. Lord, 17.
75. Croiset, qtd in Parry, "Enjambment in Homeric Verse," 251.
76. Parry, "Enjambment in Homeric Verse," 262.
77. Parry, "Oral Verse-Making I," 275.
78. Parry, "Typical Scenes," 406.
79. Homer, *Od.* 2.107.
80. Homer, 14.294.
81. Homer, 19.148.
82. Homer, 24.142.
83. Parry, "Oral Verse-Making II," 332, fn3.
84. Lord, *Singer of Tales*, 78.
85. Lord, 27.
86. Lord, 28.
87. Lord, 24.

88. Durkin, *Oxford Guide to Etymology*, 37.
89. Foley, *How to Read an Oral Poem*, 11–20.
90. Lord, *Singer of Tales*, 27.
91. Lord, 99.
92. Lord, 28.
93. Lord, 109.
94. Lord, 13.
95. Lord, 120.
96. Wittgenstein, *Philosophical Investigations*, 42e (§88).

Chapter 6

The Desk as Stage

Trying to find historical parallels to the idea that contemporary poetry might be at least in part generated through the very mechanisms we draw on to speak, we seem to have found a spectacular case, in Milman Parry and Albert Lord's demonstration that the Homeric poems were not transmitted down the centuries through myriad acts of by-heart recital, but rather recomposed on the spot, at each and every performance. And this seems to have been, and even still to be, the predominant pattern for poetic production in societies without letters, globally. Publication, transmission and creation are one and the same thing. Yet the idea that these findings might relate to contemporary practices is problematised by Parry and Lord themselves. Both see a stark distinction between traditional oral and literary poetry. In fact, the oral and the literary emerge as opposed terms in their analyses. That said, and with the exception of some of Parry's statistical comparisons, analysis is not really the right word for how either Parry or Lord approach literary poetry.[1] Both treat it as a foil for their discussions of oral poetry, advancing a number of offhand assumptions about written composition in the process, including that its inherent nature is to be planned. Over the next two chapters, we will see that there are very real reasons for their refusal to allow that oral and literary poetries are at all related. But we will also find some grounds for a rethinking.

One of Parry and Lord's key reasons for holding that oral and literary poetries have nothing in common concerns the distinct relationships these artforms bear to the concept of originality. As Lord puts it, 'There are periods and styles in which originality is *not* at a premium'.[2] 'Expression', he tells us elsewhere, is the oral poet's 'business, not originality, which, indeed, is a concept quite foreign to him and one that he would avoid, if he understood it'.[3] For the oral poet 'is not a conscious iconoclast, but a traditional creative artist'.[4] The oral poet's lack of interest in originality is, as we have seen, linked by both Parry and Lord to the functional requirements of 'rapid composing in performance'.[5] It will be worth underlining how massive those requirements are. As previously noted, Lord detected compositional rates among the Balkan poets of between 10 and 20 decasyllabic lines per minute. Equally noteworthy is the fact that those poets were not simply engaging in short bursts of creative activity. They could compose at that pace for hours on end, and even over successive days. The descriptions of all-night bardic singing throughout classical literature are pertinent. Oliver Taplin models how a performance of *The Iliad* might have proceeded: he speculates on three successive night-long sessions, ranging from six and a half to nine hours each.[6] It is hardly surprising that Parry and Lord's explanation for how it could be at all possible would focus on the swift repeatability of formulaic mechanisms.

But note too, how oddly that stress on a functionally driven unoriginality sits, in Lord's specific case, with his occasional analogies between the singer's practice and the everyday acts of learning new language and speaking. An apprentice singer learning the formulas and themes is, Lord tells us at one point, 'like a child learning words, or anyone learning a language without a school method; except that the language here being learned is the special language of poetry'.[7] He tells us at another point,

> In studying the patterns and systems of oral narrative verse, we are in reality observing the "grammar" of the poetry, a grammar superimposed, as it were, on the grammar of the language concerned. Or, to alter the image, we find a special grammar within the grammar of the language, necessitated by the versification. The formulas are the phrases and clauses and sentences of this specialized poetic grammar. The speaker of this language, once he has mastered it, does not move any more mechanically within it that we do in ordinary speech.[8]

But is everyday speaking, for all its time constraints, that necessarily conservative?

On the other hand, there does seem to be some truth in Lord's repeated claim that our contemporary literary poetries 'shrink from the habitual' and 'seek the unusual for its own sake'.[9] Their achievement in this regard has even been demonstrated experimentally. Ivan Fónagy published a lab-based study of verbal redundancy in 1961, 'redundancy' referring to the possibility of readers or listeners 'predicting the following elements of the text' on the basis of those already supplied.[10] Fónagy showed that subjects required prompting to guess 60 percent of the subsequent phonemes in a symbolist poem by Endre Adi, compared to only 33 percent of the phonemes in a newspaper article and only 29 percent in the conversation of two young girls.[11] Yuri Lotman, who cites this study, comments:

Our own experiments not only confirm the data of the Hungarian scholar, but also show that poems intuitively felt by a given informant as good were guessed with greater difficulty, that is, they have low redundancy for him. In bad poems, it grows sharply. This permits us to introduce objective criteria into an area that is most difficult for analysis and has traditionally been dealt with by the formula: *De Gustibus non disputandum est.*[12]

Jacques Rancière has theorised this drive to the unexpected at a more global level, in his characterisation of the turn that practices of verbal, visual, and plastic art have taken since the late eighteenth century. Dismissing the concept of modernism, as based on 'the completely simplistic image of a great anti-representational rupture' at the start of the twentieth century, when a break with representational strictures is just as palpable in Kant, Schiller and the Romantic artists they heralded, Rancière refers to this, our period from the Romantics to the present, as 'the aesthetic regime'.[13] It is a period in which the long-historied idea that only certain subjects are dignified enough to represent in serious arts is replaced by the idea of art as transgeneric practice which brings out, whatever the topic or medium, 'a new partition of the perceptible'.[14] The word 'new' is pertinent. In Rancière's neat phrase, 'The whole paradox of an aesthetic regime of art is that art defines itself by its very identity with non-art'.[15] This formulation evokes a type of art that demands its practitioners incorporate ever new aspects of experience, simply to maintain its identity as itself. This might happen at the level of diction, as Fónagy's experiment revealed. It might involve previously ignored or even shunned subject matter, as when Eliot included 'the typist home at teatime' in *The Waste Land*, the first time a female clerk had been treated as a subject in European letters outside light verse.[16] In the plastic arts, one finds whole new media become the vehicle for art, as when Marc Quinn freezes nine litres of his blood into a sculpture of his own head called *Self*, Damian Hirst decides to exhibit a shark, Marinetti to feed Italy spaghetti by radio.[17] Nor do the occasional 'revolts' in favour of an art of the boring and/or every day, seem to do much more than revive the dynamic Rancière identifies, bringing yet more of that which is at present extraneous to art into its fold, and so fulfilling our art's identity as somehow other to itself. An example would be John Baldessari's *I Will Not Make Any More Boring Art*, a lithograph in the MoMA collection, which Baldesssari's students created on the basis of one of his exercises and hung in his name. The line 'I will not make any more boring art' is inscribed 17 times in succession.[18] One thinks of prayer. This is not-art, and so belongs.

In contrast, an oral poet like Avdo Međedovič is 'deeply conservative' in his songs.

The strange area here has to do with how that conservatism manifests. Avdo Međedovič, 'religiously maintaining the meaning of a song' while repeating it 'verbatim', nonetheless feels free, as we have seen, to alter its order, to change its cast and to add extensive new ornament, to the point of almost tripling the size of the song.[19] Fónagy's experiment with text prediction, were it conducted upon such a population, might show that an oral epic poet like Međedovič and a modern symbolist poet like Endre Adi have more in common than Parry and Lord would lead us to believe. Are terms like originality and unoriginality really adequate to capture these kinds of nuances?

But even if it be granted that there is some relation in this regard between Homeric/Balkan poets, and the literary poets we interviewed, Lord's analysis of that 'gap between composition and reading or performance' operative within literary cultures, surely drives home the impossibility of using his or Parry's work to comprehend literary composition.[20] Lord may be offhand in his references to the 'leisure' literary poets enjoy when composing, and trivial in mocking their pretentiousness, but his capacity for formulating compelling challenges to blithe assumptions about supposed universals remains acute.[21] The following, one of the most famous passages of *The Singer of Tales*, puts severe strain on any attempt to relate the compositional practices of oral epic poets to those of poets composing for the page.

> Were we to seek to understand why a literary poet wrote what he did in a particular poem in a particular manner and form, we should not focus on the moment when he or someone else read or recited his poem to a particular audience or even on any moment when we ourselves read the poem in quiet solitude. We should instead attempt to reconstruct that moment in time when the poet wrote the lines. Obviously the moment of composition is the important one for such a study. For the oral poet the moment of composition is the performance. In the case of a literary poem there is a gap between composition and reading or performance; in the case of the oral poem this gap does not exist, because composition and performance are two aspects of the same moment. Hence, the question 'When *would* such an oral poem be performed?' has no meaning; the question should be 'When *was* the oral poem performed?' An oral poem is not composed for but in performance. The implications of this statement are both broad and deep.[22]

One can see why one of Lord's most well-known students, Gregory Nagy, would place such importance on this paragraph, and on its second-last sentence, in particular. Nagy describes the latter as the 'fundamental statement' of oral theory.[23] Widely quoted, the sentence gives in a nutshell the sharp challenge of Parry and Lord's ideas, insisting in concisely chosen words that we think again about the world we have long known: the 15,693 lines of *The Iliad,* the 12,110 of *The Odyssey*, were not composed once and for all, then later repeated by heart. Their transmission over centuries was improvised, each and every time. And this is how, throughout most of human history, verbal art has thrived. In short, the paragraph is a model of rigorous, summative thinking. And the broad distinctions it encapsulates are clearly correct. To make the obvious point: none of the poets we interviewed over 2006–2015 gave any impression of delivering anything other than a verbatim rendition of a pre-composed text, when they read their poems live. So when Marcella Polain performs the following lines live, these are the very words she will read, from the page:

our house looms bright and planetary
the neighbours pass
continual and silent

you catch in my throat
a long blue note that
plummets from me[24]

PERFORMING ON THE PAGE

It would, however, be remiss not to mention that Polain describes the composition of her poems in the very terms Lord so decisively cordons off for oral poetry. Polain told me in Perth in 2006 that her poems are composed performatively, as if she were acting them on a stage. I had been asking if it was necessary to be 'in the right mood' to compose. Or was it a matter of having no mood at all?

POLAIN. When composing I feel an openness. It's like going on stage. It's like going on stage and you have to have the same feeling of just being present. When you go on stage, you've done the rehearsal, and your body knows it, so it's a matter of putting aside any concerns about the words or the movement and entering into that space: just stepping onto the stage and just doing it. It's the same feeling.
INTERVIEWER. This is to compose?
POLAIN. To compose, yes.
INTERVIEWER. This is intriguing. People make a constant division between the performative and the creative arts on the grounds that one involves originality and the other involves some sort of rendition. Though I have encountered this

metaphor for composition before and I've thought about it as a metaphor for what I do when I write poetry.

POLAIN. Yes.

INTERVIEWER. When I write, it involves something like performance.

POLAIN. Yes.

INTERVIEWER. The question that this then begs is, is there an audience to your composing?

POLAIN. Is there an audience? I grapple with this all the time when teaching writing students. When they ask me, 'Do you write with an intended audience in mind?', I always feel I have to say 'No. I consciously have no concept of an audience'. But you see that's the same thing as going on stage. If I thought about audiences and went on stage, I would freeze. You have to have a sense of audience, but then you go out there and act as if nobody's watching you. You know they are, of course. There's a part of you that knows there are people there, but the part that you draw on to be able to do what you do has to put that knowledge aside. I don't think it's been the case for a long, long time that I really wrote without thinking that someone else is going to read it. I want people to read it. But that's really quite separate at the moment of writing. It can't be there.[25]

Our interview archive abounds with metaphors from performance, once discussion turns to composition. Recall G. C. Waldrep's statement that when writing he does not 'know more than a line or two ahead. If I know two lines ahead where the poem is going, that's unusual and strange. I don't where it's going and that's part of the fun of it, that kind of tightrope walk in the composition'.[26] Waldrep's metaphor is interesting, in the light of Polain's comments on the actor's distance from the audience. After all, tight-rope walking is not an artform we associate with interaction, though the act is, of course, performed in front of a (typically anxious) audience. One thinks of inward focus. But however that may be, Waldrep's analogy to the practice also tempers Lord's severe contrast between oral and literary poetries, artforms distinguished, as Lord would have it, on the grounds that, of the two, only the oral form is composed '*in* performance'.

We are moving into very metaphoric territory here. After all, neither Polain's nor Waldrep's analogies for composition attenuate the stark truth of Lord's observation that oral poets do not offer verbatim renditions. Nor do those oral poets revise. An Avdo Međedovič performance is first-time only. Our written performances dissimulate that condition, over the long duration of a multiply-staged compositional process involving a great deal of revision. But is it not also the case that one of the best ways to generate the feeling of a sustained, in-the-moment, utterance is to produce it in the moment? The comment might apply to revision as well.

Don Paterson's observations on composition are even more redolent of what Lord calls 'rapid composing in performance'.[27] Paterson doubles as a jazz guitarist. Asked by Kevin Brophy whether composing poetry is similar to composing music, Paterson responds that for him it is. He then has a rethink: 'One can compose to order. You can sit down and just do it. Whereas poetry you can't really do in the same way. But it's a similar process'. This leads to a further about-face, 'Oh God! No. No, really, I think the difference is that, when you are writing a poem, that's performance'.[28]

Paterson proceeds to describe playing live jazz. You spend a great deal of prior time practising, much of it mechanical: 'a lot of it is just arpeggios, practice, you know, keep the chops up'. Then there is playing: 'And when you play there should be nothing in your head, the instrument should be playing you, you should be surprising yourself continually because you are, ideally, in a Zen-like state. You've done all the prep and you just have to play. I see that as analogous to the art of poetic composition'. The poetry has its own form of practice: 'You do your reading, you think about it, you think about technique, you think about your *ars poetica*, about great, large spiritual concerns and metaphysical quibbles'. All of this prepares the poet, so that

> when the clouds part and there's nothing in your head, you can sit down and perform. You don't have to think about where a pentameter line ending goes, all your metrical tempos are part of your motor skills, you know how rhyme works, you don't have to think about it consciously. It's performative–for me. That is where the magic, if you like, if it is going to happen, will happen. It is in that state. These are analogous scenarios.[29]

Paterson added at that point that 'gigging with a guitar' and 'reading out of a book' in public have nothing in common: 'So why we use the word "gig" about a reading, when it is just reading out of a book you've already written, I don't know. But writing a poem is a gig'.[30]

One might, of course, point out that these literary poets are not composing in performance conditions at all. No one is going to get anxious at too much dead air. A poet might even forget what they are doing and just stare at the wall. And there will necessarily be a delay between the poet's writing and the reader's reception. We have not bridged the gap which Lord identifies at all. Nor have we addressed that other glaring issue here, the gulf between the composition of speech in real-time, and whatever writing practice is being referenced in these metaphors of acting, tight-rope walking, playing music live. But there are curious resonances here, all the same.

To explore them, let us hone in on the strange fact noted above, that even as Polain, Waldrep, Paterson and others describe composition in vividly performative terms, audience interaction does not seem to be the point. Paterson, for instance, responded to a question about whether he had to be in a certain mood to compose with the aphorism that Beethoven 'ascended to heaven on a ladder of frozen tears'. The process, Paterson continued, 'is cold. . . . Often you are not moved until you are your own reader. Then you realise that you have written something that moves you as a human being, but did not move you as a composer'.[31] The inward intensity described or connoted in Polain, Paterson and Waldrep's responses leads me to link them with a second set of interview responses. Though these do not concern stage-work *per se*, they do associate composing with an intense and immediate experience of the present moment, a moment that is clearly performative in nature.

Consider Eiléan Ni Chuilleanáin's reply to Kevin Brophy's question as to whether composing and editing feel like similar processes. Ni Chuilleanáin's immediate response was 'I think not. When composing you are really down in there, it flows up over your ears'. She further described it as 'descending, being plunged in and wanting to exclude everything else. It's not even like trying to get dinner ready for six people when it's ten minutes to the hour. It's more intense than that'.[32]

Maxine Chernoff spoke about being alert and open: 'You start with some active attention. But you do not know where the active attention is going to take you'.[33] I asked if this characterised the production of Chernoff's programmatic works as well, for instance, her book *Without*, a collection of 64, mostly one-page poems on things that lack (specific poems include 'Without Coherence', 'Without Heretical Texts', 'Without Number', 'Without Strangeness' and 'Without Years').[34] Chernoff commented: 'Obviously when I have a project that has a concept, I am going into it with a concept. But I do not know where the poem is going to take me, or what the poem is. It is only through writing it, that I discover that'. The poem that results will go through 'many, many dry-run drafts. I write a zillion drafts at once, and usually, by the end of a day, I have a poem that is pretty much there'. I asked if any sensory modality seemed uppermost during those moments of active attending.

CHERNOFF. The visual definitely seems to be the main one when I am sitting and writing. When I am re-reading and re-writing, the sonic comes in. It is not that my ear is dead and suddenly it is alive. It is that I look to the visual first.
INTERVIEWER. And would you be actually seeing what you are describing in your mind's eye, and working from that?
CHERNOFF. That would require things to be seeded in my mind longer than they usually are when I compose. It is quick. And there are a lot of changes, a lot of metamorphoses in my writing. I do not usually stay with one scene very long. My scenes are more based in those moments when your attention shifts, and my interest in the writing is in how one's attention shifts within a poem, to include what the poem eventually contains – but not in a single shot. I am not

doing continuous shots that add up to a poem. I am doing many quick shots, that make up the poem.[35]

We are back to an analogy between composition and staging, though here the medium is cinematic. We all know the dizzying experience of watching a film as its 'kino-eye' leaps and shifts.[36] That is Chernoff's metaphor for the sort of attention she engages in composition. It sounds like a description of being a movie much more than appearing in one. And again, note how the dialogics of the writing appear much more focussed on a conversation internal to the artist/artwork, than with any assumed figure of the audience.

Polain, Waldrep, Paterson, Ni Chuilleanáin and Chernoff's theatrical and otherwise performative analogies for writing poetry problematise Lord's picture of that gap between the composition and the performance of literary verse, while keeping decidedly intact the gap Lord identified between the occasions of a literary poem's composition and the occasions on which it is performed, that is read to an audience, or in the reader's head. We can see, all the same, how important performative and in-the-moment compositional practices are to so many of the poets we interviewed, as a sheer matter of technique.

AUTHOR BEING MULTIPLE

I will keep heading in this direction over the remainder of this chapter, aiming to provide a fuller sense of what the interviews suggest of the poets' practices, and in particular to underline their diversity. As we have just seen, some of those interview descriptions of composing tally well with the idea that the poet's words arrive (in those moments when they do arrive) with the suddenness that research at the coalface between linguistics and psychology suggests they necessarily must. But other poets set little store by that. To them, what counts is staying the course, over innumerable such instances, so much so that it would be misleading to think of their work in terms of what transpires in the immediacy of the given moment. As far as they are concerned, the poet is the one who brings that whole plethora of disparate moments together.

Parry's ideas can spark another curious parallel here. Consider his stress on the trans-individual nature of Homeric poetry, as the product of a whole culture (for Parry, writing in 1923, the word is 'race') that has composed hit and miss down the centuries to bequeath a fully fledged diction, and a coherent set of stories, to each successive generation: 'The poetry was not one in which a poet must use his own words and try as best as he might to utilize the possibilities of meter. It was a poetry which for centuries had accumulated all such possibilities – all the turns of language, all the words, phrases and effects of position, which had pleased the race'.[37] What if we were to take this idea of collective poetic composition as an image for these contemporary poets who work not for centuries but over months and years to accumulate the manifold 'turns of language, all the words, phrases and effects of position' that pleased them amid attempt after attempt, drawing on, but also ultimately negating, that two to three seconds of focal consciousness that we (as subsequent chapters shall argue) inhabit as our existential lot? Hegel wrote that 'reflection, feeling, or whatever form subjective consciousness may take is actual only in the present'.[38] True, but one can also accumulate many such presents, to construct larger continuities out of them. What else could it mean, to create a life?

Yet even for poets inclined to prioritise the aspects of their practice that involve accumulating and managing past and future moments, there is clearly still something compelling about those inspired instants, times when, at least metaphorically, 'Singing, performing and composing are facets of the same act' (Lord).[39] In spite of C. K. Williams's opposition to the Auden quotation, he mentioned experiencing them, when I asked him the same question I had put to Polain. Do you have to be 'in the right mood' to compose? Williams replied, 'I wouldn't call it mood – that's too vague a word'.[40] But he continued that 'there is definitely a condition of consciousness that allows for the composition of poetry, and it's a quite shifty condition'. Williams said that it has to do with assuming a receptivity to connections between music and meaning, two key themes in our discussion to that point, then added,

> but it's even more complex than that. Something happens to you, you never really know quite what, and your mind starts working poetically. I can't force it, I just prepare myself for it, and wait for it, and try to be patient, which is never easy. And sometimes it happens, and sometimes it doesn't. That waiting is the hardest part of my life as a poet. I've never been very patient about anything. Or anything beside writing poetry.[41]

Kenneth Goldsmith described the way in which ideas come to him for his programmatic works in terms of a similar receptivity. It is a matter of attending to what is 'spontaneously generated' in certain, unpredictable moments. 'I think some of my best ideas are spontaneously generated. Or at least, I don't know where I come up with them. I really don't. Like, "Wow, great idea, print the internet". I would say that usually they're reactive. They're reactive to something that happens in life. And then it's like: 'I've got to go and do that. Bam'''.[42] This was surprising, given Goldsmith himself describes his works as 'uncreative'. A case in point would be *Day*, a 750 page book containing Goldsmith's transcription of every single word of one day's edition of the *New York Times*.[43] He told me in response to the question about mood that the writing of such works is 'secretarial, it's closer to programming. There's no emotion involved, it's sheer drudgery, and one does not need to be in a certain mood, or to feel spontaneous at all. There's something to be done and one must get through it regardless. What I do is mechanical'. The other reason I was surprised by Goldsmith's embrace of spontaneity at this point was because his earlier response to our Auden quotation had been forthright and negative. The idea that one might come up with 'something new that has never been said or heard before' struck him as particularly 'ignorant'.[44]

Yet Goldsmith also stated that he thought it 'possible to take things that have been said before and put them together in ways that they haven't been put together before: the idea of the remix'.[45] The notion goes at least as far back as Descartes's observation that the strange entities we perceive when dreaming are simply fusions of the things we already know. Consciously fictitious images were for Descartes cases of 'remix' too: 'For indeed when painters themselves wish to represent satyrs and sirens by means of especially bizarre forms, they surely cannot assign to them utterly new natures. Rather, they simply fuse together the members of various animals'.[46] Compare linguist Wallace Chafe's comment that 'imagined experiences . . . always have some basis in reality'. If 'people have never seen unicorns, they have at least seen horses and rhinoceroses'. This sounds like a paraphrase of Descartes, and perhaps it is. But it is worth noting the far-reaching insight in the comment to follow: 'Combining them is a process not wholly different in kind from remembering'.[47]

Still responding to Auden, and now tempering his initial comment on spontaneity, Goldsmith proceeded to explain how he had the idea for *The Weather* – and thereby for the 'American trilogy' of books *Traffic*, *Weather* and *Sports*, each of which comprise the transcription of a year's daily radio reports on their respective topics. Goldsmith's friend, Alan Licht, had

> composed a little audio piece of 10/10 WINS weather reports. . . . I listened to Alan's piece and I almost cried. . . . It brought back memories of my childhood growing up in New York. It was a beautiful sound, the language had a very specific sound, and it mentioned a lot of the geography. I listened to this thing. I really reacted very strongly to it, and then said, 'I want to make a textual version of that'. And once I did that, I realised that there were other things on the radio, other types of language. So it was very internalised. All this stuff came out of memory. It came out of nostalgia. It came out of my attachment to place, to geography, being a lifelong New Yorker, the sound of radio, the accents and the voices. So that whole series derived probably from the same place where C. K. Williams writes his poems. That's actually the genesis of that project. But the output is very, very different.[48]

The irony in Goldsmith's identification with Williams on this matter of spontaneous, reactive utterance is, as we have seen, that Williams rejected the idea that suddenness counts for all that much, compared to bringing one's poem to a finish. Williams believed it the very nature of art to feel 'spontaneous, almost improvised' – but only to its readers. For in fact, those moments come about 'syllable-by-syllable'. That 'shifty condition' where 'your mind starts working poetically' may well be essential to composition, but it is otherwise not so important to Williams.

Incidentally, there was a reason Goldsmith was referring to Williams at this point. In his monograph, *Uncreative Writing: Managing Literature in the Digital Age*, Goldsmith describes how during a public lecture he gave at Princeton, 'an elderly, well known poet, steeped in modernism, stood up in the back of the auditorium and, wagging his finger at me, accused me of nihilism and of robbing poetry of its joy'.[49] When Goldsmith learned of the other poets I was interviewing, he added that Williams – the poet in question – not only attacked him in this public fashion, but also stopped in the middle of that attack, to answer a call there and then on his mobile phone. Each was surprised to learn I was also talking to the other.

'Give him a big bear hug from me', Goldsmith said.[50]

I laughed.

It would be wrong, at any rate, to overplay Goldsmith's espousal of spontaneity. What he said on the matter was strictly to do with how he generates the concept for an artwork. The content of his books is laboriously collected in the various programmatic ways those works entail. One could not ignore this self-styled 'drudgery' in any discussion of his stance on the 'spontaneously generated'.

Nor can we forget that for poets like C. D. Wright ('It is not possible to retain the child's spontaneity'), the writing is so disparately generated and rewritten that terms like 'rough draft' and 'revision' start to lose all analytic purchase.[51] Earlier we saw Wright describe composition as 'a building project, laborious, sometimes tedious', where one struggles to be 'bold enough to put a whole garage of lousy words down'. That garage is not for public display. It is the storehouse from which Wright draws her materials. But her writing is not just akin to building. It is also like painting:

WRIGHT. I like a very incisive language. At the same time, I really like a lot of texture. So that means I build up the paint. Even though I like something to be very clean, I am likewise attracted to layering.
INTERVIEWER. Can you elaborate on that?
WRIGHT. Layering in and laying in different registers of language. I am not enthralled with a smooth, overly consistent language.

INTERVIEWER. Is it something to do with giving the reader a sense of the physicality of the words?
WRIGHT. Yes, physicality. I also think that if it's not all in the same register, it makes the work more animate.
INTERVIEWER. So it is about subverting language's capacity to serve just for information? It is about getting into all those other spaces?
WRIGHT. It can be hard to get up in those spaces. Everything having been written. Everything having been said. You still have to get up in those spaces.[52]

Construction, architecture, painting, carpentry: Wright's metaphors have very little to do with stage-craft. I think of that Raymond Carver short story, where a character remarks upon cathedrals that took so long to build no individual artisan could ever have seen the full construction process to which they had devoted their entire life.[53] It has always struck me that Carver was reflecting on writing there, the way an author's slow building of something as short as a short story necessarily involves the work of innumerable past selves, whose enthusiasms and pains proved shorter than the construction itself.

Wright also referred to collecting, to inquiry, and to generational interactions:

> The words for seeing things can come later. But I make the notes on the spot. Finding the right words is a finicky, time-eating pursuit. I like words *period*. All tracks of diction. Trashy language, *haute* language, archaic language, colloquial, idiomatic, specialized. I have some facility for metaphor (my father, by the way, was keen on words too). The right words, as I said, come later. I like to move close to the edges of what I see.[54]

Note, to add a further element to our picture of contemporary practices, that in the very interview in which Marcella Polain described composing in terms of 'stepping onto the stage', she also characterised the act of writing as infinitely slow and difficult.[55] In fact, Polain sounded very like Wright at such moments. When asked how fast she wrote, Polain observed that other poets she knew would write copiously, and then have the problem of trying to reduce. But 'I've never had that problem. I can't even imagine having that problem because it's always the reverse: I'm tweezering things out'. During the composition of Polain's first book of poems, *Dumbstruck*, she wrote 'line by line. A line would come, maybe a second, and then I would have to leave it and just carry it around with me until another line or two came. Maybe four lines would come at once after that and then I would leave it, and that's the way most of that work was done. Not all of it'.[56] Actually, Polain's process had changed since *Dumbstruck*, a fact she attributed to having written a novel in the meantime. A first draft might now emerge in a single sitting. It may be that the theatrical analogy quoted at length above related solely to this newer phase in her composing. But it did not sound that way. Again and again in our interview archive one finds references to those inspired times when 'Singer, performer, composer, and poet are one'.[57] But it is also almost always the case that such reports come side by side with reference to other, more 'time-eating' (Wright) compositional modes.[58]

In some of the interviews, reports of a slower mode were relegated to the poet's past. Though describing himself as practitioner of in-the-moment composition, Don Paterson also referred to his days of hyper-revision in the late 1990s and early 2000s. A poem 'would go through 90 or a 100 drafts'. Now, on the other hand, 'I tend to write more things that I don't immediately understand because I am spending less time with them, but I don't think that's a bad thing. I think that maybe means some of the subjects are coming from a more unconscious place'. Paterson has left the days of '90 or a 100' drafts behind, in favour of a different sort of multiplicity.[59] But almost all of the other interviewees who made reference to a rapid, performative mode of composition acknowledged their practice of slower ways of working. These may be performative in their own right. Each of these modes might have multiple distinct versions. But however that might be, the main point here is that C. D. Wright and Don Paterson were rare in reporting a current practice so thoroughly one way or the other. Most poets described a mix.

Even the characterisation of Wright as a thoroughgoing reviser needs some hedging. For though she diminished the personal significance of any kind of epiphanic mode, she did indicate occasional enjoyment of it, as when I queried her about the value of spontaneity:

> That's the real deal: when something unexpected looms up. You were half unaware that you had actually prepared, or that you had so tuned your eyes and ears. It is an ultra-sweet moment. For spontaneity, much preparation. You have to be there and for adults it doesn't show up often enough. It is not possible to retain the child's spontaneity. There *are child-like* artists, who are wondrous. They may be cases of arrested development, but for spontaneity you cannot match them. Yet you aspire to be present for the times when there is a flash that you could not have laid out so specifically.[60]

So, sometimes the right words do come suddenly. But even as Wright refers to such a mode, she counters that her practice is overwhelmingly in an accretive mode, practised over multiple moments, slowly building them up.

Much more typical than the responses of either Wright or Paterson were reports of situations in which the poet composes stretches with suddenness, and yet also partakes of the kind of personally 'collective' effort noted above, corralling the multiple efforts of past selves into one and the same poem.

Rae Armantrout's practice of different compositional modes emerged in the following exchange:

INTERVIEWER. How fast do you compose?
ARMANTROUT. It really varies. Sometimes I write slowly and sometimes I write quickly. A few of my most successful poems – successful, in that a lot of people like them – I wrote very quickly. But that is not always the case. One poem I like a lot took me several months to write, and it's short. But on the other hand I have written a poem in a few hours. It really varies.[61]

The previous two chapters addressed works of textual and ethnographic scholarship for insights into how the sometime practice of rapid composing Armantrout refers to here might be humanly and/or culturally possible. The progression of this book has been to indicate something of that sudden mode's pertinence to the present scene. But the intermittency of such practices needs to be just as surely underlined, and the will power it takes to keep building works on their basis acknowledged. For it seems just as clear that the poets interviewed partake of that other 'Parryan' quality, to do with how a poem might be handed down from one self to another self of the very same poet, till finally achieving a kind of collective voice, publicly ascribed to the one individual poet, now fully responsibilised as said poem's author.

Some comment on the role the other individuals play in generating a poet's work is also called for. No discussion of the cognitive mechanisms by which people write poetry would be complete without reference to such social authorship. The interview archive is unambiguous here: the judgement of selective others is regularly drawn upon. Those significant readers help to author a poet's works as his or her own, as Williams attests in the following exchange.

INTERVIEWER. Let me ask you about the broader poetic community. What part is played in your practice by your relationship to other poets?
WILLIAMS. Over the years it's been very important to me. I've always had friends, poet friends, to whom I send my work and who criticise it and make suggestions. For many years the most important for me was Galway Kinnell. We'd work on each other's poems, as I say, judge and suggest, and Galway is a genius. I learned so much from him. The last few years we've sort of fallen away from doing that, we're more each into our own work. But I never consider a poem done until a friend has seen it and put that extra glare of light on it. It's a very strange thing – as soon as you give the poem to someone else, even before they read it, it shifts a little, it becomes slightly something else from what you had thought it was, and you begin to look at it in a slightly different way. You see your little errors and smudges, and places where you've

let yourself cheat a little bit. It's always been very crucial to me to have other poets looking at my work. Over the years there have been different poets: for a long time Steve Berg, more recently Robert Pinsky and Alan Shapiro and Alicia Ostriker. But I have to have someone looking at poems before I consider them finished.[62]

Williams's suggestion that an 'extra glare of light' is necessary for him to consider a poem 'finished' is interesting in terms of the quotation from Albert Lord that I have been considering through this chapter: 'Were we to seek to understand why a literary poet wrote what he did . . . we should not focus on the moment when he or someone else read or recited his poem to a particular audience'.[63] On the evidence of Williams's words here, recital to a first reader can be part of the reason a poet wrote what they did and, for instance, stopped changing it. Again, this does not overly diminish the power of Lord's illuminating distinction between oral and literary poets, advanced on the grounds that in the literary poet's case composition and performance are separate phenomena. But it does suggest Lord's oppositions are too rigid. Judging by the interviews, performance to others regularly contributes to the generation of literary verse.

In Kevin Young's case that 'extra glare of light' literally does come from being before an audience. We were in a café just outside the Emory campus in Atlanta, on a mid-winter day in 2014. I asked Young if there were people to whom he showed drafts.

YOUNG. Not particularly. Not until much later – I would not show drafts of individual poems, but rather a book manuscript draft. And then it is usually too late.
    I am much more a lone wolf.
INTERVIEWER. But your editor?
YOUNG. I would not send her a poem. I will never do that.
INTERVIEWER. You will send her a full manuscript.
YOUNG. Yes. I guess magazine editors can sometimes serve as that early reader. But having edited, myself, I know there are so many things to do with timing. I mean, you can send the right poem to the right person at the wrong time. There are many permutations of that. I tend to hold pretty tight to the things. I find public readings much more the place where I would try out a draft. It will be pretty far along, frankly. But that is where I work.
INTERVIEWER. Is it a matter of gauging by an audience response?
YOUNG. No.
    INTERVIEWER. It is about gauging by your response, as you hear it in public?
YOUNG. Yes. Audience response is not always the best meter.[64]

It is important to add that Young's 'lone wolf' approach does not seem to be all that common, from the evidence of the interviews. That said, Don Paterson was another poet who reported not showing drafts to anyone prior to the publication process.

Pertinently, Paterson does report having participated in a highly competitive workshop environment, back at the start of his career, in London. This was in the early 1980s: 'Really good people came along. You really had to have your shit together come Wednesday night. . . . It was a form of publication'. Paterson favours workshops when the sense of publication is so palpable: 'You worried about what these people were going to think. You take a great deal more care about it that way'. That was long ago for Paterson, and he now clearly regards it as a developmental stage.[65] In contrast, most of the interviewed poets reported that they do show work prior to publication, not as a learning strategy but, rather, as part of the very process of producing it.

What emerged from those discussions, with only very few exceptions, is that those first readers are usually very close to the poet. G. C. Waldrep, for instance, shares drafts by email 'with a few, just a very few friends, and not all the time'. He mentioned Dana Levin in Santa Fe, Ilya Kaminsky in San Diego and John Gallagher in Missouri, all poets. They 'know me intimately, they know my work intimately. They've read pretty much everything I've published'. On the other hand,

> they don't write like I do. They're not instantly approving of what I do. I have to sell it to them, I guess. Given my very different aesthetic, I try to see if I can I convince any two of them – two out of the three – to understand what I'm doing and to appreciate it. Dana and I go back and forth on line-editing all the time. With Ilya and John, it's more macro-level responses. And no, I don't take most of their direction. That's not the point. The point is to give the work to a trusted reader and get a response.[66]

This was in contrast to Waldrep's earlier experience of workshops during his Iowa MFA, and then at the Middlebury Bread Loaf Writers' Conference. In those cases, it was more a matter of sifting out 'useful bits' amid the 'boatloads of advice from people who clearly didn't understand what I was doing'.[67] Noelle Kocot found her experiences of a highly combative workshop environment at the University of Florida 'formative, in that it made me immune to criticism if I thought something was good. It made me not care. It gave me an ego of steel'.[68] Whereas for Brook Emery, starting out in workshops was 'rather good – not because of what people would say about my poetry, but because it allowed me to feel the territory a little'.[69] In general, workshopping seemed less about improving one's poems than about developing a sense of self in relation to the community one will come to inhabit.

Turning back to the first reader, or readers, the singularity of the relationship at the basis of that exchange is a consistent theme in the interviews. It is a striking fact that five of the 14 poets I interviewed over 2013–2015 stated that their first reader was, or had been in the past, their intimate partner. When this was not the case, the poet–first reader relationship was characterised by very close friendship. Rae Armantrout sends poems to Lydia Davis and Lyn Hejinian at times, but always to Ron Silliman.

> We went to college together at Berkeley. Sometimes we exchange several emails a day. We also play *Words With Friends* – an online scrabble game. I send him pretty much everything I write, and if he hates it, I will really think twice about it. Sometimes we get in arguments. But he does not send me what he writes. He just has a different process. He makes good editorial suggestions, because he has been looking at my work for so long.[70]

I have already cited C. K. Williams on his practice of sending poems out to poet friends. But Williams's 'constant first reader', he went on to say, was his wife, Catherine, who is not a poet but a jeweller.[71]

Paul Hoover's comment on the first readings which he and Maxine Chernoff used to perform on each other's work while married provides insight into why poets would so consistently elect close, rather than anonymous, first readers:

> It was a simple process. We would read it out loud, and the other person would say something like, 'Well, that bit at the end – I think you should look at that again.' Or, 'I think you have a weak beginning.' We would then read the complete work, for a second check. It was not a formalised process in which you mark up the text. That is too intrusive, and, in a way, too commanding. Knowing the other would object to weak work, we would always polish our drafts very well before presenting them.[72]

This suggests that one's awareness that a specific other will be reading one's poem might have a proleptic effect on the revising (or even composing) of it. One might start to borrow those eyes, and even something of their relation to suddenness.

Forrest Gander and C. D. Wright were the first readers of each other's poems. The couple also spent many years as co-editors of the small press, *Lost Roads*. Gander reported reading work for a number of poets as a consequence of relationships forged during those days. I asked him about that editing work. His comments have much to say about the first reader relationship, and why it might best be trusted to people who know one well.

INTERVIEWER. When you're reading manuscripts in an editorial capacity, does that feel like the same process as reading your own work? Are you using the same eyes?

GANDER. My first impulse is to say that I can't ever get that kind of objectivity on my own work. But it's also that I'm judging other people's work by what the work asks from me. I am judging it by what is particular to that person's poetics. My own work is connected to my own poetics. So they're different kinds of critiques.[73]

Later in our discussion, Gander expanded on the idea that each poet requires a personally specific critique:

GANDER. This is what Zukofsky and Pound talk about in terms of 'a measure', the idea being that one's 'measure' has to be particular. One's sincerity is identifiable and uncounterfeitable and all one's own. That's why this guy writing in this new edition of Harper's magazine, who thinks that current poets should sound like Shelley, is so ridiculous. It's not good enough to be working in the terms of someone else's sublime. You have to make your own sublime.[74]

Gander's comments help to explain why the poets we interviewed so often selected first readers from those with whom they had had close and long relationships. These are the people who have already broken through the threshold of acquaintance, and so are in a better position to judge the poem 'by what is particular to that person's poetics', as Gander put it. One knows this intuitively from reading new books. One might need to read three or four poems before realising how good they are. Similarly, it might take three or four poems to work out they are bad. A first reader is already there, at that space of unique possibility (and customary shortfall).

Another question concerned whether published critical reviews of a poet's work, or scholarship on it, had ever led to a change of practice. C. K. Williams's reply to this question was representative: 'No . . . I definitely haven't had anything written about my poems that would make me change my mind about how I do things'. I underline that this comment applied only to reviews in print. 'In private', Williams continued, 'I've had people say about a poem, "That's awful", and I know I have to start over or throw the poem away'.[75] Rae Armantrout's response to the question was also negative: a review had never lead to a change of practice. A review was generally a good thing, all the same: 'I like to get reviews, because I like people to hear about the book. Of course', she added, 'I hate to get bad reviews. But poetry does not tend to get a lot of bad reviews'. Commenting that she only started receiving bad reviews on winning the Pulitzer Prize for *Versed*, Armantrout added that 'prior to that sort of situation, if people do not like a poem, they just ignore it'.[76]

Armantrout was not the only poet to experience the U.S. reviewing culture as lacking in bite. Reviews tend to be 'puffy', Waldrep told me, while Noelle Kocot noted, 'They're not going to review your book if they don't have something stellar to say about it. After a while, it all blends into everything else'.[77] Armantrout's comment on the (post-Pulitzer) experience of receiving bad reviews was illuminating.

> Whether I really care about a bad review depends on who the reviewer is. If it is somebody whose poetry I like, and they do not like my poetry, then that hurts me. If it is somebody who is obviously coming from a very different perspective, or has different values, then it does not bother me much. Good reviews can sometimes be problematic too, because sometimes people want to categorise you in a way you do not particularly care to be categorised. Maybe they are praising you, but you still are not all that happy. It is very hard to make people happy with reviews. But you have to try to just say, 'Well, if they didn't totally trash me, they're getting the name of the book out there, so good'.[78]

The reference to potential hurt makes clear that public reviewing can certainly have intimate impacts upon a poet. But the general pragmatism of Armantrout's comments underlines that the critical directions one might take with one's art are not really what is at stake there. This is consonant with our interviews with poets in other countries, and also chimes with what Australian poets told me a decade earlier. Public, critical reviewing of one's work does not have much aesthetic input on the future productions of the poet reviewed. It is not part of the social authorship of the poems.

C. D. Wright had an interesting comment here. We were in Petaluma, CA, in a large living room, with a wide window looking over the city to the distant scree.

INTERVIEWER. What about other inputs into your work? Do you, for instance, set any store by critical reviews?
WRIGHT. A critical review, if about someone else's work, might give me ideas.
INTERVIEWER. About another's work?
WRIGHT. Yes. Some operative insight about writing.
> On the other hand, I might be reading a poet I admire a lot and part of the gratification is overridden by wondering, 'How did she do that? Is that something I can do and make my own?' I read with covetous, vested interest; with a sense that I really would like to reach such exactitude on my own terms. I want to be a virtuoso. (Ambitious). So I look to other virtuosos to figure out 'How is this done?' (Naïve.) I am interested in techniques, and strategies, artfulness put together out of somebody else's consciousness – the practical effects that I have missed, whatever offers a little idea, a wee leap to attempt.[79]

I recognise in Wright's words something of my own motivation for interviewing so many poets over the last two decades, here in Australia, and there in the States, where I lived as a child.

NOTES

1. Parry, "Oral Verse-Making I," 279–301.
2. Lord, *Singer of Tales*, 2.
3. Lord, 44–45.
4. Lord, 4.
5. Lord, 17.
6. Taplin, *Homeric Soundings*, 26–31.
7. Lord, *Singer of Tales*, 22.
8. Lord, 35–36.
9. Lord, 65.
10. Fónagy, qtd in Lotman, *Analysis of the Poetic Text*, 282, fn29.
11. Lotman, 33.
12. Lotman, 282, fn.31.
13. Rancière, "Politics and Aesthetics," 206.
14. Rancière, "Aesthetic Revolution," 140.
15. Rancière, "Politics and Aesthetics," 206.
16. Rainey, "Introduction," 22.
17. Quinn, "Self"; Hirst, "The Physical Impossibility"; Kirshenblatt-Gimblett, "Barbara Kirshenblatt-Gimblett on Edible Art."
18. Baldessari, "I Will Not Make Any More Boring Art."
19. Lord, *Singer of Tales*, 109.
20. Lord, 13.
21. Lord, 22, 65, 128.
22. Lord, 13.
23. Nagy, *Homeric Questions*, 17.
24. Polain, "when bees see blue."
25. Magee, "Marcella Polain Interview," 43.
26. Waldrep, interview by author, July 9, 2013.
27. Paterson, interview by Kevin Brophy, July 2, 2013; Lord, *Singer of Tales*, 17.
28. Paterson.
29. Paterson.
30. Paterson.
31. Paterson.
32. Ni Chuilleanáin, interview by Kevin Brophy, June 17, 2013.
33. Chernoff, interview by author, November 17, 2014.
34. Chernoff, *Without*.
35. Chernoff, interview by author, November 17, 2014.
36. Vertov, "Kinoks-Revolution."
37. Parry, "Comparative Study of Diction," 425.
38. Hegel, *Philosophy of Right*, 10.
39. Lord, *Singer of Tales*, 12.
40. Magee, "Interview with C. K. Williams," 102.
41. Magee, 102.
42. Goldsmith, interview by author, July 6, 2013.

43. Goldsmith, *Day*.
44. Goldsmith, interview by author, July 6, 2013.
45. Goldsmith.
46. Descartes, *Meditations*, 11.
47. Chafe, *Discourse, Consciousness and Time*, 33.
48. Goldsmith, interview by author, July 6, 2013.
49. Goldsmith, *Uncreative Writing*, 15.
50. Goldsmith, interview by author, July 6, 2013.
51. Wright, "An Interview."
52. Wright.
53. Carver, "Cathedral," 224.
54. Wright, "An Interview."
55. Magee, "Marcella Polain Interview," 43.
56. Magee, 40.
57. Lord, *Singer of Tales*, 13.
58. Wright, "An Interview."
59. Paterson, interview by Kevin Brophy, July 13, 2013.
60. Wright, "An Interview."
61. Armantrout, interview by author, November 11, 2014.
62. Magee, "Interview with C. K. Williams," 93–94.
63. Lord, *The Singer of Tales*, 13.
64. Young, interview by author, July 20, 2014.
65. Paterson, interview by Kevin Brophy, July 13, 2013.
66. Waldrep, interview by author, July 9, 2013.
67. Waldrep.
68. Kocot, interview by author, July 13, 2013.
69. Emery, interview by author, October 25, 2014.
70. Armantrout, interview by author, November 11, 2014.
71. Magee, "Interview with C. K. Williams," 94.
72. Hoover, interview by author, November 14, 2014.
73. Magee and Gander, "Paul Magee Interviews Forrest Gander."
74. Magee and Gander.
75. Magee, "Interview with C. K. Williams," 95.
76. Armantrout, *Versed*; Armantrout, interview by author, November 11, 2014.
77. Waldrep, interview by author, July 9, 2013; Kocot, interview by author, July 13, 2013.
78. Armantrout, interview by author, November 11, 2014.
79. Wright, "An Interview."

Chapter 7

Oral Verse in Performance

The reader might still find it hard to accept that the Homeric materials discussed over the previous two chapters could offer even loose parallels to the claims in some of our interviews. What about the formulas and formula systems, the typical arming or messenger scenes, the larger story patterns like the return, the return-rescue, the feud and so on? Surely they point to an artform that is worlds away from the verse we write and publish today? Without attempting the absurd task of equating oral and written poetries, I will argue that Homeric scholarship becomes much more available for supporting contemporary references to speech-like compositional practices among writers, once certain recent developments in the field are considered. These developments undermine the tendency of an earlier generation of Homerists to explain the extraordinary fact of 'rapid composing in performance' by treating the oral poet as mouthpiece for a pre-existing code.[1] Such mechanising trends course through Parry and Lord's writings, where they clash strangely with moments as contrary and thought-provoking as Lord's far-reaching claim, of those same formulas and themes, that 'the speaker of this language, once he [*sic*] has mastered it, does not move any more mechanically within it than we do in ordinary speech'.[2] Scholars since the 1990s have furthered the idea of a Homer who is actually just performing a variant upon speaking, often quoting this sentence of Lord's as they do so.[3] In the works of the decades since then, the author of *The Iliad* and *The Odyssey* has emerged as someone, a whole succession of someone's, who composed their formula-run utterance by way of the very aptitudes and strategies we ourselves draw on when telling stories – albeit with more of an ear to music.

Key to these developments has been the idea that the Homeric poems constitute the record, albeit in verse, of a storyteller who is thinking in the moment. Discussing the poems' distinctively processual syntax, Egbert J. Bakker notes that 'the Homeric poet, in beginning a stretch of discourse, does not yet know how he is to end it, as the text he produces is a dynamic process rather than a fixed product'.[4] *The Iliad* and *The Odyssey* appear in such work like the transcripts of a speaker who does not quite have the words ready to do his storytelling bidding, has to find them in the moment, and conveys the energy of that processual thinking into his albeit traditional lines. That is to say, the Homeric poems are being increasingly taken in contemporary scholarship as documentary evidence of an ancient Greek version of Auden's figure of the genuine speaker, finding out what that speaker has to say in the very act of saying it.

THE ART OF TELLING STORIES

Elizabeth Minchin's *Homer and the Resources of Memory: Some Applications of Cognitive Theory to The Iliad and The Odyssey*, published in 2001, is based on the explicitly Parryan premise that the two Homeric poems are 'the work of an orally-trained poet'.[5] The poems, Minchin underlines, 'were performed live'. What is more, 'it is essential to take this into account' in any study of them. Yet for Minchin the reason it is important to focus on the live, extemporised nature of the lines we now read as Homer's has little to do with finding anything mechanical in them. Rather, it is because doing so brings into sharp relief 'the close parallels that exist between "ordinary", everyday storytellings and the "special" storytelling of Homer'.[6] For Minchin, the apparently repetitious elements which Parry, Lord and their immediate followers attributed to the functional requirements of 'rapid composing in performance', are actually just more focussed versions of the kinds of practices we engage in every time we speak.[7]

Contemporary cognitive psychology provides Minchin with the means to propose an alternative model for how the Homeric poet might have composed at pace, a model more attuned to the extraordinary richness and attentiveness of the verse. Her focus is on recurrent action patterns, those scenes, in Parry's words, of 'arrival, sacrifice and eating, journeys by sea and land, arming and dressing, sleep, hesitation before decision (μερμηρίζειν) [*memērizein*], oath, and bath', whose repetitious patterns the latter identified in the two poems, and labelled 'typical scenes'.[8] Lord would subsequently call them 'themes'.[9] For Minchin, there is nothing necessarily Homeric, or even traditionally oral, about them: 'I submit that Homer's narrative patterns, namely those typical scenes or themes named by Parry and Lord (which replay in more or less detail everyday situations, procedures and speech acts), may be identified as the expressions of cognitive scripts'.[10] Minchin's point will be that the Homeric poet was just telling stories, something we also know how to practise compellingly, including late into the night.

The concept of the cognitive script has its roots in Frederick Bartlett's 1932 book, *Remembering: A Study in Experimental and Social Psychology*, and came to renewed prominence in the co-authored work of Roger C. Schank, a cognitive psychologist, and Robert A. Abelson, a theorist of artificial intelligence. Schank and Abelson's *Scripts, Plans, Goals, and Understanding: an Inquiry into Human Knowledge Structures* was published in 1977.[11] The pair were seeking to theorise how subjects store and process typical patterns of speaking and behaving, the better to operationalise them as computer code, in the days prior to our realising that machine learning actually works best when practiced along non-human lines.[12] Yet even though the overall project has been abandoned, the pair's concept of 'script' has served usefully to encapsulate Bartlett's finding that experiences 'which are similar in nature and content, such as visiting a restaurant', will not actually be stored in rich detail in our memories, but rather 'will be remembered in terms of standardised, generalised episodes, or structures of expectation'.[13] Also known as 'episodic memories', 'cognitive scripts' provide a way for the mind to minimise on the processing involved in recall, by tricking us into thinking that we remember so much more than we actually do of a given event. The generic sets of sequenced routines which scripts contain are also, Schank and Abelson argue, vital for economical communication. They have in mind the obvious fact that we can frequently allude to a single item in a generic behavioural sequence and take for granted our listeners' awareness of the rest. So a flatmate might say, 'I don't feel like eating at home tonight, let's call a restaurant' and a set of conventional expectations for what will happen next (e.g. that we will travel there, that we will be served food, that one or both of us will pay for the meal) can be taken as given. It would be otiose for that friend to explain that in addition to the phone call they would like all the things I have just listed to happen. Scripts, as Schank and Abelson put it, allow us to leave out 'the boring details'.[14] A third thing scripts do is anchor storytelling. 'Most real stories, that deal with scripts relate events that are unusual with respect to a standard script'.[15] *The night we both forgot our wallets and only realised half-way through the main course at a Michelin two-star restaurant* might, for instance, form a conversational anecdote.

Minchin offers examples of some of the cognitive scripts her readers might have at their disposal: using public transport, borrowing from the library, engaging in international travel, making a cup of tea, lighting a cigarette. Notably, even those who have never engaged in one or other of these behaviours will probably still, if belonging to the same culture, possess a script for the conventional sequences of actions it typically involves. They will also often have a sense of that scripts' various 'tracks', that is, permissible variants. They might have acquired this knowledge through witnessing others perform the actions schematised therein, they might have picked it up in general conversation, via representations in the public media or elsewhere. The key point is that a similar situation would have pertained in the Homeric poet's time. Both audience and poet would necessarily hold in memory 'scripts for setting out on a journey, preparing a meal, dressing, preparing a bed and so on; these are routines which they have often witnessed and performed. On the other hand, not every listener would know by personal experience an arming script'. But it would not be difficult, Minchin adds, for a budding singer 'to acquire this script (through the medium of epic or through stories told in ordinary conversation), since it is closely related to a dressing script'.[16] On the other hand, the dressing script, along with most of the other scripts the Homeric poet draws upon throughout the epics, would already have been acquired in the simple course of one's growing up, well before any actual apprenticeship as singer.

The apprenticeship would have focussed on the budding singer's acquisition of a received, formulaic diction and on his learning to wield it in the moment in verse. But 'there is little or no need' to postulate that extra tranche of learning Lord theorised on Parry's lead, whereby traditional singers would acquire their knowledge of set-piece 'themes' like 'setting out on a journey' or 'preparing a meal' through repeated practice, and then would go on to perform those fixed patterns live. By Minchin's account, we can give the Homeric poet 'considerably more credit for the story he chooses to tell'.[17] Far from confined to the narrow structures he learnt in singing school, the poet is telling stories with something more like the freedoms we ourselves exercise, when recounting interesting happenings. For 'we all have these skills and we all use them, although not with the conspicuous success of the great singer of oral epic in the ancient world'.[18] To put this in terms of our wallet-forgetting anecdote, we all have the ability to recount that kind of thoroughly 'scripted' experience spontaneously, eliciting different degrees of audience engagement in the process, depending on the quality of our improvising.

Minchin's Homer has no need for rote themes – just the capacity to tell a story with interest, one whose outlines he and his audience already know, and to do so in verse. As for how that interest is generated, this is a good place to problematise Lord's claim that the oral poet, confined to formulaic utterance by the need to compose his poem on the spot, 'makes no conscious effort to break the traditional phrases and incidents'.[19] Compare Schank and Abelson's above-mentioned observation that the stories we tell to divert each other in conversation are mainly about moments when script-based expectations are violated. Minchin concurs. She provides a close reading of Book 23 of *The Iliad*, that lengthy account of the funeral games which Achilleus stages for Patroklos, one book prior to the former's rapprochement with Priamos. Her analysis focuses on the evidence Book 23 provides for the existence of an ancient Greek contest script (*'The prizes are set up/A challenge is announced/*

The competitors come forward' etc.), as well as other culturally specific scripts, including one for harnessing horses, another for setting out on a journey, a third for taking pursuit, plus scripts for exhorting, threatening, protesting, having a chariot accident, consoling, renouncing and accepting.[20] But just as relevant as any description of these conventional themes is Minchin's insistence that what motors the drama in these lines are the moments when expectations based on these scripts are violated. One of the high points of Book 23 is when the young Artilochos, flush with a desire to win, breaks with the given sequence for a chariot race by wantonly cutting Menelaos's chariot off, thereby arousing the latter's great anger.[21] In fact, Homer constantly arouses tension through narratives that serve to 'break the traditional . . . incidents'. Minchin's analysis of scripts transforms at this point into something else altogether. For these are the moments at which one pushes the contents of a given schema to breaking point, substituting for structure the surprises of art. In Minchin's sharp phrase, the Homeric poet works 'not so much *from* memory, but *with* memory'.[22] We draw on the codified behavioural patterns which our memories provide, not just to navigate the world around us, but to put a glitch in that world, for the sake of a story – and we do so live.

THE ART OF KEYING ONE'S AUDIENCE

John Miles Foley also focusses on the link between our everyday communicative practices and the work of the oral poet, improvising live. This leads him to revise our understandings of the formulaic aspect of the Homeric poet's diction. Foley concurs with Parry and Lord, in holding that 'traditional phraseology and narrative patterning seem to be characteristic of oral and oral-derived epics around the world and throughout history'.[23] But he also believes that if one wishes to understand Homeric, South Slav and other such cultures of oral performance, one needs to go beyond this simple and readily observable fact. It is just as important to think through why an audience would want to listen to a poem composed that way in the first place. In Foley's view, almost all of the criticisms directed at Parry and Lord's work can be traced to this 'single shortcoming of Oral Theory in its initial form: a virtually exclusive attention to composition at expense of reception'. Parry and Lord 'naturally concentrated on the apparent miracle of how a preliterate poet could have produced such an imposing pair of monuments' without writing. But this led them, when it came to Homer's diction, to accept 'Parry's mechanical notion of an "essential idea," namely, that "swift-footed Achilles" meant simply Achilles, "ox-eyed Hera" merely Hera'.[24]

Foley is referring to the claim in Parry's 1928 doctoral thesis, *The Traditional Epithet in Homer*, that a repetitious phrase like *boōpis Hēra* (ox-eyed Hera) can in any given case be reduced to the 'essential idea' for which it stands: 'What is essential . . . is what remains after all the stylistic superfluity has been stripped from it'. Parry's example is *ēmos d' ērigeneia phanē rhododaktulos Ēos* (When rosy-fingered Dawn, child of morning, first appeared). Parry claims that the 'essential idea' of this often-repeated line is simply 'when day broke'.[25] *The Odyssey* contains 20 instances of it, *The Iliad* two, plus three cases where the formula's concluding phrase *rhododaktulos Ēos* (rosy-fingered Dawn) rounds off an otherwise distinct line. The relentlessness with which the poet of *The Odyssey* resorts to this formula lends a certain reasonableness to Parry's contention that the line is actually just an unit of code, expressing in the metrical space available something much simpler: an idea like 'at first light'. If a shorter space required filling, a shorter formula would do just as well, provided its 'essential idea' be the same. One can see how this concept of 'the essential idea' might lead to images of the Homeric poet as a type of 'assembly-line worker' (Ong, criticising the implications of Parry's approach), and even a 'conformist poet' (Minchin, likewise), one whose formulas and themes served as little more than 'prefabricated, multi-purpose units of composition'.[26] Why would anyone want to listen to such a performance?

Foley's way out of this impasse involves deeper exploration of the communicative context in which oral poetry is composed and delivered. His theory of 'traditional referentiality' holds that formulas and formula systems should be understood as 'indexes of traditional meaning', pointers to something much weightier, and at the same time much more contextually alert, than Parry's 'essential ideas'.[27] Recall the famous epithet-phrase *polutlas dios Odusseus* (much-suffering, God-like Odysseus), which appears 38 times across the two poems, as noted above. By Parry's account, this repetitious phrase does little more than convey an 'essential idea' like 'the Ithacan leader' in conveniently metrical form. Foley, on the other hand, argues that hearing such an epithet in a live performance will call to an audience's mind 'the entire heroic portrayal, complete with its mythic history and contradictions, as known to the tradition and signalled by this phrase'.[28] The poet's invocation of *polutlas dios Odusseus* (much-suffering, God-like Odysseus) keys an audience's listening, by drawing in as context all the previous utterances of those words, and generating expectations based upon them.

The artistic value of such 'traditional referentiality' is best demonstrated when we turn to phrases like *hupodra idōn* (looking darkly), which is found 17 times in *The Iliad*, nine times in *The Odyssey*. Thirteen and seven of those times respectively, this two-word phrase comes embedded in the larger *d' ar' hupodra idōn prosephē* (looking darkly then said) formula we explored in chapter 5. The reader may recall Parry's table, reproduced in chapter 5, with its open slots to either side, for person addressed and speaker, respectively. One of the examples we saw there was the following:

ton d' ar' hupodra idōn prosephē podas ōkus Achilleus
Swift-footed Achilleus looking darkly then said to him [29]

The two-word phrase at the core of this line, *hupodra idōn*, is conventionally translated 'looking darkly'. By Foley's reckoning, the phrase is more accurately understood in terms of the use it performs, which is to build suspense. The invariable reason a Homeric character will be described as *hupodra idōn* (looking darkly) is because that hero or God is taking offence at another's rudeness. The phrase indicates this, and at the same time it alerts the listener to the impending onset of a particular type of dramatic scene – one in which the consequences of a superhuman being taking offence will play themselves out. By keying listeners in to the drama about to unfold, 'framing the singularity of the immediate situation in a resonant traditional context', such phrases are 'not building blocks, but speech acts', raising tensions.[30] This analysis leads Foley to the conclusion that, far from being mechanical, formulas and formula systems are the drivers of a 'uniquely empowering medium, full of traditional implication at every level'.[31]

Foley's interpretation of the formulaic language that Parry identified across the two epics accepts its omnipresence, at the same time that it shows that the poets using such a 'traditional register' are by no means 'constrained at the level of diction'. Rather, 'their phraseology naturally reaches beyond the present moment or situation to the immanent network of traditional implication'.[32]

In making these claims, Foley certainly brings the audience into the equation, where Parry and Lord left their enjoyment of this seemingly mechanical art so opaque. It is by this same token clear that what Foley is doing, in advancing this argument, is returning to the ideas Lord so tantalisingly advanced in chapter 3 of *The Singer of Tales*: 'The speaker of this language, once he has mastered it, does not move any more mechanically within it than we do in ordinary speech'.[33] After all, our speech is replete with formulas and formula systems too: for example 'by the same token', 'after all', and 'I'm so glad to see you'. Some of these pre-fabricated expressions include elements just as archaic and (to the speaker) inexplicable as Homer's. Etymologist Philip Durkin suggests as much: 'It is questionable how far most speakers ever stop to analyse idiomatic expressions such as *to catch up on, to give (something) up, to leave off (doing something), on the one hand . . . on the other hand, to run (someone) to ground*'.[34] *Hand*, for instance, is there in *on the one hand* because it once meant *side* (as in *the side of a gate*, which as late as 1548 could be referred to as 'the hande of the gate') while *to run (someone) to ground* came to us from fox-hunting.[35] But who now breaks either of these phrases into their component parts, whether to generate, or to understand them? Perhaps poets occasionally do. But my point for now is that our general inability to do anything but accept such phrases as pre-given formulas when speaking English does not stop us deploying them with all sorts of contextual nuance and implication, irony being a case in point. Who is to say that formulaic phrases have to be mechanical in use?

Not only was the Homeric poet speaking on the spot, he was generating all the complexity we associate with a vivid public speaker:

All fell silent and hung from his lips.[36]

THE ART OF THINKING BY SPEAKING

An in-the-moment Homer emerges even more clearly from Egbert J. Bakker's work. His contribution focuses on Homer's syntax, and specifically on the manner in which the poet links his clauses together, as a sequence of loosely connected bursts of language.

To put that approach in context, Bakker is critiquing, and at the same time pinpointing the grain of truth in, a whole tranche of nineteenth- and twentieth-century arguments attributing a pre-intellectual character to the oral poet's thinking. Those arguments make much of Homer's recourse to formulas. But they focus with just as much vigour on Homer's supposedly unsophisticated way of linking them into sequences of lines. As Maurice Croiset, a Hellenist of the Belle Epoque, put it: 'Complicated groupings of ideas are absolutely unknown to Homeric poetry. . . . The ordinary law of this naïve and clear style is juxtaposition. When, contrary to custom, the sentence happens to grow long, the successive ideas join on to one another in the order that they occur to the mind'.[37] Croiset's reflections on Homeric syntax are echoed in Walter J. Ong's more recent, and still widely quoted, claims that the thinking (not just the lineation!) of people without writing is:

(i) Additive rather than subordinative
(ii) Aggregative rather than analytic
(iii) Redundant or 'copious'
(iv) Conservative or traditionalist
(v) Close to the human lifeworld
(vi) Agonistically toned
(vii) Empathetic and participatory rather than objectively distanced
(viii) Homeostatic
(ix) Situational rather than abstract[38]

and so on. Ruth Finnegan deflates this kind of wild extrapolating by pointing to the Limba language spoken in Sierra Leone, which exists in solely oral form: in Limba, you use *hu* as a prefix to create abstract nouns.[39] Go figure. But Bakker's response is even more acute.

Bakker argues that the bursts of loosely connected syntax characteristic of Homer's verse reflect the brief chunks in which any speaker will necessarily parcel out their words, when engaged in the dynamic flow of speech, 'situational', 'abstract' or otherwise. We speak in short spurts, known to linguists as 'intonation units' (a.k.a. 'idea units' or 'tone units'), and the connections between these typically clause-length units are often rather loose. The idea was foreshadowed in the introduction to this book, where we saw Heinrich von Kleist, and then a pair of contemporary linguists, discourse upon 'the gradual production of thoughts whilst speaking', that is the staggering of speech into short, sub-sentential units, due to the fact that, in Pawley and Syder's words, 'the largest unit of novel discourse that can be fully encoded in one coding operation is a single clause of eight to ten words'.[40]

The following transcript provides a further example of the highly localised, one might even say myopic, nature of real-time speech production. It constitutes an excerpt from an interview subject's description of a short film. The film involved a boy falling off a bicycle and thereby dropping his load, a basket of pears. Here is the subject's description of that moment in the film, as transcribed by linguist Wallace Chafe. Each line represents a distinct burst of speech.

(a) [.69] A--nd and you look at them,
(b) and and they see him,
(c) and they come up,
(d) [.95] a--nd without saying anything,
(e) there's no speech in the whole movie.
(f) [.6] Without saying anything,
(g) [.6] they .. um--.. help him .. put the pears back in the basket.[41]

Note how often the speaker resorts to the word *and* to begin their next utterance. Note, too, the double hyphens, which stand in this transcript for a lengthening of sounds. So when the speaker utters 'A--nd' they are engaging in the same delaying strategy which Kleist reports, in indicating that when he is not sure what to say next, he will often 'dwell lengthily on the conjunctions'. This will serve to gain him time 'for the fabrication of my idea in the workshop of my mind'.[42] Finally, note how independent, and even isolated, these nonetheless sequential chunks appear. Bakker explains that producing a discourse on the spot involves high processing demands, whoever the speaker, whatever the tongue. For this reason, spoken discourse will tend to manifest in the kind of loosely connected, and nascently rhythmic, sequences of clauses observed above. The staggered nature of Homer's utterance is, in other words, representative of speakers more generally.

So Bakker retains the seed of value in Croiset, Parry and others' observations on the supposedly primitive nature of Homer's syntax. The two Homeric epics are indeed characterised by progressions of loosely linked clauses. But this has nothing to do with any purportedly pre-literate mindset. Rather it demonstrates that each was composed as a live performance, through the very mechanisms which we ourselves engage when speaking. 'Such properties will appear in some form in any spoken discourse, including that of the highly literate scholar when he or she speaks and does not write'.[43] You might say that 'we all speak in an oral style' Bakker quips.[44] For Homer's poetry is actually 'closer to a transcript' of everyday, conversational language, such as linguists record for professional study, 'than it is to a written text as we conceive of it'.[45]

Bakker's strategy for demonstrating this dramatic assertion is to compare the syntactic moves in a passage of *The Iliad* to the speech patterns of a present-day North American conversationalist, as transcribed by Chafe. I will reproduce the salient contours of that comparison here. Bakker starts with a hyper-literal translation of the first seven lines of *The Iliad*, Book 1, which he offers so as to show us 'more accurately what happens in the Greek' than our literary versions tend to.[46] For those translations will invariably make it look like the Homeric poet was trying to produce a polished piece of writing, with all the grammatical balances we expect from a 'good writer'. In particular, it will look as if Homer composed in 'fully formed' sentences. One actually has to fudge the syntax to translate him that way. In fact, Homer's lines segment much more naturally into pairs of intonation units, those typically clause-length chunks in which we actually speak, than they do into sentences. Segment the lines into the intonational chunks in which one would have uttered them and you realise that the spurts in which Homer 'wrote' obey a quite different order of syntax to that enshrined in 'proper' ancient Greek, one much more to do with working out what one is going to say in the very moments of saying it. That is to say, the process makes you realise that Homer's syntax is characterised by a thoroughgoing suddenness.

(1a)	*mēnin aeide thea*	Sing of the wrath, Goddess,
(1b)	*Pēlēiadeō Achilēos*	of Achilleus, son of Peleus,
(2a)	*oulomenēn*	the accursed <wrath>,
(2b)	*hē muri Achaiois alge ethēke*	that caused numerous woes for the Achaians,
(3a)	*pollas d' iphthimous psuchas*	and many valiant souls,

(3b)	*Aidi proiapsen*	<it> sent <them> forth to Hades,
(4a)	*hērōōn*	<souls> of heroes,
(4b)	*autous de elōria teuche kunessin*	and themselves as prey it put to the dogs,
(5a)	*oiōnoisi te pasi*	and to all the birds,
(5b)	*Dios d' eteleito boulē*	and the will of Zeus was fulfilled,
(6a)	*ex hou dē ta prōta*	<starting> from the moment at which for the first time
(6b)	*diastētēn erisante*	<they> stood apart in quarrel,
(7a)	*Atreidēs te anax andrōn*	Atreus's son, lord of men,
(7b)	*kai dios Achilleus*	and godlike Achilleus[47]

We traditionally put a full stop at the end of these seven lines, as being the first sentence of *The Iliad*. Bakker is not so sure. 'Is it really a sentence in our sense, with a beginning and an end?'[48] What Bakker finds there is much more like the loosely connected chunks of speech which the albeit chauvinist Croiset observed.

To see what Bakker is getting at, in questioning whether Homer's famous opening lines actually constitute a sentence ('in our sense'), focus in on chunk (5b) *Dios d' eteleito boulē* (and the will of Zeus was fulfilled). The thing that troubles our conventional assumption that we are dealing with a sentence here is that in written discourse, the ancient Greek word *d'* (and) typically serves to link items 'that are situated on the same syntactic level'.[49] But how would that work here? Are we meant to put (5b) on the same syntactic level as the imperative that opens this apparent sentence at (1a) *mēnin aeide thea* (Sing of the wrath, goddess)? That would give us something of the order of *Sing of the wrath, Goddess and the will of Zeus was fulfilled*. Obviously that jars. Could (5b) instead represent an item in the list of things (*Sing of x, y and z*) that the poet is beseeching the Goddess to sing? *Sing of the wrath that did this, the wrath that did that and the will of Zeus was fulfilled*. That also jars. But what other options are there? Unit (5b) simply does not fit into the syntactical structure of the overall sentence of which it is supposed to be a part.

Call it an 'aside' and it suddenly more or less works.

In a sea of asides. For actually, (4a) *hērōōn* (<souls> of heroes) feels quite tacked-on as a result of Bakker's attempt to convey 'more accurately what happens in the Greek' as well – as if it just came to the speaker in that moment, a second attempt at describing the 'valiant souls' already qualified two lines back.

(3a)	*pollas d' iphthimous psuchas*	and many valiant souls,
(3b)	*Aidi proiapsen*	<it> sent <them> forth to Hades,

(4a)   *hērōōn*   <souls> of heroes,
(4b)   *autous de elōria teuche kunessin*   and themselves as prey it put to the dogs,
(5a)   *oiōnoisi te pasi*   and to all the birds,
(5b)   *Dios d' eteleito boulē*   and the will of Zeus was fulfilled,

But to review Homer's approach to (4a) in this manner is to see that (5a) *oiōnoisi te pasi* (and to all the birds) has an ad hoc feel to it too, as if it were an afterthought to the idea of warriors given to the dogs in (4b), itself something of a second-go at the idea of sending all these souls to Hades. Once you start looking this way, you realise that (2a) *oulomenēn* (the accursed <wrath>) seems quite haphazard as well, as if the poet is having another attempt at the 'wrath' that has already been referred to in (1a) *mēnin aeide thea* (Sing of the wrath, Goddess), and that might, in a more globally mastered discourse, have been qualified at first mention. The closer we get to Homer's syntax, the more compelling the conclusion becomes: the speaker is coming to his thought, bit by bit, even as he composes it. His is not 'a sentence in our sense' at all. 'What the text actually gives us are a series of short speech units that are more or less loosely connected syntactically. By themselves, if approached without prejudice or foreknowledge as to their content, these units do not do much more than guiding our attention through a series of island-like ideas'.[50] Only that fact has nothing to do with any primitivity in the Homeric poet's thinking. It is simply that when speaking in the moment, we make grammatical decisions in a much more local manner. We too speak in loosely co-ordinated chains of clauses. The Homeric poet is speaking off the cuff, as any of us do in conversation – only in verse, and with huge energy and poise.

I turn to Bakker's comparator text, to drive home his point that 'we all speak in an oral style'.[51] To reiterate, the units into which the following transcript is segmented represent the short bursts in which we compose our speech live, a fact readily observable to anyone who decides to listen out for those bursts in the next conversation. By Chafe's statistics, intonation units have a median (i.e. average) length of 4.84 words in English, and a modal (i.e. most frequent) length of 4.[52] He also points out that they stay within a narrow range, rarely reaching more than 10 or so words in English. The fact that these statistics vary by language, and that that variance depends on the amount of information the language packs into its words, reflects Chafe's further contention that we are not simply dealing with respiratory phenomena, caused by the sheer need to breathe regularly, here, but rather with evolutionarily given constraints on how much information our brains can process in any given conversational moment. More on the intonation unit and its relation to the writing of poetry in Part III. Suffice to note for the moment that our speaking proceeds in short, more or less five-word bursts, and that each line in the conversational transcript below, as in the English and Greek ones above, represents another such intonation unit. Of Chafe's various transcription conventions, I will simply note here that the most important of them, for the purpose of sounding out the text, are that an equals sign (=) indicates 'lengthening of the preceding vowel or consonant', while an acute (e.g. the 'ó' in 'óne day') represents a 'primary accent (a pitch deviation accompanied by loudness or lengthening)', and a grave (e.g. the 'à' in 'càrrying my gárbage') represents a 'secondary accent (a pitch deviation without loudness or lengthening)'.[53] It will help in reading this, even in silence, to give prominent stress to the primaries and less but still some stress to the secondaries. It is surprising how vivid, and even how regionally specific, a transcript can become from attention to this small matter.

(a) Like óne day I was just
(b) . . I was . . uh càrrying my gárbage,
(c) to the gárbage dùmp.
(d) . . . And this gùy came bỳ on a mótorcyle.
(e) And thèn he went bàck in the óther dirèction,
(f) and wènt back in the óther dirèction,
(g) . . I was stìll càrrying my gárbage.
(h) And thén,
(i) . . I'm wálking =,
(j) . . like bàck to my hóuse and,
(k) . . this . . . mòtorcycle gets sló = wer and slówer and slówer,
(l) . . . and lìke it's like . . ró = lling,
(m) and fínally this gùy is sàying,
(n) . . . I lóve you.
(o) . . I lóve you.
(p) . . I lóve you.[54]

To grasp the workings of this speaker's syntax, it will help to know that a full stop in a linguistic transcript of this nature does not represent any judgement about grammatical completion or coherence on the part of the transcriber. It stands for the way speakers themselves mark what they see as the end of a thought, by descending in pitch. A comma, on the other hand, represents the rising or maintenance of pitch by which we in English, as in so many other languages, indicate that our thought is not yet complete.[55] One hears this intonational contour with particular vividness when speakers are ticking off items in a list. On the other hand, the complete thought which the speaker indicated with a descending pitch at unit (c) would seem to be a scene-setting one:

(a) Like óne day I was just
(b) .. I was .. uh càrrying my gárbage,
(c) to the gárbage dùmp.

The point of producing a sentence-final intonation contour at the end of (c) is that the speaker feels that sufficient information has been conveyed for their listener to feel oriented in the scenario. Similar analyses could be made of the decision to descend in pitch at the end of the next unit –

(d) ... And this gùy came bỳ on a mótorcyle.

– and then again after the three units that follow that one:

(e) And thèn he went bàck in the óther dirèction,
(f) and wènt back in the óther dirèction,
(g) .. I was stìll càrrying my gárbage.

The first of these sequences, unit (d), was judged a complete thought because it introduced the antagonist, the second, units (e) –(g), because it conveyed sufficient detail for the listener to grasp that antagonist's first notable act, which was to reverse his motorcycle. So we have scene-setting, introduction of antagonist, and then an act that marks the initial breaking of the script for expected behaviour in such circumstances. To think of sentencehood, in speech, as the retrospective product of a one-time decision that enough has been said to convey some such narratival or argumentative function serves to demonstrate the logic behind strings of words that from any prose perspective seems outrightly surreal. After all, the third of these sentences, transcribed without lines, would read *And then he went back in the other direction and went back in the other direction, I was still carrying my garbage.* We are simply not dealing with prose here. This is, of course, Bakker's point. As in Homer, the speaker's compositional decisions occur at the level of the intonation unit, and are only really logical when encountered at that level.

For further insight into the stylistic features which this literate speaker's monologue shares with Homer's apparently 'naïve' style, focus in, again, on the speaker's use of that highly revealing word *and*. Five of the 16 intonation units in this transcript begin 'And'. As in Homer's case, the effect can hardly be called literary. Much of the reason we feel we are dealing with something other than publishable prose here is, as pointed out in the Homeric case above, that these initial *ands* do not perform the conjunction's typical (albeit not exclusive) literary role of coordinating units on the same syntactic level. It is rather that they, much like the 'and' ending unit (j) ('like bàck to my hóuse and'), are the speaker's way of announcing that something more is to come. The upshot of their pervasiveness through the transcript is that the text as a whole feels just as 'primitive and crudely repetitive' as lines 1–7 of the *Iliad* did, following Bakker's attempt to convey 'more accurately what happens in the Greek'.[56] That is not to say that the conjunction acts the same way across these two very different languages.[57] The Homeric poet actually has two *ands* at his disposal. On the one hand, there is *kai* (and), which coordinates units on the same syntactic level:

(6b) *diastētēn erisante*   <they> stood apart in quarrel,

(7a) *Atreidēs te anax andrōn*   Atreus's son, lord of men,

(7b) *kai dios Achilleus*   and godlike Achilleus

But Homer also has at his disposal the above-noted *de* (it elides to *d'* before a vowel, and always comes as second item in the phrase). *de* does service in Homeric (but not later) Greek for this other *and* meaning that we have started to unpack, the colloquial one that indicates the start of another step in the speaker's discourse, as they move through a succession of ideas. English speakers, in contrast, use one and the same word for both functions.[58]

The words are differently calibrated across the two languages, but it is important to realise that the English *and* in the second of these meanings actually presents a very accurate, that is functionally equivalent, translation of Homer's *de*. The reason a functional equivalent for that Homeric usage of *de* can be found in a language as far removed in time and space as modern English is highly revealing, and has to do with the cognitive constraints touched upon above. There are limits on how much we can process in any given moment of real-time speech production, and this is an issue with which all spoken languages have to contend. Hence the relative translatability that pertains to the Homeric *de*, our colloquial *and*, and their equivalents in other tongues. We find ourselves constantly in a position, whatever the language, where the most convenient way to connect the next chunk of thought is with a conjunction equivalent to 'and the next thing I have to say is'. In Bakker's words, such an *and* 'serves the purpose of *continuation*: it signals that "more is to come," that the unit in question is part of a chain of ideas verbalized. In short, the passage is a *process* rather than a product, a written text'.[59]

The speaker's description of this motorcycle incident comprises, in sum, 'a series of short speech units that are more or less loosely connected syntactically'. It is, in this regard, strikingly similar to lines 1–7 of Book 1, Homer's famous 'first sentence'. The transcript, just like Homer's text, evidences a speaking in the moment. Both composers – the one a Greek poet from something like the Archaic period, the other a twentieth-century North American conversationalist – are finding their words in the very act of saying them. For the *Iliad* and *The Odyssey* are like linguistic transcripts of conversational speech. Or at least, they are much closer to that, than to 'to a written text as we conceive of it'.[60] So Bakker demonstrates his contention that the Homeric poet was composing his far from 'naïve' work in real-time, just as it came to his lips.

Actually, Bakker has a further point to make about this so revealing little word *and*, a point with significant bearing on the question of whether a real-time poetic thinking is at all possible. It emerges from his discussion of one of the *androktasía*, or 'man-to-man slaying', scenes that bestrew *The Iliad*, which is of course a poem about rage, violence and pity, as much as a document of how speech emerges in the living moment.[61] I will try to recreate the scene.

We are in Book 16, at lines 346–350. Once more, Bakker has divided the lines into their likely intonation units. Note how many of these units begin with a *de* (and):

(346a)	*to d' antikru*	and right through,
(346b)	*doru chalkeon exeperēse*	the bronze spear, it pierced
(347a)	*nerthen hup' egkephaloio*	from below under the brain,
(347b)	*kessase d' ar' ostea leuka*	and it splintered the white bones,
(348a)	*ek d' etinachthen odontes*	and the teeth, they were shaken out
(348b)	*eneplēsthen de hoi amphō*	and they were filled, the both
(349a)	*haimatos ophthalmoi*	eyes with blood,
(349b)	*to d' ana stoma kai kata rhinas*	and through the mouth and the nostrils
(350a)	*prēse chanōn*	he blew gaping
(350b)	*thanatou de melan vephos amphekalupsen*	and the black cloud of death covered [him] round.[62]

The point Bakker has to make here is that the continuative conjunction we have been discussing (the Homeric *de*/our colloquial use of *and*) only superficially represents the chronological sequencing of events in a story ('and then . . . , and then . . . , and then . . . '), however much this might seem to be its meaning in cases like this slaying scene. Bakker puts it this way: 'What we have here are not so much narrative statements asserting temporal sequence as descriptive visual details as they pass through the speaker's consciousness'.[63] A moment's reflection makes this subtle point clear. Some of the details of what the warrior, Erymas, is experiencing in this passage are being narrated sequentially, to represent distinct stages of suffering, as the spear makes its gruesome way into his skull. But, actually, that is not true of all of these stages. From the moment Erymas's 'white bones' have been 'splintered', the remaining impacts (upon the teeth, the eyes, the mouth and the nostrils) are all clearly occurring simultaneously. The progression marked by the three *de* forms in those cases is not that of events occurring in a temporal sequence, but rather a progression in the narrator's consciousness, as he successively choses the next item to bring into focus and name.

It is a point Bakker will make about spoken discourse in general. In exegeting his work, we have seen a number of examples of texts where, in place of any so-called 'balanced' sentences, we encounter 'loosely connected. . . island-like ideas': twice, in recent English passages that we know were spoken, and twice in ancient Greek passages that Bakker insists read as if spoken. For Bakker, such texts serve to illustrate the following fact:

> The concept of the sentence . . . the primary stylistic unit of written discourse and the principal domain for the operation of written syntax, is much less relevant in spoken discourse. Speakers may regularly produce sentences . . . but the syntax of their speech is the syntax of the intonation unit as it reflects the flow of ideas through their consciousness.[64]

When we put this proposition against the notion that certain Homeric and/or spoken forms such as the continuative *and* look 'primitive and crudely repetitive' from the perspective of writing, we see that Bakker's point is very much the opposite: these usages are quite literally thoughtful.[65] For the spoken grammar that looks so inadequate from the perspective of written syntax simply reflects a different mode of linguistic organisation, one based around the demands of a highly localised and ongoing intellectual process. Homer is not interested in composing sentences whose balanced internal relations will be apparent on the page. Rather, he is generating 'the kind of structure that is connected with *movement*, the flow of ideas through consciousness'.[66]

Spoken language is organised differently to the written. But the terms we use to describe it, nevertheless, often betray a prejudice towards a sentence-based syntax. For Bakker, categorical terms like parataxis (typically used to refer to the chaining of simple clauses via conjunctions like the continuative *and*) are a case in point. Implying a set of fixed practices, such terms obscure the online and improvised nature of what is really going on in any moment of spoken utterance: 'we serve the restless, processual nature of Homeric discourse better when we replace "parataxis" with words denoting not so much stylistic or syntactic *properties* of the text, as the narrator's *activities* on the path of speech. Hence the word "parataxis" may be reformulated as continuation or progression, a new step on the path of speech'.[67] With this rejection of the term 'parataxis', and even the very concept of style, we can see something of the stark challenge that Bakker's work poses. The Homer who emerges from it is a real-time speaker, rigorously focussed at the level of immediate consciousness, ever shifting from one burst of intense focus to the next.

A suddenness is everywhere.

SPEECH WRITTEN DOWN?

To conclude our survey of the Audenesque character that the Homeric poet has assumed in recent scholarship, I return to the question of writing. What gives a thinker like Bakker the licence to assume that Homer's epic verse is *speech written down*? As he so provocatively puts it, 'the written form in which it has come down to us is closer to a transcript such as Chafe's rendering of his taped discourses than it is to a written text as we conceive of it'.[68]

Bakker's way of showing that the kind of verbatim transcribing he attributes to the Homeric corpus might be possible is to cite medievalist M.T. Clanchy, who argues that, in the emergent literacy of eleventh-century CE England, it was common for authors to write by dictation. Even more to the point, Clanchy shows it was common for authors to dictate without actually knowing, in our terms, how to write at all. The latter was a task for specialists, there to transcribe those 'writers'. Exegeting Clanchy, Bakker comments that 'writing in the sense of composition was a *form of speaking*, a matter of *voice*, separated from writing in the technological sense, which was the *transcription* of the sound produced by the voice'.[69] What is more, the one with the training to read such a text would aim not so much to sift it for its message, but rather to 'restore the medium of the original message' by giving voice to it, whether to himself or to the others who wanted to read (i.e. to hear) it.[70] So a listener might 'read' a text without actually knowing, in our terms, how to read at all. Bakker takes Clanchy's expansion of our conceptions of what writing and reading might entail, to propose that something similar probably pertained to the emerging literacy of the era in which the Homeric poems were transcribed. 'What I am suggesting is that the dictating bard "wrote" by his own standards, and "spoke" by ours'.[71] The upshot of this line of thinking is that the inscription of *The Iliad* 'was meant to represent *The Iliad* in its essential quality of speech and performance, and to be as such a normative model for re-enactment'.[72] Clanchy's work shows that such a practice of *writing by speaking* and *reading by re-enacting* is at least possible. Bakker considers that in the early ancient Greek context it would have been highly likely.

But here the Homerists come to a halt. Or rather, they make clear, as Bakker himself does, that even if *The Iliad* and *The Odyssey* were products of the sort of writing practices Clanchy describes, 'there is no reason to suppose that the first transcripts were anything like the text we possess today'.[73] Bakker claims that the metrical regularity of the two poems in particular 'cannot be due to transcription as a one-time event, the creation of an unedited transcript of a performance, to be copied as is into the future'.[74] Like Gregory Nagy, Bakker hypothesises a process of 'textualisation', whereby transcripts were successively ironed out to achieve their current rhythmic finish. Yet he adds that such a 'textualisation of the Homeric tradition has been only a very partial one'. For in their 'typical segmentation and syntactic progression', the two epics have 'remained remarkably close to speech'.[75]

Bakker's grounds for his claims about the spokenness of the poems thus remain essentially Parryan. Even though we cannot reconstruct the exact stages by which *The Iliad* and *The Odyssey* were brought to writing, we can surmise from the internal evidence of Homer's diction that they are records of live improvisation. But one can hardly have certainty on texts that are two and a half thousand or more years old, as Bakker reminds us in his essay 'How Oral is Oral Composition'?[76] The essay offers a close reading of lines 390–413 of Book 6 of *The Iliad*, which describe how Andromache runs to meet Hektor as he approaches the Skaian gates, having almost forgotten his pressing wish to see her, as he gets closer to the battle:

She came to him there, and beside her went an attendant carrying
the boy in the fold of her bosom, a little child, only a baby,
Hektor's son, the admired, beautiful as a star shining,
whom Hektor called Skamandrios, but all of the others
Astyanax – lord of the city. Since Hektor alone saved Ilion.[77]

In his reading of these lines, Bakker focusses on the striking and masterly way Homer's syntax continues over the line break in a number of the Greek verses of this and the surrounding passages, an effect Bakker believes should be understood in terms of oral delivery, much more than from any visual, or otherwise page-based point of view. But what counts for our purposes is Bakker's concluding, somewhat melancholy comment on the evidentiary value any such passage bears for the one who would speculate on the genesis of the two written texts we read as Homer's: 'We will never know how close the passage is to the textless performance of the singer of tales – perhaps less close than we would like it to be'.[78]

The exact nature of Homer's textualisation is outside the concerns of this book. What is well within them, however, is the possibility that there might be a contemporary register of writing as alive to the impress of real-time poetic thinking as is Homer's.

NOTES

1. Lord, *Singer of Tales*, 17.

2. Lord, 36.//
3. For example, Foley, *Homer's Traditional Art* 6; Cánovas and Antović, "Formulaic Creativity," 69; Bakker, *Poetry in Speech*, 15 fn. 25.
4. Bakker, "Homeric Discourse and Enjambment," 17.
5. Minchin, *Resources of Memory*, 3.
6. Minchin, 7.
7. Lord, *Singer of Tales*, 17.
8. Parry, "Typical Scenes," 404.
9. Lord, *Singer of Tales*, 69–98.
10. Minchin, *Resources of Memory*, 39.
11. Bartlett, *Remembering*; Schank and Ableson, *Scripts, Plans, Goals*.
12. Chater, *Mind is Flat*, 24–27.
13. Minchin, *Resources of Memory*, 13.
14. Schank and Ableson, *Scripts, Plans, Goals*, 41.
15. Schank and Ableson, 45.
16. Minchin, *Resources of Memory*, 39–40.
17. Minchin, 42.
18. Minchin, 30.
19. Lord, *Singer of Tales*, 2.
20. Minchin, *Resources of Memory*, 43; 51–69.
21. Minchin, 58–61; 67–69.
22. Minchin, 29.
23. Foley, "Epic as Genre," 182.
24. Foley, "Oral Tradition and its Implications," 164.
25. Parry, "Traditional Epithet," 13.
26. Ong, *Orality and Literacy*, 22; Minchin, *Resources of Memory*, 5; 42.
27. Foley, "Oral Tradition and its Implications," 167.
28. Foley, 167–168.
29. Homer, *Il.* 1.148.
30. Foley, "Oral Tradition and its Implications," 168; Foley, *Homer's Traditional Art*, 33.
31. Foley, "Oral Tradition and its Implications," 170.
32. Foley, *Homer's Traditional Art*, 25.
33. Lord, *Singer of Tales*, 36.
34. Durkin, *Oxford Guide to Etymology*, 42.
35. Durkin, 42; *Oxford English Dictionary*, s.v. "Hand." https://www-oed-com.virtual.anu.edu.au/view/Entry/83801
36. Virgil, *Aeneid* 2.1 (my translation).
37. Croiset, qtd in Parry, "Enjambment in Homeric Verse," 251.
38. Ong, *Orality and Literacy*, 37, 38, 39, 41, 42, 43, 45, 46, 49.
39. Finnegan, "Speech, Language and Non-Literacy," 111.
40. Pawley and Syder, "Two Puzzles," 202.
41. Speaker 1, qtd in Chafe, "Deployment of Consciousness," 35. Chafe's transcription conventions are listed on 301, and explained on xv; see too, the discussion in the body of the text below.

42. Kleist, "Gradual Production of Thoughts," 405.
43. Bakker, "Study of Homeric Discourse," 288.
44. Bakker, *Poetry in Speech*, 43.
45. Bakker, "Study of Homeric Discourse," 292.
46. Bakker, 292.
47. Homer, *Il.* 1.1–7, translated by Bakker, 291–292 (my numbering).
48. Bakker, 292.
49. Bakker, "Homeric Discourse and Enjambment," 4.
50. Bakker, "Study of Homeric Discourse," 292.
51. Bakker, *Poetry in Speech*, 43.
52. Chafe, *Discourse, Consciousness and Time*, 65.
53. Chafe, xiii. See that page for the full transcription conventions.
54. Anon., qtd in Bakker, "Study of Homeric Discourse," 289–290. For the original, see Chafe, *Discourse, Consciousness and Time*, 208.
55. Chafe, xiii.
56. Bakker, "The Study of Homeric Discourse," 292; Bakker, *Poetry in Speech*, 70.
57. Bakker, *Poetry in Speech*, 71–73.
58. Schiffrin, *Discourse Markers*, 128.
59. Bakker, "The Study of Homeric Discourse," 290–291.
60. Bakker, 292.
61. Bakker, *Poetry in Speech*, 57
62. Homer, *Il.* 16.346–350, translated by Bakker, *Poetry in Speech*, 68–69 (my numbering).
63. Bakker, *Poetry in Speech*, 69
64. Bakker, 49.
65. Bakker, 70.
66. Bakker, "Study of Homeric Discourse," 298.
67. Bakker, *Poetry in Speech*, 62.
68. Bakker, "Study of Homeric Discourse," 292.
69. Bakker, *Poetry in Speech*, 26.
70. Bakker, 30.
71. Bakker, 26.
72. Bakker, 31.
73. Bakker, 208.
74. Bakker, 209.
75. Bakker, 210.
76. Bakker, "How Oral is Oral Composition?"
77. Lattimore, *The Iliad of Homer*, 163–164 (*Il.*, 6.399–403).
78. Bakker, "How Oral is Oral Composition?", 50.

Part III

WRITING IS SPEAKING

Chapter 8

Not-Quite Speech

Derek Attridge's *Poetic Rhythm: An Introduction* opens with an experiment. Attridge asks us to read the following sentence 'like the beginning of a long novel, silently, aiming to get the gist of it as efficiently as possible': 'O there is blessing in this gentle breeze that blows from the green fields and from the clouds and from the sky: it beats against my cheek, and seems half-conscious of the joy it gives'.[1] Whether intended or not, there is a page break at this point in Attridge's book. Over the page, Attridge asks us to read the same sentence again, but this time with Wordsworth's actual lineation. This time you should read the lines slowly, he instructs, 'letting the sound and movement of the words carry you along'[2]:

O there is blessing in this gentle breeze
That blows from the green fields and from the clouds
And from the sky: it beats against my cheek,
And seems half-conscious of the joy it gives.[3]

Attridge intends the difference in the reader's experience of these two arrangements of the same words to convey the fact that poetry, far more than prose – far more than even the same words in prose – 'takes place'.[4]

The sentence that opens Wordsworth's 1805 version of *The Prelude* 'takes place', when we read it in its original form, unfolding in lines of poetry. We find ourselves drawn to pause slightly at the end of the first line, as we do at the end of all lines, if for no other reason than the time the eye needs to flick back to the other margin. In this case, that compulsory pause gives us the space 'to comprehend and respond' to the poem's opening announcement. And it is only after such a pause, however slight, that we move on 'to discover and take pleasure in the sources of the breeze in the line that follows', focussing now on the fact that it is a breeze '[t]hat blows from the green fields and from the clouds'. Read as the start of the third line, 'And from the sky' feels much more like an event in time as well, an afterthought to the naming of those first two sources, and by the same token, something of an effusion. The mid-line colon after 'sky' in that same line seems redolent of Wordsworth's in-the-moment experience as well, a moment of stasis prior to the experience of the breeze's sudden arrival, as it 'beats against my cheek'. The impact is thus 'rendered verbally as it happens experientially'. The fourth line, which felt simply fanciful in prose, takes on energy from the fact of its lineation as well.

And seems half-conscious of the joy it gives

now arrives as a sudden playful imagining, the next step in the speaker's darting thought. So these lines function as '*as poetry*, enacting for us as we speak the words an experience, a happening in time, that is physical and emotional and mental all at once'.[5]

Note how Wordsworth's *ands* change status in the course of Attridge's prose to verse experiment. In the prose version, each served to coordinate, if slightly oddly, syntactic units of the same order, for instance, 'from the green fields and from the clouds and from the sky'. Yet a poem is 'not simply a statement but a movement in thought' (Attridge). Here are the lines again:

O there is blessing in this gentle breeze
That blows from the green fields and from the clouds
And from the sky: it beats against my cheek,
And seems half-conscious of the joy it gives.[6]

Once back into lines, the 'And' at the start of the third line takes on something of that processual, colloquial meaning discussed in the previous chapter, in relation to lines 1–7 of Book 1 of *The Iliad*, and the two transcripts of contemporary, conversational English also cited there. That is to say, it now means something much more like 'and the next thing that comes to mind is'. Attridge implies this shift in its functioning, without ever mentioning the conjunction *per se*. He writes that this third line, once read *as a line*, 'enacts the overflowing exuberance of the speaker's feelings, as yet another natural source is added to the list'.[7] A similar reading can clearly be made of the 'And' beginning line 4. The conjunction heralds a further moment in the speaker's perception. But the caesura which a reader is likely to observe after 'green fields' in line 2 imports a similar, if less prominent, effect to the conjunction heading the final phrase of that line as well. It adds a touch of afterthought ('and the next thing that comes to mind') to Wordsworth's 'and from the clouds' as well.

Egbert Bakker's argument, to recall, was that such an *and*, pervasive in conversation, and pervasive in Homer, serves not so much to join like items, but rather to mark a new step on the path of thought. We feel the speaker in the process of reaching for the next thought whenever we encounter the *de* (and *continuative*) conjunction in Homer, as we do whenever a speaker uses this same type of *and* to initiate a new clause when conversing in English. Bakker's broader point was that speaking 'represents the consciousness of the speaker in a more direct way than written discourse does the consciousness of writers'.[8] In many ways, Attridge is making the same point, though he is attributing this same property of providing insight into conscious experience to Wordsworth's verse. The poet's grammar is speaking. It is thinking aloud.

Linguists Andrew Pawley and Frances Hodgetts Syder remind us of the risky, spurt-by-spurt way in which speech proceeds:

> when speakers commit themselves to a multiclause sentence, they take a gamble. Being able to compose only a bit at a time, a speaker must gamble on being able to formulate an acceptably fluent and coherent continuation and completion of the construction. One might draw an analogy with a novelist who undertakes to write a novel to be written and published in weekly instalments.[9]

Is there not something like that in these opening lines of *The Prelude*, their segmentation and even the use of conjunctions so redolent of the graduated, risky way we produce speech in-the-moment? But does that mean that Wordsworth must have written the lines in that very fashion, as an on-the-spot gamble with what might emerge, even as he uttered them?

Georg Christoph Lichtenberg: 'I have drawn from the well of language many a thought which I did not have and could not put into words'.[10]

Novalis:

> What is most proper to language, no one knows: that it merely concerns itself with itself. That is why it is such a wonderful and fruitful mystery – that if someone merely speaks in order to speak, one pronounces precisely the most splendid and original truths. . . . Out of this arises the hate that so many earnest people have against language. They notice its wilfulness.[11]

Can we conclude, from the evidence of his syntax, that Wordsworth when writing these opening lines of the 1805 *Prelude* was trusting himself to whatever surprises language and the world might bring in those instants? Is this what published poems effectively record?

Why not draw that conclusion, given the evidence that we have just seen for the existence of an extraordinary capacity for improvising poetic thought in the moment, evidence ingrained in the very contours of the two Homeric poems' syntax? *The Iliad* and *The Odyssey* were 'not composed *for* but *in* performance' (Lord).[12] Nor should we forget – in pondering the possibility that we might indeed have a document of real-time speech in our hands in these first four lines of *The Prelude* – the bevy of poets in our interview archive who insisted on both the spontaneity and the orality of their practice. Recall Don Paterson's response to the Auden quotation. A poem 'is almost a documentary record of an epiphany that has taken place in the course of its own making. . . . You have to come to the page with nothing, an urge to speak – as Auden says – without really knowing why'.[13] I underline Paterson's use of the word 'speak' here, an approving reiteration of Auden's own word-choice. In putting it that way, the pair enrol themselves in that list of major modern poets who insist upon the spokenness of the poetic line. For William Carlos Williams, 'Speech is the fountain of the line'.[14] Robert Frost wanted a diction that was 'not bookish' but 'caught fresh from the mouths of people'.[15] Ezra Pound would have a poetry 'stripped of its perdamnable rhetoric . . . a speech without inversions'.[16] Behind all of them one finds Wordsworth, that Wordsworth who aimed to present in verse 'as far as possible, a selection of the language really spoken by men [*sic*]'.[17]

Wordsworth's 'as far as possible' invites pause here. As he states elsewhere in the Preface to the *Lyrical Ballads*, the poet 'is only selecting from the real language of men (or, which amounts to the same thing, composing accurately in the spirit of such selection)'.[18] It is also worth noting that the instances of *and* in those first four lines of *The Prelude*, although evocative of a processual usage by dint of their place in the line, still retain the power to coordinate items of the same syntactic order. Hence the ease with which Attridge can perform his poetry-to-prose experiment, something that would be far harder to carry off with the conversational materials we have considered so far. The first four lines of *The Prelude* have spokenness, but they are not quite speech. In fact, to find aspects of Wordsworth's diction redolent of vivid, in-the-moment speaking may be less illuminating of his compositional practices than it initially appears.

PARRYAN LITERARY CRITICISM?

What corroboration can be found for the seemingly fanciful idea that literary poetry might be composed in real-time, just like speech itself? And if it is not, why did so many of the poets interviewed over 2013–2015 respond positively to Auden's provocative suggestion that it might be? There is evidence of the (at least occasional) practice of rapid, performative composing among Romantic and modernist poets. There is even better documented evidence that Homeric poetry was composed live on the spot, and that this served as its very means of transmission down to the point at which writing spread among the ancient Greeks. A key if not sole proof of this, for Milman Parry and his epigones, was the extemporaneous quality of Homeric syntax, so strangely redolent of contemporary transcripts of how we ourselves speak, as we reach for the next clause to capture our emergent meaning, in a clause-by-clause advance that only sometimes adds up to a 'correct' sentence. Could the syntactic qualities of our verse be interpreted in a similar fashion?

Contemporary critics regularly praise its processual qualities. Here is Robert Hass, on Lowell's 'The Quaker Graveyard in Nantucket':

> In the speed of the writing, the syntax comes apart: it dissolves into emotion, into music and into the subterranean connections between images. Throughout the poem, it is characteristic that the important associations occur in subordinate clauses or in compounds so breathless that you have to sort your way quite consciously back to the starting point.[19]

Hass gives us a Lowell whose impassioned act of writing seems inferable from the way the sentences form on the page. 'Poetic thinking', Helen Vendler writes, 'cannot, and does not, obliterate or disavow the reflections it engages in en route'.[20] This is in the course of her analysis of Yeats's 'The Circus Animals' Desertion'. Where Hass will write of Lowell, 'The main clause is a pushing off place and the poem makes its meaning out of its momentum', Vendler, in the same set of lectures where she comments on the living qualities of Yeats's verse, will praise Pope's *Essay on Man* for displaying 'the mobility of a mind as it operates at full tilt'.[21] Poetry for her *is* thinking: 'From the "Carbonates" that poets leave behind, we can deduce as Dickinson asserts, the "fire [that] was," a fire as intellectual in its light as it is passionate in its heat'.[22] But is it really possible to tell, from the processual qualities of their diction alone, that poets' lines have emerged from a real-time act of attentive utterance? Or is it that Vendler and Hass are simply speaking figuratively in all these instances, in the manner which literary criticism by convention allows: we simply pretend the poet wrote under these passions, because their poem conveys them? For Hass, it is Lowell's 'absolute attention to feeling at that moment in the poem's process' that stands out, line by line.[23] But is he really referring to Lowell there? Is his subject not rather the illusion of a self, fabricated by Lowell, over the course of what was most likely numerous distinct sittings? Do any of these texts really amount to a demonstration that the poets in question produced their lines through something like a real-time utterance?

I would answer with a qualified 'No'. Bakker's argument as to the extemporaneous composing we can infer from Homer's in-the-moment syntax is broadly convincing, given it concerns the inscription of an ongoing oral tradition of 'rapid composing in performance' during an epoch of emergent literacy.[24] The very task, as Bakker argues by analogy to medieval writing practices, would be to fix speech in flight, and allow for its recreation as such. But when it comes to poets working in a long-established literary culture, the power of convention in contouring what feels 'caught fresh from the mouths of people' has to be taken into account. The truth is that what feels 'speech-like' on the page to us is quite distinct from the various ways in which we *do* speak. 'What people actually say is very different from what they think they say', Michael Halliday and Christian Matthiessen note.[25] Hence the estranging quality of transcripts of actual speech, especially when these are presented as blocks of prose, rather than lineated according to the intonation units in which that language actually emerged. Such diction can seem, from a certain uncanny perspective, not to represent how we speak at all. The upshot is that to capture the real-time feel of speaking and thinking in verse, a poet will necessarily avoid many of the most characteristic aspects of how we do speak. For what looks speech-like to us is a matter of literary convention. The position I have just sketched will not, however, be the end of the matter and, in fact, is just where things start to get interesting. For writing, in all its various modes, constitutes a kind of 'speaking', all the same.

SPEECH-LIKE BY CONVENTION

Spoken language has features that do not work in the same way, when they appear in writing. Eleanor Berry provides a compelling demonstration of this fact. The Frost and Williams comments on the closeness of poetry to speech cited above are from her article, 'Modern American Poetry and Modern American Speech'. Berry also quotes T.S. Eliot's rather more circumspect version of what poetry shares with speech: 'No poetry, of course, is ever exactly the same speech that the poet talks and hears: but it has to be in such relation to the speech of his time that the listener or reader can say "that is how I should talk, if I could talk poetry"'.[26] With Frost, Williams and Eliot's statements on the spokenness of the best poetry on the table, Berry looks at six explicit representations of conversational speech in their actual poems. The passages she analyses include a narration by one of the witches in Frost's 'Two Witches', one of Williams's first person monologues, and Eliot's presentation, towards the end of Part II of *The Waste Land*, of a working-class woman's bar-room monologue about her absent friend, Lil.[27] Berry contrasts the direct speech in these passages with the picture of naturally occurring speech that has emerged in contemporary linguistics, since the spread of affordable recording devices in the 1950s. In effect, her strategy is the same as Bakker's, but the result in her case is the direct opposite: the experiment serves to underline how far literary poetry's apparently spoken syntax is from actual speech.

Recall the continuative *and* ('and then the next thing I have to say is') discussed at a number of points above – most recently in our pointing out something akin to it in the first four lines of *The Prelude*. It will be worth underlining how pervasive this *and* is in conversation. One of Wallace Chafe's archives involves a set of 1,000 intonation units (again, the bursts in which we speak, often, but not invariably, coextensive with clauses) produced by 11 different speakers during dinner party conversations: some 23 percent of those units included a continuative *and*, most typically at the start of the intonation unit.[28] Interestingly, and again *pace* Croiset and Ong, those speakers were all academics. Berry's point, in contrast, is that there are no instances of this type of *and* in the six supposedly conversational poems she analyses.[29]

To approach the next of her contrasts, note the common conversational phenomenon of afterthought. As Chafe puts it, 'It happens over and over again that a speaker will indicate with sentence-final intonation that she has achieved the goal of communicating a center of interest, only to double back and rescan the same center of interest for one or more additional pieces of information'.[30] 'Center of interest' was Chafe's term, at that point in his work, for the hazy webs of memory and argument that come to mind, whenever we have some particular idea we want to communicate. We will later see him address the matter in terms of 'semi-active consciousness' and 'topic'. As for the afterthoughts that indicate we are still nagged by something that our earlier efforts at speaking have failed to convey, such afterthoughts are pervasive in conversational corpora and common in Homer as well; we saw examples in the first seven lines of *The Iliad*, where their presence served to ground Bakker's point that the Homeric poems really were generated in the act of real-time speaking. For speakers do not 'achieve the expression of a series of centres of interest without some trouble' (Chafe).[31] Afterthought emerges 'over and over again' in conversation.[32] Yet its presence is minimal in the six conversational poems Berry surveys. She finds one instance in *The Waste Land* passage, and one in the Williams poem. Her comment is pertinent: 'One such instance apparently serves to establish or reinforce that the text in question represents unplanned speech. More such instances, being much more noticeable to a reader than to a participant in a conversation, would be distracting'.[33]

For a third contrast, consider Chafe's reference to 'sentence-final intonation' in his definition of 'afterthought' above. He is alluding to the above-mentioned fact that in English, as in so many other languages, we descend in pitch as we come to the end of a sentence. For we certainly do use sentences in conversation, however much transcripts might seem to belie their centrality to our speech. In this sonic fashion, the speaker indicates that he or she 'has achieved the goal of communicating a center of interest'.[34] It is just that the multi-clausal strings we bring to a close in this fashion do not necessarily display the kinds of balances we expect in our prose. For the following is a sentence, thus defined: 'Uh, well, that's an interesting question, and that, you're quite right, monolithic technology would never offer that'.[35] A speaker's use of sentence-final intonation over the final words of this string is unremarkable in speech, where the context, the placement of pauses and the transience of our two-three second focus of conscious attention will allow it more or less to work. The results are often very strange, and rarely artistic, when printed. There are no such sentences in the poems Berry analyses, which seek, after all, to sound like speech.[36]

The high degree of repetitiveness in the two conversational transcripts cited in chapter 7 constitutes a fourth typical feature that literary attempts to embody a speech-like diction will necessarily avoid. The first of those transcripts ('(a) [.69] A—nd and you look at them,/(b) and and they see him,/ (c) and they come up') featured six instances of 'and' (including two of 'and they') in the first 16 words, while 'without saying anything' appeared twice in the full 40 words as well. Berry remarks of a similar transcript: 'Such repetitions and replacements of words and afterthoughts are not particularly noticeable to participants in a conversation – the need to produce and process speech in real time, which tends to bring them about, tends also to obscure them'.[37] We do not overly notice our own repetitiveness, caught up as we are in the very act of generating our speech. Nor do we tend to notice it when comprehending another's speech. Berry's point is that these repetitions stand out very prominently on the page, to the point that they simply do not sound conversational at all.

It will be worth elaborating on some of the functions which repetition serves for conversationalists. We have just seen Berry relate the pervasive repetition in our speech to the high processing demands of real-time speech production. But conversational repetition serves key intersubjective functions as well. For Deborah Tannen, repetition is one of the great drivers of conversation. Here, to cite one of her examples, is how a friend responded to her request that she be allowed to record their dinner party:

PETER. Just to see if we say anything interesting?
DEBORAH. No. Just to see how you say nothing interesting.
PETER. Oh. Well I – hardly ever say nothing interesting.[38]

Commenting on the 'astonishing rhythmic and iconic coordination that can be observed when people interact face to face', Tannen argues that one of the key ways such 'ensemble' effects come about is through the close-coming repetition of prior phrasing.[39] It gets a rhythm going. If you found yourself sounding this transcript out in your head while reading it, you may well agree that a key part of the success of such exchanges is in the speakers' timing.

You might also agree with me that the comparative awkwardness of Peter's final comment is as much a matter of the jarring rhythm as anything else. That is because wit *is* rhythm, rhythm and meaning combined. But those rhythmic features do not merely serve to platform witty remarks. When Tannen claims that 'rhythm is as basic to conversation as it is to musical performance', she has all modes of conversation in mind. As an intuitive demonstration of that broader point, she reminds us of the way two speakers can sometimes be observed trying to speak at exactly the same time, after a pause in conversation. It is because they are 'on time'.[40] But the point for us to draw from all this is that repeating what has just been said is a key way of effecting that kind of onward-moving pulse. It gets a rhythm going; more precisely, it serves to bring out the rhythmic contours in what has just been said. Repetition keeps us attentive to each other's speech rhythms, engaged in what is to come next.

Other functions which close-coming phrasal repetition performs in conversation include providing listeners with a means to demonstrate attentive 'listenership', and giving them further ways to assume a role as participant in the exchange.[41] In both cases, 'parroting' the others' words is not about repeating the same message at all. Actually, such repetition regularly provides speakers with an economic way to advance distinct positions on a common topic. This might involve making minor variations to the words, but it can just as well be a matter of varying the emotional tone of another's words, even as one repeats them. Again, it would seem that the ephemerality of words as they are heard, and the subtly shifting nature of intersubjective contexts, stops us in such cases from feeling like we are just hearing the same thing, over and over. Repetition can even platform discovery: 'Ongoing discourse is . . . woven of the threads of prior talk. When fishing for words, speakers cast a net in the immediately surrounding waters of conversation'.[42]

But however innate to speaking it is, the point is that there is far, far less repetition of words and phrases in the twentieth-century poems Berry analyses. Even more to the point, when it does appear, 'the repetition creates a highly formal tone: the language seems more poetic than conversational'.[43] Doubtless for this reason, William Carlos Williams's poetic representation of conversational narrative almost entirely avoids it. There is more repetition in Frost's *The Witch of Coös*, and the fascinating effect, as Berry notes, is not to make the speakers in that poem sound more conversational, but rather to make the poem as a whole feel 'more formal and rehearsed', which seems to have been Frost's very point.[44] The poem feels 'closer to ritual speech'.[45]

I have emphasised poets' desire for their work to feel in-the-moment, as if emergent in the narrator's here and now. But obviously aspects of their work also seek to create recursive, ritualising effects. This is apparent in Berry's major example of conversation-like repetition, the passage from Part II of *The*

Waste Land ('A Game of Chess') where Eliot has an anonymous woman in a bar recount her exchange with the absent Lil.

You ought to be ashamed, I said, to look so antique.
(And her only thirty-one.)
I can't help it, she said, pulling a long face,
It's them pills I took, to bring it off, she said.
(She's had five already, and nearly died of young George.)
The chemist said it would be alright, but I've never been the same.
You *are* a proper fool, I said.
Well, if Albert won't leave you alone, there it is, I said,
What you get married for if you don't want children?
HURRY UP PLEASE IT'S TIME[46]

It is worth noting how conversational these lines actually are. Eliot's ear is acute and there are numerous features we could point to. There are, for instance, six complement clauses in these 10 lines. A complement clause is a *that* clause (with or without the actual word *that*) following upon a verb of saying, thinking or knowing. Each of the speaker's *I said* and *she saids* in this excerpt is linked to a complement clause, and the following line contains a complement clause ('it would be all right') as well:

The chemist said it would be all right, but I've never been the same.

According to Douglas Biber and Camilla Vásquez's statistical work on the large Longman corpus of spoken and written English, such clauses are five times more common in speech than in conversation. The '*that* omission' characterizing every single one of the complement clauses in this passage is markedly conversational as well, occurring 80 percent of the time a complement clause is used in a spoken context, by Biber and Vásquez's statistics.[47] But what is just as characteristically conversational as Eliot's deployment of complement clauses with '*that* omission' is the fact is that his speaker repeats the word *said* so often, in such a short space. Yet this third fact has some quite paradoxical effects. For the result of representing this kind of everyday repetitiveness in a poem serves, as Berry points out, to ritualise it. The repeated instances of *said* give the impression 'that Eliot's text, even where representing informal conversation, is part of a thoroughly formal poem'.[48]

Note, in this same regard, the effect of the 'HURRY UP PLEASE IT'S TIME' call one encounters once here and another four times over the surrounding lines. Tonally and thematically, the utterance feels more akin to the Marvell allusion at the start of Part III ('But at my back in a cold blast I hear/The rattle of the bones, and chuckle spread from ear to ear') than to any actual bar-room announcement.[49] This capitalised instruction to 'HURRY UP PLEASE IT'S TIME' comes across as essentially freighted and ironic, even though these are the very words one hears in such a bar every night, repeated as many, if not more, times. Again, the repetition that is so every day in spoken exchanges becomes, in the forcefield of the poem, that which most draws attention to itself as artificed.

The upshot is that the poets who most wish to link poetry to orality will avoid the kinds of everyday repetitions that are essential to it. Repetition is simply not how you convey the impression of a thought that has emerged in the moment, as if spontaneously ('how I should talk, if I could talk poetry'). When poets do avail themselves of such phrasal repetition, it will be to formalise things, as in Frost's case, or to estrange them, as in Eliot's ('and chuckle spread from ear to ear'). These are essential effects, to be sure. But too many of them will get in the way of what Attridge has described as 'the mobile forward-moving energy that animates almost every literary work'.[50] In particular, it will hinder our sense that we are dealing with a text emerging in the here and now.

Berry also looks at hedges: *like, sort of, kind of*. One of Chafe's studies shows hedges appearing eight times more often in samples of conversation than in samples of academic prose.[51] There is only one hedge in the six poems Berry analyses, a *sort of* in the Frost. As with Eliot's sole usage of a continuative 'And' in the bar room passage above, it seems clear that any more than one hedge 'would be distracting'.[52]

Nor are there any fillers (*um, oh, ah, uh*) in Berry's sample of conversational poems. They would look artificial.

NOTES

1. Attridge, *Poetic Rhythm*, 1.
2. Attridge, 1–2.
3. Wordsworth, qtd in Attridge, 2.
4. Attridge, 2.
5. Attridge, 2.
6. Wordsworth, qtd in Attridge, 2.
7. Attridge, 2.
8. Bakker, *Poetry in Speech*, 45.
9. Pawley and Syder, "One-Clause-at-a Time," 195.
10. Lichtenberg, qtd in Auden, "Words and the Word," 105.
11. Novalis, qtd in Hamacher, "95 Theses," 30.
12. Lord, *Singer of Tales*, 13.
13. Paterson, interview by Kevin Brophy, July 2, 2013.
14. Williams, qtd in Berry, "Modern American Poetry," 47–48.
15. Frost, qtd in Berry, 47.
16. Pound, "A Retrospect," 11–12.

17. Wordsworth and Coleridge, "Preface," 29.
18. Wordsworth and Coleridge, 38.
19. Hass, "Lowell's Graveyard," 10.
20. Vendler, *Poets Thinking*, 107.
21. Hass, "Lowell's Graveyard," 10; Vendler, *Poets Thinking*, 28.
22. Vendler, 9.
23. Hass, "Lowell's Graveyard," 16.
24. Lord, *The Singer of Tales*, 17.
25. Halliday and Matthiessen, *Functional Grammar*, 51.
26. Eliot, qtd in Berry, "Modern American Poetry," 47.
27. Berry, 50.
28. Chafe, "Linking Intonation Units," 10.
29. Berry, "Modern American Poetry," 51.
30. Chafe, "Deployment of Consciousness," 35.
31. Chafe, 33.
32. Chafe, 35.
33. Berry, "Modern American Poetry," 52.
34. Chafe, "Deployment of Consciousness," 28.
35. Anon. qtd in Berry, "Modern American Poetry," 58
36. Berry, 58.
37. Berry, 51.
38. Tannen, *Talking Voices*, 71. Tannen's transcription conventions are listed at 193.
39. Tannen, 32.
40. Tannen, 33.
41. Tannen, 61.
42. Tannen, 83.
43. Berry, "Modern American Poetry," 52.
44. Berry, 50.
45. Berry, 53.
46. Eliot, *Waste Land*, 139 (2.156–165).
47. Biber and Vásquez, "Writing and Speaking," 541.
48. Berry, "Modern American Poetry," 55.
49. Eliot, *Waste Land*, 70 (3.195–196).
50. Attridge, "Phrasing and Repetition," 39.
51. Chafe, "Evidentiality," 270.
52. Berry, "Modern American Poetry," 52.

Chapter 9

Writing as 'Oral Dictated'

A final illustration of how generally oblivious people are to the stark differences between how we speak and how we represent speech in writing (not to mention theatre, film, television, etc.) begins personally. However much I read linguistic analyses of real-time speech production, I continue to receive a shock, whenever I see how my own speaking looks on the page, stripped of most of the prosodic and other information that helped it to make sense at the time. I am referring to the verbatim interview files which I receive back from the transcribers, and then have the task of 'brushing up' for approval by my interviewees. One's eyes instantly alight on narcissistically wounding excerpts like the following:

INTERVIEWER. Well it's probably a question there whether poetics is a constantly shifting thing for it to be real, or if it's possible to have a single poetics, a consistent poetics, would that be a contradiction in terms perhaps?

At such moments, I take heart from Geoffrey Leech and Jan Svartvik's suggestion that any transcript will look 'less rambling' if broken into the intonation units in which it was actually uttered.[1] For, of course, that is how it was generated and heard at the time, as a series of spurt-like units, along the lines of

Well it's probably a question there,
whether poetics is a constantly shifting thing,
for it to be real, –
or if it's possible to have a single poetics,
a consistent poetics,
would that be a contradiction in terms perhaps?

Another important factor as to why such words seemed acceptable and intelligible at the time would be the context in which they were delivered. I will call the poet to whom I put the above question (was it even a question?) Poet A. Poet A had been telling me about the pile of notes where they keep all the various thoughts they write down on poetics, adding that many of those notes actually contradict each other. In responding to that comment, I was trying to make the Nietzschean point that to admit multiplicity and contradiction into our conception of an object might be the best way to stay true to it. Here is how the poet responded to my proposal in turn:

POET A. Yeah, oh I think so, yeah, the thousand flowers bloom business, I think you're stuck with the fact that . . . <u>and</u> it would be deadly, <u>and</u> I think that's what I worry about when any particular school of poetics or something becomes particularly dominant <u>and</u> especially if they have dominant . . . enters the academies <u>and</u> enters especially these creative writing schools <u>and</u> so people start doing this, but neglect the value in other things or just dismiss it. I think this ... yeah, there's very many different ways <u>and</u> again, I think it depends a lot on the particular poet's personality and perceptions <u>and</u> how they do things.

We find a number of the characteristically oral features discussed above in this short transcript, which includes four fillers (two cases of 'yeah', two of 'oh') and four complement clauses (e.g. 'I think you're stuck with the fact'), while '*that* omission' is a feature of all but one of these same clauses.[2] We also find a predominance of continuative *ands* over coordinating ones: seven versus one. I have underlined those continuative *ands* (and left without underline the only coordinating one, in 'personality and perceptions') to emphasise this particularly conversational feature. But I have also done so to aid the reader's comprehension, on the grounds that indicating where the continuative *ands* appear will usually show where intonation units begin, and with that, something of the logic of the speaker's discourse.[3]

Yet however much one elucidates the logic, it seems fair to say that a sense of linguistic impoverishment remains – just as it pertains to the patrician Eliot's representation of bar-room speech in Part II of *The Waste Land*, for all the incantatory quality of the speaker's repetitions. That is, of course, why I have anonymized Poet A's transcript. A responsible interviewer necessarily translates these sorts of passages into a written register if a name is to be attached to them, and then on the basis of that 'brushed up' version seeks permissions to cite. Not to translate the words into prose amounts to a flagrant misrepresentation, for as Michael Halliday notes of such purportedly verbatim texts, texts, the 'formlessness of speech is an artefact of the transcription; if a written text is reproduced with all the planning processes left in, then it too will appear formless'.[4] The fascinating implication of Halliday's comment is that we simply do not hear the 'hesitations and "false starts"' that appear in a transcript when listening to the same discourse face-to-face.[5] Actually, it is not the same discourse. One might expatiate here on the way certain journalists will leave such characteristically oral features in, when it is a matter of quoting a disliked politician, or a speaker from a maligned class, or ethnicity – the primitivist discourses referenced in Part II, à propos the evaluation of Homer's syntax, find all sorts of way to retain currency. The point that concerns us here, however, is that the reason verbatim citations of speech are so potentially discriminatory is that we are generally ignorant of the differing tendencies of spoken and written language, though we hear, and what is more, produce strings of words like Poet A's every day. (The irony here is that A's ideas on poetry and writing were among the most intellectually compelling of any to emerge in my 15 years of interviewing poets. For me to draw on Nietzsche in the course of our interactions was simply a way of trying to keep up.)

As a further, practical testimony to the distance spoken discourse bears from the image of it in our books and newspapers, plays and films, and even from our immediate perception of it, consider the amount of work it takes to convert a transcript like that cited above into citable prose. A key issue concerns the so-called 'false starts'. It is fiendishly difficult to work out whether curtailed strings – like 'I think you're stuck with the fact that . . . and it would be deadly, and I think that's what I worry about' – contain information that does need to be somehow represented in the final, full-sentence, version, or whether those words really are 'false starts', that is false to the speaker's actual point, and so need be scrapped. After all, those curtailed words might well represent a genuine proposition, in elliptical form, a proposition perhaps inferable from context, in the manner of A's earlier nod to 'the thousand flowers bloom business'.

There is a deeper point to be made here as well. In the 1930s, Lev Vygotsky pointed out that intimate couples, speaking aloud to each other, will often feel licensed to talk in a 'condensed, abbreviated' way, on the grounds that through long familiarity each already has a good grasp of what the other most likely intends to say. Vygotsky makes the observation in the course of a discourse on the 'inner speech' that runs through our minds. He believes it is often similarly elliptical. We more or less 'know' what we have in mind, even as we tell ourselves something, and for that reason we can verbalise the idea in our heads (i.e. think it) in a 'maximally compact' way, just as the couple can speak in that 'maximally compact' way to each other out loud.[6] Let us grant that Vygotsky is correct in his observation on the occurrence of 'condensed, abbreviated' diction in intimate conversation, and that he is further correct in his diagnosis of the prevalence of 'condensed, abbreviated' diction in inner speech, that is thought (elsewhere, he suggests that his researches concern phenomena 'as unknown to science as the other side of the moon').[7] We might then be entitled to claim that the 'false starts' in Poet A's diction are actually not 'false starts' at all, in the sense of the beginnings of thoughts that lead nowhere, but rather 'condensed, abbreviated' ideas. That would be to suggest that Poet A is quite literally thinking aloud at such moments, his speaking as immediate to the concepts it expresses as thinking them would itself be.

Perhaps Vygotsky would have come to the same conclusion, had he lived into the era of mechanical recording devices, and realized how pervasive speech fragments are and how much communication proceeds by way of them, including among relative strangers. Just 30 years into the era in which such devices became common, Wallace Chafe and Jane Danielewicz were arguing that all spoken discourse has the 'thinking-aloud' property to which I have just alluded: 'speaking has the advantage of providing a more direct expression of ongoing thought processes. For listeners, as well as for us investigators, speaking makes available a more direct window on the mind in action'.[8] From such a perspective, Poet A really would seem to be engaging in 'the gradual production of thoughts whilst speaking', a phenomenon so often valorised as genuinely poetic.

To return, however, to the argument advanced over the previous chapter, the language which conveys Poet A's thoughts so immediately does not seem to be of the kind that could ever actually appear in poems.

SPEAKING FOR THE PAGE

The chapters of this book would seem to have come some way toward the notion that composing poetry in a real-time, speech-like manner might be a feasible cultural practice. The important complication introduced in the previous chapter is that even were literary poets to compose with something like the immediacy of real-time speaking, they would still have to avoid many of the most characteristic features of how we actually do speak and think in the moment. Yet there is something in the idea of writing having to avoid such features that doesn't quite ring true. Whoever thinks to themselves, while writing, 'I must try to avoid putting too many *umms* in this sentence'? Who – even more to the point – ever says 'umm', or 'ahhhh' to themselves, hesitating in the middle of the sentence they are trying to compose? The unlikeliness of that scenario will lead us to a somewhat paradoxical position. A writing that would aspire to a spoken immediacy may well lack many of the most characteristic features of oral utterance. But writing, in all its modes, constitutes a form of speaking, all the same.

To make the experiment of trying to allow as many *and*-initial clauses, *sort ofs*, *ummms* and afterthoughts into an act of writing is an interesting way of underlining this point. The only way to do so, it seems to me, is to put on some sort of colloquial voice, act it out in one's head, and write down what emerges there. What that thought-experiment reveals, however, is that this is just the sort of role-playing we perform when we write in any case. We shift into whatever particular voice the context demands, use it to say in our heads whatever it is we want to write, and copy those words down. The previous chapter argued that one's writing voice, however naturalised it may come to feel to the writer, is never quite the same as the one we use when speaking aloud. There are almost never any *um*s or *ah*s there, far, far fewer clauses beginning with a continuative *and*, and nothing like the amount of repetition. Those features of everyday speaking are simply not there for the writer, to the point where one would somehow elect to leave them out. But that does not stop the voice we adopt when writing from constituting a type of subvocal or otherwise imagined speaking. Even in the composition of the most academic of prose, we say the words to ourselves as our very means of generating them.

Vygotsky's term 'inner speech' was used above for what Maria L. Slowiaczek and Charles Clifton Jr describe as 'the subjective experience of hearing a voice in one's head'.[9] Others label it self-talk, covert speech, voice imagery, articulatory imagery, auditory verbal imagery and inner monologue.[10] We also, if somewhat loosely, just call it 'thinking'. Rather than writing having nothing to do with uttering words, the truer picture is that, when writing, we speak the words in our heads, as thoughts, so as to compose them, and we do so in the specific and highly elaborated ways of speaking we have fashioned for the page. We speak them to ourselves, in our heads, and just occasionally out loud. Writing is, in other words, an experience of suddenness. We intend – strive towards – a certain hazily present idea and the words rise up in our minds as we do so. We might plan out their general contours, and work with a formulaic diction, but just what exact words we will say in our heads are not knowable in advance of the very moment of saying them there, so as to then further modify and/or write them down. There are, of course, nuances in the case of the speech-impaired, that we will come to shortly, though they only prove the rule. Writing is not the opposite of speaking, but rather a slowed-down, expanded and generally subvocal version of that activity, that we then transcribe.

An initial way of demonstrating these assertions will be to show that one can speak out loud – in real time – in a very different register to that of the speech transcripts we have seen so far, one much closer to the sort of language we find on the printed page. It is something interviewers know on a very practical level. Transcripts like the one which follows are far easier to 'brush up' for publication. My analysis will be as follows: this next interviewee, whom I will call Poet B, is engaged in the kind of speaking one would typically perform in one's head when producing prose. An immediate indice of that will be how much easier it is to understand the transcript. Establishing this will further underline just how fast one can compose, at least when it is a matter of prose. In fact, one can speak prose – or rather, a somewhat chaotic and restricted form of it. After all, that is just how we write it, by saying it to ourselves in our heads, albeit with multiple recalibrations, then writing it down.

Here is a question I posed towards the end of my interview with Poet B, followed by that poet's response. I will underline the continuative *and*s, and leave without underline the coordinating one ('go out and dig'), with the same two-fold purpose as in Poet A's case, above: (1) to bring out a key feature of conversational speech; and (2) to assist with the reader's comprehension, by giving an indication of some of the intonational breaks that served to make this discourse sound 'natural' when it was uttered.

INTERVIEWER. Okay. Um. There's just two more questions here. <u>And</u> the first one is asking about the differences between you in the act of writing a poem and you at other times, the times between poems, if you like. Like whether you feel you're a different self in those . . . .

POET B. Yeah, that's a good question. I mean you would think I would have a better understanding of that. I mean part of me thinks I'm a rather consistent um personality ah but actually um until fairly recently I'd always been afraid of a lot of things. I kind of got over that in a very late blooming way um <u>and</u> writing was a place where I felt quite free <u>and</u> even though I find it really, really hard to write, still finding it really, really hard to write . . . it's much easier to clean, I love to clean when I don't want to write or something like that, you know, just go out and dig in the dirt or something but yeah, writing is still I think a free space. I do feel, at least initially, that I can say anything. I can put . . . anything I can find the word for I can put it down <u>and</u> you have to have at least a little more social inhibition when you move about in the world <u>and</u> so there's some there's definitely a distinction but I kind of think that people who read what I've written probably know me as well as I know myself in some ways. That I'm more revealing than I intend to be in my work <u>and</u> I think a lot of writers are revealed in their writing in ways that are unbeknownst to them.

Evidently, this excerpt has many of the features typical of conversational speech. Poet B utters six *and*s, all but one of them continuative. There are 10 hedges is the poet's response ('a lot' (twice), 'kind of' (twice), 'or something' (twice), 'a little', 'fairly', 'in some ways', 'quite'). There are nine fillers ('um' (thrice), 'yeah' (twice), 'I mean' (twice), 'ah', 'you know'). There is significant repetition here as well: 'I can' (four times), 'really, really hard to write' (twice), 'to clean' (twice). These features have all been associated with spoken language, and their prevalence in that medium attributed to the processing constraints of real-time speech production. As I noted of the continuative *and* earlier, when producing speech in the moment we find ourselves constantly in a position where the most convenient way to generate the next chunk of thought is by availing ourselves of familiar, finely honed devices of this order. Hence Douglas Biber and Camilla Vásquez's somewhat paradoxical claim that, for all their potential stylistic variety, 'spoken registers tend to be relatively oral'.[11]

But note the features that indicate something else is going on here as well. Earlier I cited Biber and Vásquez's finding that speakers drop *that* from complement clauses 80 percent of the time. Poet B omits *that* only 50 percent of the time here. Note too, that however prominent Poet B's use of the continuative *and*, these usages tend to initiate a passable prose sentence (one has to ignore the current punctuation markers to see this). Even more significantly, the poet's repairs are easily disentangled ('I can put . . . anything I can find the word for . . . down'). This is true of even the most seemingly garbled part of the excerpt:

and even though I find it really, really hard to write, still finding it really, really hard to write . . . it's much easier to clean, I love to clean when I don't want to write or something like that, you know, just go out and dig in the dirt or something but yeah, *writing is still I think a free space.*

By italicising the relevant words, I have tried to bring out the fact that Poet B is, for all the lengthy and whimsical aside, maintaining the kind of sentence structure that does service in prose. Poet B is speaking rather as one would, when composing prose for the page.

The following discourse would, on the other hand, seem at first glance quite markedly oral. It begins with a characteristically conversational *and*, and is replete with the kinds of repairs that indicate multiple, in the moment, recalibrations. I will call this interviewee Poet C:

And I think this was one of the problems of with say a lot of avant-garde poetry was that – particularly language poetry, was that it was assumed . . . the – the ego of the author assumed, that everybody was going to read every word of it, when in fact nobody did, and they were very disappointed by that, you know, that that it wasn't read closely.

Poet C is clearly speaking, rather than writing these lines.

The impression of orality in this poet's discourse is amplified when we take on board Michael Halliday's observation that a spoken discourse will tend to present us with an intricacy of verbal relations, as opposed to the contrasting density of noun-usage observable (at least as a broad tendency) in written discourse.[12] For instance, a string like 'one of the problems . . . was that it was assumed' would generally feature fewer verbs in prose-writing, particularly at the scholarly end of the scale, where writers tend to deploy nouns like 'assumption' instead: 'the problem was the assumption'. Whether delivered orally or in writing, verbs, especially when they are active, tend to require one to name the doers and the done to, and this is particularly the case in English. That is to say, our verbs tend, unlike nouns, to bring actors and objects in their wake. Perhaps for these same reasons, Poet C feels drawn, at the price of some dysfluency, including a whole flip in mood from passive to active, to find a subject for the assuming that they have just mentioned ('one of the problems . . . was that . . . it was assumed ... the the ego of the author assumed'). A scholarly writer would likely go straight for 'the problem was the assumption', skating over all such tricky questions of agency. Anyone tasked with editing scholarly writing knows the obfuscations that scholarship's excessive reliance upon nouns can serve to licence.[13] Halliday's summation of these contrasts is that 'in the spoken language, the unit of organization is the clause. . . But in the written language the organizing unit becomes the noun, or rather the nominal group'.[14] We see that characteristically spoken preference for verbal formulations, with named agents driving them, in Poet C's discourse here, and especially in the very repairs to which the poet subjects it.

But what is just as important to note is that, however 'relatively oral' aspects of Poet C's diction are, the poet is nonetheless producing an easily recognizable prose sentence pattern. The very repairs that seem to garble the poet's words actually in each case maintain a coherent link back to a recognizably prose structure. For the upshot of the repairs analysed above is not only to clarify who is doing what to whom. They simultaneously serve to reinstate a prose sentence structure, allowing the transcriber with relative ease to extract a sentence like

> One of the problems with a lot of avant-garde poetry (and in particular with language poetry) was that the author egotistically assumed that everybody was going to read every word of it.

Might we not conclude that these are the sorts of repairs the speaker would practise when writing prose? That would amount to arguing that Poet C is speaking as they would when composing prose for the page. If so, it would explain why it was, once more, so relatively easy to 'brush up' Poet C's text for citation, as it was in Poet B's case, and in vivid contrast to how things were with Poet A's.

One could draw a thick line through the 30 research interviews which I have conducted with poets in the course of this project, had professionally transcribed into 'verbatim' prose, and then proceeded to prepare for authorial approval. On one side would be the interviews like Poet B and Poet C's, which took some 12 hours apiece to translate into a citable text; on the other, would be transcripts like that of Poet A, which took at least 40 hours and required minute attention to detail. This stark division also characterized the three interviews which I conducted with writers of scholarly prose in 2018. Two of those interviews took some 12 hours each, the other some 40–50 hours to prepare. That all 33 of these interviewees have their own unique speaking styles goes without saying. But the sharp division into two groups remains and only makes sense on the grounds that one group of these 33 interviewees were *speaking for the page*, as if they were actually writing, and the other group not.

I realise that one would typically describe these subjects' respective speaking styles in different terms. One might say that Poet B and C's speech was oral in its 'medium' but literate in its 'conception'.[15] Or that those poets were communicating in quite markedly literary and/or expository speech registers.[16] Such analyses have the advantage of underlining that there is no one single 'spoken style', a point Halliday himself, for all the broad contrasts he draws between the spoken and the written, is keen to make.[17] But what such terms fail to capture is that all writing is initially oral, albeit just spoken in our heads. Certain interviewees provide an insight into this fact, by the skill with which they manage to generate on the spot the kinds of verbal strings that can more or less do service on the page. For Poets B and C were certainly speaking to me. But they were speaking just as much to the recording device; they were speaking to the device as if it were the self taking their words down, when they compose prose for the page. That is because writing *is* speaking: a slowed-down, expanded and generally subvocal version of it.

HEARING WHILE READING

The next point to make is that we all intuitively treat writing as a form of speaking – a speaking for the page – when we are reading it. Reflection on the phenomenon of silent reading will serve to make this clear. For Eudora Welty, 'Ever since I was first read to, then started reading to myself, there has never been a line read that I didn't *hear*. As my eyes followed the sentence a voice was saying it silently to me'.[18] We speak the words to ourselves, as we read them. Then again, we do not always do so. Any academic reader knows how to skim read. The intermittency with which we give inner voice to the words we read has led some reading scientists to suggest that actually, 'skilful reading' might not require 'phonological coding' at all. It might be that proficient readers develop forms of 'direct access' that take us straight from the visual representation of a word 'to an entry in the mental lexicon'.[19] Other scientists have countered such claims with experiments showing, for instance, that test subjects in a high-speed categorisation trial were more likely to list the silently read word 'rows' as a type of 'flower', than the orthographically similar word, 'robs'.[20] Subjects must on some level have been sounding the words out for the homophone (rows/rose) to trip them up. Such seemingly convincing examples are met with contrary studies that point, for instance, to the reading prowess displayed by certain subjects who are phonologically impaired to the point of lacking inner speech altogether.[21] But what both sides of that debate have consistently agreed upon, while disagreeing about its relevance to their own model of normative silent reading, is that readers will tend to give 'inner voice' to texts they find hard to comprehend. We sound such texts out in our heads, in an effort 'to get what the writer is saying'. One rarely pauses to ask why.

It is worth dwelling on this every day, but rather curious, phenomenon, because there is something quite revealing in it. The first thing to note is that one of the key reasons we stumble in reading is that so little of our sonic grammar is marked on the page. For even though 'intonation contours and sentence rhythms provide patterns which group words into phrases and highlight new and important information', very little of that sonic grammar is encoded in our writing system.[22] Noting this, Slowiaczek and Clifton argue that what we are effectively doing, in sounding out sentences that stump us, is performatively guessing at that missing code. Take a typical 'garden path' sentence:

The old man the boat.

Reading this on the page, we might start wondering why we have an old man, a boat and no verb. The problem does not arise when we utter it aloud, however, because in such a case we lengthen the duration of *old* and rise in pitch on *man*, to indicate a phrasal boundary between the two, and thus convey that *man* is here used as a verb (to control, to sail, to staff). As in most such cases, the sentence is only 'garden path' when we encounter it in print, without the usual sonic clues. Pausing in such a case, to sound out various possibilities, provides us with the means to discover and settle upon the one that makes the most contextual sense. We subvocalise when stumped. The same research suggests that we also invariably subvocalise when we know that the writing – not just one sentence, but the piece as a whole – will be complex or involved. Performatively guessing at the sonic code obviously helps us make sense in these cases as well. So, when it is a matter of reading some multiply-qualified sentence of theoretical prose, let us say some Charles Saunders Peirce, we intuit from the portion of the sentence we have read so far which upcoming clauses are parentheses, shift (albeit just in our heads) to the lower, and more narrow, pitch range by which we indicate asides when speaking, and then at the end of the parenthesis shift back up to our previous pitch to resume the main line of the syntax. Multiple parentheses can thus be embedded in one sentence and the main train of meaning will still ring out clearly. We are particularly given to 'singing' in this manner when reading philosophy. In sum, what an author means is inseparable from our sense of how they said it while writing it. We all know this, if only intuitively. Why else recreate it in our heads as speech at those moments of encountered or expected difficulty?

There is also the way we use prosody to signify emotion. As Peter Myers explains and, indeed, graphs:

> the more attitudes, feelings and tones of voice there are in a person's speech, the more it tends to be musical. Whether solicitous or rebuking, ironic or affectionate, the tones give rise to tunes. If there is no attitude or tone expressed – 'John Smith was born in 1924' – there is no tune. It is the attitude of exasperation that might give the melody of, for example,

>   will
>   that?'[23]
>   saying
>   stop
>   you please
> 'O

This must be one of the reasons why we normally subvocalise literary works, and in particular why we as a rule sound out dialogue in our heads.[24] Without sounding out a character's utterances, it becomes very hard to grasp their emotions!

Whenever we encounter difficulty, complexity or drama in a text, the assumption guiding our reading comes into the open: everything we read is the product of a kind of speaking. Assumptions can, of course, be wrong. In this case, I suspect that our own experience as writers has a profound influence on the way we try to restore a difficult text to a spoken original, making the matter much more than simply assumed. We know by personal experience that composition is really an act of inner speaking.

We know it experimentally as well. In one of the most well-known demonstrations, cognitive psychologists N. Ann Chenoweth and John R. Hayes asked three sets of subjects to type sentences in response to a set of stimuli, in the presence of a metronome ticking at 120 beats per minute. One group were given no other instruction, the second asked to tap their foot in time with the metronome while writing, and the third to say 'tap' in time with the metronome, again while writing. The last of these conditions is known as 'articulatory suppression' and it has been used widely in experiments on the cognitive dimensions of reading and writing, for such vocalisation makes it very difficult for a subject to produce and hear their own inner speech. Tapping one's foot obviously presents no such difficulties and had little more effect on the second group's capacity to compose than the metronome itself. For the third group, on the other hand, having to say 'tap' again and again 'slowed the rate of writing, increased mechanical errors, sharply reduced P-burst [intonation unit] length, and increased the perceived difficulty of the writing task'.[25] Ronald Kellog likewise found that encumbering writers with a concurrent visual/spatial task is far less disruptive than imposing a verbal one upon them.[26] But he and his colleagues, Thierry Olive and Annie Piolat, did make the intriguing, additional finding that concurrent visual recognition tasks do significantly interfere when subjects are asked to write down definitions of concrete (but not abstract) nouns.[27] The 'mind's eye' does indeed seem to have a role in composition, when it is a matter of finding words for (imagined) percepts. The point, at any rate, is that experiments in the cognitivist tradition have corroborated the claim that composition requires the use of inner speech.

A case in point, aphasia is typically accompanied by agraphia. An exception, on the other hand, would seem to be provided by those rare cases of phonologically impaired individuals who lack outer and inner speech but can nonetheless write. In a much-cited study, David N. Levine, Ronald Calvanio and Alice Popovics describe a 54-year subject who has lost all phonological capacity as the result of a stroke but can perform the short-term memory tasks associated with the everyday practice of saying something in your head over and over so as not to forget it (a phone number, a licence plate number). What is more, that subject could not only write 'single words but full sentences showing a lucid and coherent organisation of thought'.[28] Levine and his colleagues argue that in their subject's case these verbal skills are 'all mediated by visual imagery'.[29] In fact, something like this must apply to spelling itself, whoever the writer, given our general capacity to inscribe homophones correctly, that is to write 'I wear clothes' rather than 'I where clothes'. The case of deaf writers adds another level of complexity. Clearly many with acquired deafness retain inner speech and hearing, and draw on both to write.[30] The congenitally deaf, for their part, would appear to write on the basis of their inner visual imagery of the words alone. Yet what that might mean is interestingly qualified by studies of ideation among that population. Various psychological and neurological studies of inner sign among the deaf suggest, for instance, that 'it would be a mistake to imagine that deaf voices will activate visual parts of the brain in the same way that hearing peoples' voices are associated with auditory parts'.[31] Mairéad MacSweeney and her colleagues accordingly found through neuroimaging studies that when congenitally deaf subjects process signs, they draw not so much on the right hemisphere locations 'specialized for visuo-spatial functions', but rather on the left temporal regions of the brain that are 'typically privileged for processing heard speech'.[32] Their conclusion is that 'in the absence of auditory experience, this area becomes attuned to vision rather than audition'.[33] When writing, such subjects speak by generating the look of the words, just as when reading, they hear with their eyes. Writing is speaking.

'WORKED OVER SPEAKING'

But even if so, we would still seem to have an impossible gap to ford between the proto-prose sentences we have seen Poets B and C produce in their real-time speaking and the sentences writers see fit to publish, sentences characterised, among other things, by the absence of the hedges, fillers and dysfluencies that pervaded those two poets' interview transcripts, however much they approximated to prose. Any attempt to claim that writing is at core speaking needs to make sense of the fact that fillers like *ummm* and *ah* almost never come into our heads in the first place, as we sit and write. Are we really still 'speaking' at such times?

Wallace Chafe argues that we are. Chafe does, nonetheless, identify great differences between writing and speaking. Key among the ways the two activities differ for Chafe is that writing is far more 'worked over'.[34] Chafe adds that 'worked over' is not a very satisfactory term, but he can find no better. On that same page he notes that unlike speaking 'writing has to be taught and the average person never really learns to do it very well'.[35] Now on one level, the 'worked over' quality to which Chafe refers concerns the fact that we tend to revise our initial drafts on later occasions. As illustration, he confesses to having put over a dozen drafts into the very chapter we are reading.[36] The experience of encountering such a statement in the course of a monograph is uncanny, and redolent of the liar's paradox. It is worth adding that Chafe's writing is a model of lucidity: somebody has finally turned on the lights. Actually, it is a revised-12-times somebody. In short, we would seem to be quite far from the idea that writing emerges in the manner of speech, when dwelling on this aspect of writing's 'worked over' quality, typically labelled 'revision' and understood to happen retrospective to a first drafting. But Chafe has a subtler point to make here, that will take us right back to the idea that writing is a kind of real-time speaking, with suddenness at its core.

The 'worked over' quality Chafe attributes to writing is not just a matter of the revisions we perform days and weeks after our initial writing, to produce a 12-times revised document that pretends to proceed from one and the same speech situation.[37] That 'worked over' quality is a feature of what happens during the initial moments of composition as well. Observing that the average speed of spoken English, with pauses, approximates to 180 words per minute, Chafe notes that due to simple matters of motor-function, writing in all its modes necessarily proceeds much more slowly. Typing might come in at a third of that speed, if it is a matter of copying a pre-existing text. Coming up with new words will clearly be much slower. Chafe's estimate is that handwriting or typing new sentences might proceed at approximately a tenth of the speed of speaking, some 18 words per minute.[38] This is a rough estimate, assuming a more or less unbroken composing, and however one might want to temper the figure to account for varying practices among the plethora of different writers, there is a key point that holds here regardless. It is that written composition will always, for simple mechanical causes, be much slower than the composition of real-time speech. This is the reason writers feel no pressure to avoid those *umms*, *ahs* and *a--nds* that intersperse our speaking, and why such words so rapidly appear as artifice when put (not left, but rather put) in a writing. We know that *um*, *ah* and the like simply do not come to mind as we write. They are not part of how one says a string of words to oneself, when working out what to put down next. Due to the mechanically induced delays just noted, we are simply not that pressed for time. Chafe's further point is that that relative time delay makes for certain opportunities:

> what is happening in our thoughts during all that extra time? It is doubtful that very much of our cognitive capacity has to be devoted to the mechanical activity of writing itself, at least after we get beyond the first grade. In writing, it would seem, our thoughts must constantly get ahead of our expression of them in a way to which we are totally unaccustomed when we speak. . . . The result is that we have time to integrate a succession of ideas into a single linguistic unit in a way that is not available to us in speaking. In speaking, we normally produce one idea unit [intonation unit] at a time. That is apparently about all we have the capacity to pay attention to, and if we try to think about much more than that we are likely to get into trouble.[39]

Pawley and Syder's 'one-clause-at-a-time' hypothesis was mentioned in the Introduction for its insight into the severe constraints on real-time processing when we speak, and the continual suddenness to which that plight leads. We do not know the exact words we are about to utter till the second or two before, and often not even until the very moment of, uttering them. Chafe's reference to 'trouble' at the end of this quotation is a reminder of the limited purview imposed upon us, and the contorted utterances this can lead to, as witnessed in the various transcripts of naturally occurring speech cited to this point. Chafe's claim about writing, however, is that the mechanical constraint of having to take the time to write the words down obviates many of these issues. It has the effect of providing additional processing power, by freeing up more time.

Some of that surplus time evidently goes into creating a denser type of intonation unit, and a greater coherence between units, than is possible when speaking. The fact that readers can read so much faster (some 200–400 words per minute, by Chafe's estimate) than we can speak (again, up to approximately 180), that they can scan ahead to grasp the shape of the sentence and, what is more, that they can always go back and reread, is clearly part of this picture as well. For it means we can pack more into our utterance and still be intelligible. In Chafe's words, 'the abnormal quickness of reading fits together with the abnormal slowness of writing to foster a kind of language in which ideas are combined to form more complex idea units and sentences'.[40] Halliday makes the important rider, in criticism of Chafe's characterisation of the written product as 'more complex', that spoken and written language 'tend to display different kinds of complexity; each of them is more complex in its own way' than the other.[41] Halliday points to the statement 'It'll've been going to've been being tested every day for the past fortnight soon', which he overheard at one point: it comprises 'five serial tense choices, present in past in future in past in future, and is also passive'.[42] Such multi-tense formulations are 'very difficult to construct consciously ... and they are equally hard to process when you are reading', but arise spontaneously and seem comprehensible enough in spoken contexts.[43] A discourse that tends towards an intricacy of verbal relations certainly has its own complexities. But the point for us here concerns the unique affordances of writing. It is not simply that a writer has time for retrospective revision. Writing is also more 'worked over' at the point of production. One can work and rework a phrase, before putting it down.

Turning to the devices by which scholarly writers act, as Chafe and his colleague, Jane Danielewicz, put it, to 'increase the size of their intonation units' when they come to write, their small corpus of academic speakers and writers shows that in published papers the very same subjects use twice as many prepositional phrases, over three times as many attributive adjectives, four times as much nominalisation and five times as many participles as they do in their conversations – including when those conversations are on academic topics.[44] 'None of these devices is cognitively difficult', Chafe and Danielewicz add, 'but combining them in quantity evidently requires the extra time and care available to a writer'.[45] It 'appears that the necessarily rapid production of spoken language consistently produces a less varied vocabulary as well'.[46] The 'worked-over' quality facilitated by the page has the effect of inducing us to pack our expressions with more of a certain type of detail, even as the 'speaker', and the cognitive faculties they draw upon, remain the same.

It is worth adding that Chafe and Danielewicz's sample is small by contemporary standards, and that their study is distant enough from us in time to have included handwritten letters in its sampling. The broad brush of its findings has, however, been more recently confirmed. Writing in 2008, on the basis of an archive that is one thousand times larger than that Chafe and Danielewicz had at their disposal in the late 1980s, and of much broader social composition, Biber and Vásquez corroborate the general outlines of the academic writing/colloquial conversation ratios which I have just tabled, and with it Halliday's earlier finding that what predominates in English-language conversation is the 'dense use of short, simple clauses'.[47] Just as pertinently, Biber and Vásquez echo the insistence of all three linguistics, Chafe, Danielewicz and Halliday, that there is no one-size-fits-all model for either writing or speaking. After all, 'there is an extremely wide range of variation among written registers, because writers can choose to employ linguistic features associated with stereotypical speech'. But they also agree that speakers' choices are narrower in this regard, for the 'real-time production circumstances' of extemporaneous speech militate against it exercising a similar freedom, in relation to written registers.[48] We come once more to the notion that speaking puts us much more in the constrained space of the immediate moment, the very thing valorised in our verse. In contrast, writers have the capacity to expand upon that same moment, even as they fashion something like it for the reader to raise from the page in the course of their reading.

Now just as writings can vary vastly in their syntactic features, the time one will take for writing a given sentence can vary greatly as well, being potentially as long as the breath one has remaining. Yet even as constraint in that direction relaxes, it is clear from Chafe's various writings on the topic – their tenor overall, and also that explicit estimation of an average 18 words per minute when one is handwriting – that his normative model for written composition is not some infinitely slow accretion of word on word, but something much more like a simultaneously slowed down and yet expanded form of speaking, a speaking one practises (most typically) in one's own head, and simultaneously transcribes for the page.

Studies in the cognitivist tradition yet again serve to corroborate these theses. David S. Kaufer, John R. Hayes and Linda S. Flower have, for instance, tracked subjects' compositional practices by asking them to 'think aloud' as they write prose sentences. Such an approach shows writers generating short bursts of language that they proceed to comment upon and modify in further bursts, till eventually arriving at serviceable sentences.[49] Here is an example of a subject performing such a 'think aloud' protocol, while writing:

> ok. . . . the summer after tenth grade . . . I and oh . . . I and . . . no . . . twenty seven students . . . and I . . . from my school district . . . that sounds kinds of

awkward . . . would it be twenty-seven students from my school district and I . . . but then I was part of the school . . . oh but if I said from my school district . . . the summer after tenth grade . . . twenty seven students from my school district . . . and I . . . went to France . . . for two weeks.

Here is the sentence that the subject in this fashion wrote down:

The summer after tenth grade, 27 students from my school district and I went to France for two weeks.[50]

To reflect on the artificiality of the product we generate through such means – artificial because of the image of fluent, one-time thought it conveys to the reader – is a curious matter. Could we not describe prose as a *heroic* form of speaking? After all, no one can ever quite speak the way our prose does, in real-time. On the other hand, one can, with practice, get better and better at speaking that way – for the page, and also even out loud. At certain times, one can 'get on a roll'.

DICTATION

The curious thing is that Albert Lord discovered something similar to Chafe's theory of writing's 'worked-over' quality, in his interactions with illiterate Balkan singers. As well as recording singers live on twin turntables connected by a toggle switch (this invention, commissioned by Parry, allowed the several minutes of recording-time, which was all that phonographs could then manage, to be extended indefinitely), Parry and Lord at times asked singers to dictate.[51] This would be a far less natural scenario, for it would require that they repeatedly halt their live composing, while waiting for the team's scribe, Nikola Vujnović – himself a singer, but literate – to catch up. Singers would also often be stopped by Vujnović in turn, whenever he felt a line was not true to the tradition. Lord comments that the extended pauses this process entailed could severely disable a singer 'accustomed to rapid-fire association and composition'.[52] Yet though composing was often vitiated by dictation, at other times it could lead to a poem better than those recorded live. This was especially so with singers of Međedovič's calibre. Lord comments: 'The texts thus obtained are in a sense special; they are not those of a normal performance, yet they are purely oral, and at their best they are finer than those of normal performance. They are not "transitional" but are in a class by themselves'.[53] Lord conjectures, on this basis, that our two Homeric poems were written down through some such process, at the hands of an informed listener. He is explicit on this: 'They are *oral dictated texts*'.[54]

There has been much criticism of this theory of Lord's, on the grounds that we simply have no way of knowing how Homer's works actually reached the page.[55] Yet what Lord's discussion of the oral dictated texts he and Parry gathered in the former Yugoslavia does do, regardless of its relation to Homer *per se*, is further corroborate the validity of Wallace Chafe's contention that the decrease in speed attendant upon the act of writing might serve to facilitate a more 'worked over' diction, that nonetheless remains in key qualities live. The fact that Lord is describing a team of poet and scribe, whereas the poets in our archive are referring to a solitary practice, is perhaps less of an objection to the links I am making than one might think. As Charles Saunders Peirce notes, 'a person is not absolutely an individual. His thoughts are what he is "saying to himself," that is, is saying to that other self that is just coming into life in the flow of time. When one reasons, it is that critical self one is trying to persuade; and all thought whatsoever is a sign, and is mostly of the nature of language'.[56] That critical self might well have pen in hand. It may even put conscious criticism aside for a while, the better to allow the unfamiliar in what is emerging to emerge, particularly when those selves as a whole are under the sway of a rhythm.

Literary works are in this sense 'oral dictated' texts, like almost all human writings. But poems are somewhat different in this regard. In what follows we will see ways in which the passage from inner speech to transcribing hand might be even more immediate for the poet than for the writer of prose, for all the fact that neither author has any real way of knowing exactly what words will come, in what order, till those words speak out suddenly in their minds.

NOTES

1. Leech and Svartvik, *Communicative Grammar*, 22.
2. Biber and Vásquez, "Writing and Speaking," 541.
3. The transcript, excepting the underlining, is as received from the transcription company. The same is true of the excerpts from Poet B and Poet C's interviews, cited below.
4. Halliday, *Spoken and Written Language*, 77.
5. Halliday, 90.
6. Vygotsky, *Thought and Language*, 99.
7. Vygotsky, 153.
8. Chafe and Danielewicz, *Properties*, 10.
9. Slowiaczek and Clifton, "Subvocalization," 573; Vygotsky, *Thought and Language*, 99.
10. Alderson-Day and Fernyhough, "Inner Speech," 931.
11. Biber and Vásquez, "Writing and Speaking," 546.
12. Halliday, *Spoken and Written Language*, 61–87.
13. Labov, "Non-Standard English," 16–18.

14. Halliday, "'They'd Been Going To've Been Paying Me All This Time'," 153.
15. Bakker, "How Oral is Oral Composition?" 40.
16. Halliday *Spoken and Written Language*, 44–45; Biber and Vásquez, "Writing and Speaking," 537; Biber and Conrad, *Register, Genre and Style*, 86.
17. Halliday *Spoken and Written Language*, 61–87.
18. Welty, qtd in Chafe, "Punctuation and the Prosody," 396.
19. Van Orden and Kloos, "Question of Phonology."
20. Van Orden, "A Rows is a Rose."
21. Levine, Calvanio and Popovics, "Absence of Inner Speech."
22. Slowiaczek and Clifton, "Subvocalization," 581.
23. Myers, *Sound of Finnegans Wake*, xii.
24. Yao, Belin and Scheepers, "Direct versus Indirect Speech."
25. Chenoweth and Hayes, "Inner Voice in Writing," 112.
26. Kellog, "Working Memory Components."
27. Kellog, Olive and Piolat, "Verbal, Visual and Spatial," 384.
28. Levine, Calvanio and Popovics, "Absence of Inner Speech," 405.
29. Levine, Calvanio and Popovics, 408.
30. Clark "Deaf Poets," 6.
31. Fernyhough, *Voices Within*, 228.
32. MacSweeney et al., "Neural Systems," 1583.
33. MacSweeney et al., 1590.
34. Chafe, *Discourse, Consciousness and Time*, 43.
35. Chafe, 44.
36. Chafe, 43.
37. De Biasi, "What is a Literary Draft?," 35.
38. Chafe, "Integration and Involvement," 36–37.
39. Chafe, 37.
40. Chafe, 37.
41. Halliday, "Spoken and Written Modes," 66.
42. Halliday, "'They'd Been Going To've Been Paying Me All This Time'," 135.
43. Halliday, 139.
44. Chafe and Danielewicz, *Properties*, 15.
45. Chafe and Danielewicz, 19.
46. Chafe and Danielewicz, 8.
47. Biber and Vásquez, "Writing and Speaking," 539.
48. Biber and Vásquez, 537.
49. Kaufer, Hayes and Flower, "Composing Written Sentences," 1986.
50. This transcript, from Kaufer, Hayes and Flower's earlier work, appears in Chenoweth and Hayes, "Fluency in Writing," 82.
51. Nagy and Mitchell, "Introduction," x.
52. Lord, *Singer of Tales*, 128.
53. Lord, 125.
54. Lord, 149.
55. Foley, "Oral Dictated," 602–603.
56. Peirce, "Essentials of Pragmatism," 258.

Chapter 10

Consciousness as a Window of Three Seconds

I interviewed Alison Croggon in Port Melbourne, in 2006:

INTERVIEWER. So when you're in the process of composition, do the words come to you as single word units, as phrases, or as whole lines?
CROGGON. It always comes to me in lines. Does it come to you in lines?
INTERVIEWER. Yes. Lines and words.
CROGGON. Very seldom words on their own, for me. Usually a line will come, and then another, and another, and another. The lines float up – you're always reduced to speaking quite vaguely about these things because it is a bit mysterious. You're not sure where they come from. But they occur. For me, they're usually triggered by some kind of rhythm. I mean something that I hear innerly.
INTERVIEWER. Does it ever feel like someone else is doing the writing?
CROGGON. It always feels like I'm doing it. But it feels like I'm listening to some other part of me, that's not always available. I almost feel like there's a door in there. If I could open it up all the time, I would write every thought.[1]

Croggon writes by that door. It was noted in the first chapter that when poets speak of having 'an idea for a poem', they are often referring to an actual line or phrase *from that poem*. Something similar might be detected in Croggon's use of the word 'thought', in the comment, 'I would write every thought'. That thought is not a plan to execute, but an actual line. Things 'float up', as Croggon puts it, in her professedly vague metaphor. And yet she underlines that what comes to her in this rhythmic, line-by-line fashion, sounds out in her consciousness. Further, she is the one generating the sounds. Croggon is describing how during composition she speaks to herself in sudden, rhythmic lines, that she piece-by-piece transcribes.

To further explore what might be going in such an 'oral dictated' scenario, note that there are no references to sentence-construction in Croggon's discussion of how she writes poetry, neither in this passage nor elsewhere in the interview. The only times Croggon uses the word 'sentence' in the interview are in relation to her prose-writings. This lacuna is pertinent to our inquiry into the capacity for poetic lines to emerge through the kind of speech-compositional processes Auden describes in the quotation we put to the poets. For conversationalists do not seem to have the crafting of sentences uppermost in their minds either. As Chafe comments, sentences 'do not always emerge from ordinary speaking with compelling clarity'.[2] The speaker's most immediate focus is on the intonation unit, that prosodic-cum-cognitive unit we have tracked through various contexts to this point. My point will be that conversational speakers are in this regard much closer to poets, than they are to prose writers.

It is interesting to compare Croggon's focus on lines with what Derek Attridge told me about his own focal unit of composition, when I interviewed him about his prose-writing in 2018. To put this in context, I was talking to Attridge in the course of a pilot study towards a separate project on the relationship between academic writing (so-called 'writing up') and discovery. My colleague, Lucy Neave, and I aim to test whether the composition of research reports serves as a distinct means of inquiry in scholarship and science, just as composing – however one does compose – clearly does for poets and novelists.[3] This will see us asking scholars and scientists some of the very questions that were put to poets in the interview research discussed through this book. For instance, do academics ever feel surprised by what emerges as they write? For the pilot study, I interviewed Derek Attridge, Hannah Sullivan and Michael Hoey, all of whose scholarly work is cited in these pages. One of the key points of difference between poets and scholars that emerged from those interviews had to do with the compositional function of the sentence.

We were in York, in March 2018, just days after unseasonal storms had blanketed the United Kingdom in swathes of ice and snow. Asked whether he feels he is the same person in the act of writing as he is at other times, Attridge replied, much like the poets, that he does not feel like 'a different person' when he writes. 'But I feel less present as a person, in a way, because of the feeling of giving myself over to the writing and the thinking'. This comment led to the following exchange:

INTERVIEWER. Could that be because one has to become so supple to the material, to allow it to speak?
ATTRIDGE. I don't know. I think, for me, it is bound up with getting the style right. Which is odd. It's not just the ideas. It is actually the language. Once I

am inside the sentence, the rest of the world ceases to exist. I am in there. I am trying to make it work the way it wants to work. I was going to say 'the way I want it to work.' But it's not even like that. It is not me wanting it to – it is that the sentence is developing itself, and I want to make sure it gets exactly what it wants. It's a strange thing.[4]

That these three scholars often sounded like the poets whose interviews I have discussed through this book was certainly thought-provoking. The most broad parallel was that Attridge, Hoey and Sullivan each confirmed that for them the act of writing serves to elicit many of the findings which such communications are assumed merely to report. But key points of difference to the poets transpired as well, especially, as noted above, in relation to the sentence.

The sentence emerged as a key compositional unit for all three scholars. Its centrality is apparent in the comment cited above and it is just as clear in Attridge's description of how he embraced the new technology of word-processing, when it started to spread in the 1980s. A key element in his enthusiasm at the time was for the way the word-processor allowed him to reformulate things 'at a sentence-by-sentence level': 'The capacity to just shift the words around, try the sentence this way, see that it still doesn't sound quite right, try it another way, place this paragraph after that one, add in a new thought . . . all of those things used to be so laborious. Now I can do them in an instant'. We see paragraphs enter the picture here too. But actually, the main comment Attridge made on them in the course of the interview was 'Paragraphing is intuitive for me'.[5] These echoed comments by my other two interviewees. Hannah Sullivan discussed paragraphs in similar terms, recognising their importance to writing, but finding their generation to all intents and purposes automatic. 'I don't really have much to say about the topic', she stated.[6] Michael Hoey, the linguist of the three, has written articles on how paragraphs function. But he too reported generating them more or less 'intuitively' in the course of his writing.[7] Sentences clearly claimed more of these three thinkers' attention.

The significance of the sentence was apparent in Sullivan's response to a question on what pleasure she finds in scholarly writing:

> I think it's the pleasure of making things clear to yourself that have previously been murky, things which seem important. There is also the pleasure of finding moderately elegant sentences to express those things. Perhaps there is also a rhetorical pleasure in feeling that I am going to convince the reader – that person out there – once and for all, that this is the way that it is. The sense that the writing will be found persuasive.[8]

There are a number of interesting contrasts we might draw here. For instance, only one of the 30 poets I have interviewed over the last 15 years spoke of persuasion as a compositional aim: 'A fair amount of argument is part of the fabric of my writing', C. D. Wright said.[9] Much closer to what the poets told me of their motives was this idea of clarifying what is personally murky – though intensifying the mystery, and transmitting it to others in that form could be as much as or even more of a goal. But the chief matter I want to point to in the excerpt above is Sullivan's reference to 'finding moderately elegant sentences'.

I commented that Croggon made no reference to sentence-construction when discussing her poetry – though she used the word 'sentence' twice in that interview, when conversation strayed onto the fantasy novels she also writes.[10] That pattern is borne out in the 29 other interviews I have conducted with poets. When I asked them about their writing practices, sentence-construction almost never came up. I will put some numbers to this. Ten of the poets I have cited to this point (Eileán Ni Chuilleanáin, Kenneth Goldsmith, Noelle Kocot, Medbh McGuckian, Don Paterson, Marcella Polain, G. C Waldrep, Ian Wedde, C. K. Williams, C. D. Wright) did not use the words 'sentence' or 'sentences' at all during our discussions, even though composition was a key topic. Forrest Gander used 'sentence' once, in relation to the novelist, Robert Coover. Brook Emery used it once too – or rather, he voiced it in the course of a quotation, which he clearly approved, from Marianne Moore: 'In a poem the excitement has to maintain itself. I am governed by the pull of the sentence as the pull of a fabric is governed by gravity'.[11] Aileen Kelly said the word 'sentence' twice, Paul Hoover three times and Maxine Chernoff seven, most of these in the course of discussing her prose poetry. Two of Rae Armantrout's four usages of 'sentence' concerned prose poetry as well, hers and Lyn Hejinian's. The other two uses were in response to an explicit question I asked her on the topic. It was her ultra-short lines that had me curious:

INTERVIEWER. I am intrigued by the role of sentences in your compositions. I am wondering if you would always in one sitting get the full movement of the sentence? Would you ever stop halfway?

ARMANTROUT. I probably would get at least a sentence. I might want to go back and revise it later. But I do not picture stopping in the middle of a sentence.[12]

Armantrout laughed as she said this, I assume because the thought struck her as unlikely. But I also want to note that my conversation with Armantrout on sentences ended there. There just did not seem to be all that more to explore. This is in contrast to the word 'line'/'lines' which Armantrout used seven times in discussing her writing and editing, none of these cases in response to questions containing the word. Excluding such possibly elicited cases, we find Chernoff using the word 'line' or 'lines' 19 times, Emery 18 times,

Paterson 12, Hoover 11, Waldrep and Williams five each, Gander four, Ni Chuilleanáin three, Kocot once, and Wright, Polain and McGuckian zero times. I should add that when Sullivan, who is a celebrated poet in her own right, referred to her poetry-writing, the word she used was not 'sentence', but 'line'.[13]

My reading of these emphases is that the model of completed thought we associate with the sentence might well function as a kind of gravitational device for the poetic line, somewhat as Marianne Moore describes it. But it is the line itself that is uppermost in the compositional moment. My data are merely suggestive, of course. But they add detail to the picture that is starting to emerge here: contemporary poetic composition is focussed on something much closer to the bursts of language in which we actually speak, than is prose-writing.

On the other hand, both can involve an advance into the unknown. Hoey told me that

> sometimes I will write something and think, 'Yes, that seems true. Do I have the evidence to support it?' I will then go away and perform an analysis of some data, to see whether I'm right. . . . Quite often, it will be that an analogy strikes me. I will use that analogy, and the more I explore it, the more it will open insights for me, which I then incorporate.[14]

Hoey is, of course, touching upon a profound poetic theme here, in line with the counter-intuitive findings of our pilot study more generally. Poets may not be the only ones who write to find out what it is they have to say on a topic.

But it is equally important to stress that there was nothing in these three scholars' accounts of their sentence-focussed prose composition that equates to what Noelle Kocot told me in Pennsylvania in 2013: 'Usually, I'll be going through the day, carrying a little notebook, and a line will come into my head'.[15] Nor did I hear anything like Claire Gaskin's comment, six years earlier in Richmond, Melbourne, on how she catches occasional dream-lines: 'you wake up with a line, a dream-line, that's fully composed'.[16] Sentences, in contrast, do not seem to arrive whole. What is more, they are often composed at a remove from the thoughts driving them. This was apparent from Hoey's observation that he would generally have the sequence of propositions structuring any of his oral presentations clearly worked out beforehand: 'But I never know the sentence structure I am going to use, or anything of that order'. Likewise, having said that 'I quite often write things in my head before I write them down' Hoey clarified, 'I am not talking about the sentences. But I will have each of the propositions in my head, and know the way in which they are going to fit together'.[17] The suddenness of that future speaking – and the exact words it will bring in the live context of an oral presentation or act of writing – is clearly less vital to the formulation of the ideas than it would be in the case of a poet. One might recall too, at this point, Sullivan's distinction between the pleasure of 'making things clear to yourself that have previously been murky, things which seem important' and 'the pleasure of finding moderately elegant sentences to express those things'.[18] Obviously the two blend into one in key regards, but the fact of the matter is that, as far as prose goes, it still makes sense to distinguish between sentences and the ideas they express.

The Pear Stories is illuminating here. Led by Wallace Chafe in the late 1970s, this research project saw Chafe and his colleagues eliciting verbal accounts of the contents of a short, silent film about a boy who steals some pears. One of these accounts was cited in chapter 7, and then again more briefly in chapter 8. Among the study's strategies was to have participants re-describe that film at periodic intervals. So, having described its contents anywhere from five to 25 minutes after first viewing it, subjects were asked to describe their memory of the film six weeks later, and then a whole year later.[19] What Chafe found through studying the transcripts later confirms the distinction between sentence and propositional content that we saw Hoey and Sullivan articulate above. For the sentences which speakers used to describe the film displayed little consistency over these intervals. On the other hand, the consistency of the ideational content within the intonation units making those sentences up was 'impressively robust'. These findings confirmed Chafe's sense that, as he later put it, 'the boundaries of sentences are assigned in the course of particular verbalisations and, unlike foci of consciousness, do not represent units of perception, storage, or remembering'.[20] The implication is that we do not perceive, store or remember in sentences, but rather in the spurt-like intonation units tracked in both Homer's Greek and the conversational transcripts cited above. This would explain why prose writers like Hoey, Sullivan and Attridge will describe the sentence *not* as their unit of memory or fore-planning ('I never know the sentence structure I am going to use'), but rather as the focus of an active elaboration ('Once I am inside the sentence, the rest of the world ceases to exist. I am in there. I am trying to make it work the way it wants to work'). It would also explain why, again in Chafe's words, 'consistently successful sentence construction is possible only under the more leisurely circumstances associated with writing'.[21]

There is more to say here. Certain template constructions allow speakers and writers alike to sketch out the form, if not the exact content, of multi-clausal units in advance of saying them, and so to achieve greater in-the-moment fluency and even sentence coherence, than these preliminary remarks would seem to suggest. Any lecturer knows these strategies, as does any writer. Also, one can always, as previously noted, 'get on a roll'. Particularly at the insistence of a rhythm. It remains the case that sentences of any length do not arrive fully formed. But thoughts can.

Swimming in Minus

Still dark at seven in the morning,
Melbourne winter, and the St Kilda ocean
separates me from my skin-wrapped bones.
Like Descartes, who refused
to believe his body
his own.
The thinking words in his mind were him.
Deserving the property title that is cogito.
If I can think then I'm still alive.[22]

SPOKEN THOUGHT

Certainly, not all thought is verbal. Inner speech might even turn out to be a rarer phenomenon than a common wisdom would have it. Psychologist Russell Hurlburt and his colleagues have for over 40 years been eliciting introspective reports on inner speech through a 'descriptive experience sampling' technique. The technique involves giving participants a wearable device which at unpredictable times will beep to prompt them to take notes on whatever thoughts were in their minds over the preceding seconds. These notes are unpacked in an 'expositional interview' the following day. Contrary to earlier claims in the literature that 'Human beings talk to themselves every moment of the waking day' and that 'inner speech is an *almost continuous* aspect of self-presence', a review of 51 individuals across two separate studies from 2008 and 2010 found that Hurlburt's subjects were on average engaged in inner speaking 23 percent of the time.[23]

But however frequent or infrequent inner speech may be, the question that concerns us involves the type of inner speaking one engages in, when generating a poem. Sentence formation is clearly not the central issue here, nor the sharp rent between thought and form which prose sentence protocols inspire. We might start our inquiry into this aspect of poetic composition by somewhat rhetorically asking whether the same rent applies to thinking itself. When we think verbally, saying the thoughts to ourselves as we do, do we already have a plan for what to think in mind? Isn't the experience of verbal thinking much more like *thinking by speaking*, discovering exactly what it is one thinks in the act of innerly articulating it? We suggested as much in the Introduction, also noting that the results are, of course, often predictable. We can add at this point that the connection we have seen so many poets make between poetry and speaking might well be attributed to the fact that thought itself speaks suddenly (and the poet transcribes). That is to say, poetry has a close relation to speaking because that is how we think it up in our heads.

To put further nuance into that picture, it seems that there are ways – not so much to plan, but rather – to predispose one's thinking towards certain things, for instance, by reading on a topic. I cited Claire Gaskin earlier, on how one might 'wake up with a line, a dream-line that's fully composed'. Gaskin explained:

> At different times in my life, I've actually been able to train myself to go to sleep and wake up with a fully composed line. And they're the best lines, you know, because they bypass surface logic and have a logic of their own. They often summarise all I've been thinking and reading. So they come out of my thinking but they're not a shortcut, because it takes a lot of work to train yourself to do that.[24]

Ted Hughes describes something perhaps similar. He calls it 'headlong concentrated improvisation on a set theme', and as his name for it indicates, the practice has a rather more direct relation to an intended topic than the dreaming Gaskin describes.[25] The idea is to imagine what you are writing about, as intensely as possible. One is not to think about that thing, so much as 'live it'. The following will sound as if Hughes is directing us to a palpable, real-world encounter, but he means that the students he is addressing are to imagine the experience: 'Just look at it, touch it, smell it, turn yourself into it. When you do this, the words look after themselves, like magic'. That is to say, Hughes's instruction to students is to focus on bringing an object intensely to mind, and while doing so, allow whatever words that come to them, simply to arise. He adds that the moment those words feel right to the object, the student is to write them down, a new line for each fresh utterance.

> After a bit of practice, and after telling yourself a few times that you do not care how other people have written about this thing, this is the way you find it; and after telling yourself you are going to use any old word that comes into your head so long as it seems right at the moment of writing it down, you will surprise yourself. You will read back through what you have written and you will get a shock.[26]

One might also hear echoes of Gaskin and Hughes's techniques in a discussion I had with Aileen Kelly. She had been talking about how she would at times imitate things when composing, to get into the feel of whatever she was trying to describe. I asked her if she felt there was a link between composing and acting. It was an odd question, I admitted, because when you are acting someone else has typically provided the script. But was there a link?

Only if you're thinking of a role-playing process whereby the actors are generating the script. Acting for writing poetry is more like that – you feel your way through the experience and the words get generated in the process. I don't have a sense that somebody else is doing the writing. There are times, however, when I look back at a poem and think, did I really write that? Where did that come from?[27]

Kelly is referring to the generation of art, but there are ways in which her observations on the act of poetic composition have something thoroughly everyday about them. There is something of this in Gaskin and Hughes's comments too. Are we not constantly training our minds on topics and letting 'the words get generated in the process', simply so as to speak? Doubtless this is the case with unfamiliar topics, in which case an element of strain enters the picture. But does it not also hold for things we know full well, as they come up in conversation? We direct our mind to the phenomenon, start to speak and the words come to our service (when not tripping us up) as we do.

To tackle this from another angle, if Hurlburt and his colleagues really are correct in holding that inner speaking is a much less frequent phenomenon than a common wisdom would have it, could that be because so much of our thinking occurs out loud, in the very act of speaking to others?

TOPIC

To return to our consideration on what distinguishes the kind of dictation (to self) a poet engages in from that of a prose writer, consider how Hannah Sullivan described the composition of 'The Sandpit after Rain', when our interview strayed from the writing of her scholarly books and articles, to her verse.[28] 'Then . . . I came up with the first line. I was sitting downstairs in the kitchen. It was to do with a kind of voice, a choppiness. The first line is *Things happened in the wrong order, out of nature.* There was something about the sound of that, the choppiness, that allowed me to continue to write'.[29] Note that even though this first line *is* a sentence, that is not how Sullivan seems to think of it. Her description is in general at a far remove from the exploratory, gradual and recursive processes of sentence-formation which prose-writing would seem to involve.

We have repeatedly seen poets refer to having an idea that will do service in a poem and finding the words for it as one and the same act. That music is integral to this process is clear in Sullivan's comment here: it was the 'sound' of that first line, its 'choppiness' that 'allowed' her 'to continue to write'. This chapter opened with comments from Alison Croggon that headed in the same direction. I will turn to this essential consideration shortly. But to round out our picture of the type of ideational work composing involves we first need to focus on a different type of choppiness, to do with the bursts in which we generate speech. For what poets seem to cleave to much more closely than prose writers is our experience of the 'gradual production of thoughts whilst speaking', and the related fact that 'it is not we who know things but pre-eminently a certain *condition* of ours which knows'.[30] I am citing from the Kleistean essay which opened this volume, but our key reference over the final pages of this chapter will be Wallace Chafe, who offers a very similar observation to Kleist: however it is that we mentally model the things around us, 'only one small piece of that model can be *active* at one time. At any given moment the mind can focus on no more than a small segment of everything it "knows"'.[31]

Chafe's discussion of writing's 'worked over' nature has already provided us with the means to clarify the kind of speaking we perform when engaged in the 'oral dictated' act of writing. To give some context to those ideas, Chafe began as a linguistic field worker in the 1950s, publishing a grammar, a vocabulary and a number of studies of Seneca, one of the indigenous languages spoken in New York State, over the following decade. From the 1970s, Chafe's interests came increasingly to focus on questions to do with the interface between consciousness and language production. His answers to then are keenly related to our experience of the immediate moment. Hence the relevance of his work to a book on suddenness and the composition of poetic thought, even though Chafe has little to say about poetry *per se*. What he does suggest is that our thought when speaking is focussed at, and in key ways confined to, the intonation unit, and that this severe constraint reflects limits on our cognitive powers more generally.

As for why our thinking is so localised, even as we are aware of our own much broader views of things, Chafe speculates that the reason is ultimately biological: 'the evolution of the human mind has left us with abilities that are incomplete'. In any given moment, our mind 'embraces just enough information to be effective in terms of the human organism's basic needs – to make it aware of food, danger, a mate, or whatever'.[32] Yet that is not the only kind of cognition available to us, our brains having over those same millions of years of evolution ballooned into something much more powerful.

> We are ... physically designed to deal with only a very small amount of information at one time, the amount that can be comprehended in one focus of active consciousness. In the meantime, in concert with the remarkable growth of the human cortex, the capacity of our minds to store and manipulate ideas has greatly increased. Our powers of remembering and imagining have far outstripped those of other creatures. But this development has failed to include any increase in the capacity of active consciousness, which presumably remains as limited today as it was before the brain evolved to its present state.[33]

Our thinking remains narrowly focussed on just a few elements, in a short pocket of time.

Others have canvassed these themes as well. Vyvyan Evans discusses the 'perceptual moment', whereby our disparate thoughts and sensory impressions get bound into a palpable sense of immediate reality:

> This temporal interval allows us to update our awareness of our environment: every two-three seconds our felt sense of *now* is updated. And crucially, many important aspects of our ongoing experience are thereby made possible.
>
> To be perceivable, ongoing activities must occur within this three-second outer window. For example, the reversal rate of ambiguous images . . . lies within this window: every two-three seconds the [Rubin's vase] image will shift from a vase to two faces, and vice versa.[34]

For their part, cognitive psychologists, Morten H. Christiansen and Nick Chater, refer to a 'now or never bottleneck' on mental processes that 'arises from general principles of perceptuo-motor processing and memory' and fundamentally shapes not just our use of language but the very form language itself takes.[35]

Chafe concurs, arguing, as we have seen, that we compose not in terms of full-sentences but rather in the choppy, two to three second bursts we have followed him in calling 'intonation units'. Michael Halliday calls the equivalent unit in his studies the 'tone group', and adds that this prosodically detectable speech unit represents 'one quantum of the message . . . the way the speaker is organising it as he goes along'.[36] This echoes David Crystal's earlier identification of the 'tone unit' as 'the fundamental unit of neural encoding'.[37] Geoffrey Leech and Jan Svartvik also use 'tone unit'.[38] All are referring to the same basic phenomenon, though Chafe relates it, as we have seen, to evolutionarily given cognitive limitations.

One of the upshots of the biological angle Chafe offers on the matter is to illuminate the intonation unit's relevance to the felt experience of reading verse. It is certainly notable that lineated poems, when good, induce in their readers such a frequent sense of the pleasures and fears they sense in their own bodies, and such frequent intimation of the closeness of time. The previous three chapters have, under the influence of Chafe's work, implied that a prime reason for this is that poetic verse's prosody, foremost its lineation and caesurae, reflect the segmentation of our conscious speaking, thinking and perceiving far more vividly than does prose. To use a psychological terminology, one might say that the poetic line, like the intonation unit itself, brings us up close to 'the phonological loop', those few seconds of echoic memory that allows us to preserve the words we are hearing or speaking in a kind of holding pattern while we put them together as a coherent unit of meaning. Sequence is momentarily suspended by synchrony, in what may be our one actual intimation of eternity. Poetry makes that condition palpable – though we might also discern it from conversation. Then again, there is something a little uncomfortable in dwelling on how graduated our speaking, and by extension our articulated thinking, actually is. As Descartes, the foremost philosopher of the pulse-like nature of the perceptual moment and the threats this bears to identity, put it so acutely, 'It does not follow from the fact that I existed a short time ago that I must exist now'.[39] Were Chafe transcribing, Descartes's most famous statement would probably look something like this:

(a) Je pense,
(b) donc je suis.[40]

There are actually two intonation units there. The same point can be made of the Latin version the philosopher went on to publish in the 1644 *Principia Philosophiae*, also with comma, also thereby providing evidence of its internal constitution as a pair of distinct utterances, passed off as the one singular and infrangible insight: *ego cogito, ergo sum*.[41] The somewhat unusual *cogito* we find in the 1641 *Meditations* – *ego sum, ego existo* – can be analysed, that is broken down, in similar terms.[42] (Not that Descartes would have been overly concerned to find his cogito in two parts, his accompanying proofs of God's existence vastly more important, at least in his view, and more than enough by same reckoning to guarantee the persistence of the thinker's personal identity over time and therefore a stable foundation for knowledge.)[43] We tracked a version of this same identity-undermining phenomenon – consciousness as a window of three seconds – through Kleist's essay on 'The Gradual Production of Thoughts whilst Speaking' in the introductory pages of this book, and then in terms of Pawley and Syder's pathbreaking work, which described our constrained cognitive lot in terms of a one-clause-at-a-time limit on forward coding. The value of discussing that constraint in terms of 'intonation units', as Chafe does, is that it makes allowance for the fact that not all such bursts are clauses. However that might be, this is the space of suddenness, as it manifests in our everyday communication.

My contention, to repeat, is that verse is composed in a way that cleaves much more closely to this primary, evolutionarily given, segmentation of conscious experience effecting speech, thought and perception alike, than prose does. Prose proceeds otherwise, in a manner much further from its compositional source.

But what can Chafe's work tell us about how poems' broader contours might come about? How can his theory of a speaking subject 'physically designed to deal with only a very small amount of information at one time' help us, for instance, to explain Wordsworth's capacity to keep dwelling on the 'blessing' of 'that gentle breeze' over successive lines, that breeze

That blows from the green fields and from the clouds
And from the sky: it beats against my cheek,
And seems half-conscious of the joy it brings.[44]

How does one manage that kind of real-time coherence? How does one not simply lose the plot when composing, or for that matter speaking, given the narrow, three second window of consciousness itself?

We come to 'semi-active consciousness', the concept in Chafe's work that decisively separates him from the other linguists cited here, not to mention most psychologists, social theorists and philosophers – with the rare exception of William James, as we shall see.[45] What the concept of 'semi-active consciousness' brings to the table is the obvious fact that our cognitive plight never feels quite so desperate as the calamitous situation evoked à propos Descartes above, where not even a full sentence seems within our immediate ken. The point for Chafe is that the knowledge we bear cannot simply be divided into (1) that which is activated into consciousness and (2) that which remains hidden in memory. There is also the way a hazy cluster of thoughts and evaluations will come to mind whenever a given topic is raised: neither quite active or inactive, this material exists in a semi-active state. Its semi-active contents are only hazily present, till we start 'scanning' them into verbal focus.[46] Semi-active consciousness may not offer a rigorous enough platform for Descartes's project of founding all knowledge, but not all of us – to say the least – require such certainties.[47] As for how such 'scanning' might function in practice, consider the following transcript, which again proceeds from the *Pear Stories* project, and once more involves a subject's recollections of a short, silent film about a boy riding a bicycle with a basketful of pears. It will help to bring the phenomenon of semi-active consciousness to life in this case if the reader is prepared to pause after each unit, and roughly to observe the timings in square brackets as well. They represent pauses, in fractions of a second:

(a) [.75] And [.25] on his way,
(b) riding,
(c) he comes across another [.3] bicyclist, [.25] bicyclist,
(d) it's a young woman,
(e) [.5] and [1.15] for some reason she catches his attention,
(f) and he's [.4] turning his head,
(g) ... behind him,
(h) looking at her,

(i) and [.2] there's a rock in the r road,
(j) and he [.25] hits it with his bike,
(k) and falls.
(l) [.3] A--nd then [.7] his um [1.15] pears go all over the road.[48]

It seems clear from any performance of these 'lines' that the speaker is bringing to light successive facets of a till then hazily present memory, scene by scene. I was referring to this same 'scanning' phenomenon in the Introduction, when suggesting that at each point in the course of a spoken or written compositional act we intend – strive towards – a hazily present object and we say/hear ourselves say the words we have for it. The reason that kind of finding is possible is that we exist in 'a limited area of fully active consciousness surrounded by a penumbra of ideas in a semi-active state', and we reveal them as we speak, intonation unit by intonation unit.[49] We might surprise ourselves by what emerges from it in the process, but what Chafe calls semi-active consciousness is by the same token the locus of whatever coherence our discourse does manage to possess. After all, we do manage – for all our inability to form a seamless *cogito* – to hold and maintain conversations.

'One of the things that seems intuitively true of conversations is that they focus on different topics'.[50] Adopting the everyday term 'topic' for analytic use, Chafe continues, 'We can think of each such topic as an aggregate of coherently related events, states and referents that are held together in some form in the speaker's semi-active consciousness'.[51] In other words, a topic is a unit of memory. Not that it is necessarily clear to us precisely what our topic is. For a topic is also a unit of desire. Chafe quotes William James on the thinker's plight:

> In all our voluntary thinking there is some topic or subject about which all the members of the thought revolve. Half the time this topic is a problem, a gap we cannot yet fill with a definite picture, word or phrase, but which . . . influences us in an intensely active and determinate psychic way. Whatever may be the images and phrases that pass before us, we feel their relation to this aching gap. To fill it is our thought's destiny. Some bring us nearer to that consummation. Some the gap negates as quite irrelevant. Each swims in a felt fringe of relations of which the aforesaid gap is the term.[52]

The close relation Chafe posits, between the topics we bring semi-actively to mind and this experience of James's 'aching gap', evokes Auden's comments on 'when we genuinely speak', and most particularly the idea that during such times (really, it is during any time) 'we do not have the words to do our bidding, we have to find them'. By the same token, it explains how a poet might write, that is, engage in inner speech, in the various manners we have fashioned for the page, with the express aim of finding out what they 'have in mind'. Actually, it explains how a scholar or scientist might do so too.

Vygotsky also seems to have had a notion of a semi-active state, observing of the 'condensed, abbreviated' way that thoughts often come to us, that 'A speaker often takes several minutes to disclose one thought. In his mind the whole thought is present at once, but in speech it has to be developed successively. A thought may be compared to a cloud shedding a shower of words'.[53] It is always possible that Descartes' *cogito* came to him in this 'condensed, abbreviated' form, and that the qualms I have related above solely concern its unpacking. Perhaps, but in that case, the point is that to have certainty about what one thinks, one has to do just that – unpack it, and see what survives. Vygotsky's 'cloud' metaphor suggests a knowledge in the mind that is present but not quite consciously present. It may not allow for Cartesian certainty, but that 'certain condition of ours that knows' (Kleist), which Chafe refers to as 'semi-active consciousness', otherwise keeps us more or less on theme. At the same time, the idealisations surrounding practices of speaking and writing would seem to help fill the gaps in coherence these somewhat ramshackle processes invariably generate.

For a further angle on those gaps, we can focus on Chafe's description of conversation as a phenomenon characterised by sequences of topics, during which 'one or more individuals talk about the same thing'.[54] Pointing out that topic development can be a collaborative matter in conversation and, on the other hand, that there can be contest over whose topic will prevail, Chafe makes the important, further point that the production of spoken and written language alike, even the most monologic, is always attendant upon the producer's model, however obtuse, of where their listeners are at. On the basis of this last observation, we might suggest that the 'aching gap' James identifies at the core of any topic is just as much about our discourse's opening to its imagined audience. To recall Jacques Lacan's insistence that unconscious desire manifests just where we are not, in the Other ('Man's [sic] desire is the desire of the Other') is apposite.[55]

This discussion of the concept of 'topic' may, nonetheless, seem to run counter to some of the poets' comments. We have now seen numerous instances where a poet asserts that they will never write with a topic in mind. But here I return to James's observations on the 'aching gap': James helps us to see that not grasping entirely what one thinks of a phenomenon is closer to having a topic than we might imagine. Conversely, that 'aching gap' might assume centrality in one's grasp of a matter. Having 'an idea' for a poem in the sense discussed back in chapter 1, that is a line or half-line that seems promising, may well function in this manner. One's topic is *Where might this go?* To quote Jan Owen, with whom I spoke at Aldinga Beach in South Australia, back in 2006, 'I'll often begin a poem because I know something and want to know more'. Her aim is to be in the kind of space where knowing opens onto the unknown: 'if I can be true to some of the details, and to the feeling, I can suggest something that might be understood: the strangeness of things. Their otherness'. Owen proceeded to talk about travel, but her comments clearly also relate to composition: 'Bad things can happen and marvellous things can too. You simply are more awake. That's a very important word for me. Alert and awake. That's why I write: to wake up and find who, where, why, what'.[56]

The idea that one might take an uncertain complex of ideas and treat it as one's very topic, scanning through whatever words it makes available, chunk-by-chunk, finding out just what those ideas are by innerly voicing them, seems related to Sullivan's comments on starting the poem, whose first line I cited above: 'There was something about the sound of that, the choppiness, that allowed me to continue to write'.[57] Sullivan had thereby found a topic, a 'something about the sound of that', that could serve to propel her into the composition.

That cloudy 'topic' might likewise comprise an uncertainty as to what one is feeling. Here is how Rae Armantrout explained it, when I asked about the link between composing and emotion.

INTERVIEWER. You referred before, when talking about composition, to an uncertainty about an emotion, and said that composition might involve a search for that emotion. Can you talk more about that?

ARMANTROUT. I think the emotion part is front-loaded. This is going to sound incredibly vague, because it is a little bit vague to me too: but often the way a poem starts with me is just with a vague feeling that is associated with something. Let's say I was in a car and I was passing something on the street. All of a sudden I get a particular feeling. It is usually a complex of things setting me off, not just that sight. Then I start teasing it out. This is vague, but it is like the feeling is sitting in the middle and there are things arrayed around it, that are connected to it somehow. That is how it is in the beginning, most of the time. As the composition goes on, things get more rational, and critical.

INTERVIEWER. It might be these things are impossible to generalise, by their very nature. But I am wondering if those initial feelings tend to be discordant in relation to the object? Could that be what sparks you off?

ARMANTROUT. Probably sometimes. If I always understood it, then it wouldn't be poetry! But I think that is probably true. There is sometimes a sense of discord. And disquiet.[58]

We can conclude this discussion of Chafe's concept of semi-active consciousness with a comment on his idiosyncratic terminology. It 'would not be too misleading', he notes, to relate key elements of his theory to the well-established psychological concepts like 'short-term' and 'long-term memory'.⁵⁹ One can also see the relevance of Alan Baddeley's concept of 'working memory'. I mentioned the 'phonological loop' component of Baddeley's widely accepted model above.⁶⁰ These terms might stand in for the way Chafe describes thoughts as either 'activated' in consciousness, as for instance, when verbalised in an intonation unit (e.g. when the words 'donc je suis' come to mind), or 'inactive'. The reason Chafe nonetheless eschews labels like 'working memory' is 'partly because of their possible implication that memory is a place. . . . One of the endearing qualities of Frederic Bartlett (1932) is the fact that his book was titled not *Memory* but *Remembering*'.⁶¹ As it happens, Chafe draws on Bartlett's concept of schemata to encompass the culturally given dimensions of the topics we 'navigate' in speaking.⁶² Concepts like ideology (in, say, Žižek's sense), or discourse (as in Foucault or Butler's work), might also do service here. It is clear that the world and its interests speak through us, and especially in our most seemingly private concerns. But what both the psychologists and the thinkers of those critical categories by and large lack is the concept of a knowledge that is only hazily present to consciousness. What we have not 'so obviously allowed for', since James, is the concept of 'a semi-active state', the phenomenon Chafe names with his term 'semi-active consciousness'.⁶³ That is to say, our psychological and social-theoretical analyses tend to lack a sense of the subject's conscious opening to the unknown.

I would suggest that Wordsworth's famous reference to composition as a form of 'spontaneous overflow' would have occasioned far less twentieth- and twenty-first-century dismissal as incurably Romantic, had our intellectual armature included a concept like Chafe's 'semi-active consciousness'. For Wordsworth makes explicit that what one accesses through a process of 'spontaneous overflow' is in key ways already present: 'For all good poetry is the spontaneous overflow of powerful feelings: and though this be true, Poems to which any value can be attached were never produced on any variety of subjects but by a man [*sic*] who, being possessed of more than usual organic sensibility, had also thought long and deeply'.⁶⁴ By Chafe's account, what the poet must have in their head at such a point of felicitous composing is a topic. For as he puts it so estrangingly in one of his last publications, 'a topic can be seen as a conceptual unit that is too large to be accommodated within the limited capacity of fully active consciousness'.⁶⁵

NOTES

1. Croggon, interview by author, April 24, 2007.
2. Chafe, "Consciousness and Language," 141.

3. Neave, "What Constitutes Discovery?"; Magee, "Writing as Discovery."
4. Attridge, interview by author, March 12, 2018.
5. Attridge.
6. Sullivan, interview by author, February 26, 2018.
7. Hoey, interview by author, March 6, 2018.
8. Sullivan, interview by author, February 26, 2018.
9. Wright, "An Interview."
10. Croggon, interview by author, April 24, 2007.
11. Moore, qtd in Emery, interview by author, October 25, 2014.
12. Armantrout, interview by author, November 11, 2014.
13. Sullivan, interview by author, February 26, 2018.
14. Hoey, interview by author, March 6, 2018.
15. Kocot, interview by author, July 13, 2013.
16. Gaskin, interview by author, January 20, 2007.
17. Hoey, interview by author, March 6, 2018.
18. Sullivan, interview by author, February 26, 2018.
19. Chafe, ed., *Pear Stories*, xiv.
20. Chafe, *Discourse, Consciousness and Time*, 143.
21. Chafe, 141.
22. Magee, "Swimming in Minus."
23. Hurlburt, Heavey and Kelsey, "Phenomenology of Inner Speaking," 1487; 1483.
24. Gaskin, interview by author, January 20, 2007.
25. Hughes, *Poetry in the Making*, 23.
26. Hughes, 18–19.
27. Kelly, interview by author, April 30, 2007.
28. Sullivan, *Three Poems*.
29. Sullivan, interview by author, February 26, 2018.
30. Kleist, "Gradual Production of Thoughts," 408.
31. Chafe, *Discourse, Consciousness and Time*, 28.
32. Chafe, 140.
33. Chafe, 140.
34. Evans, *The Crucible of Language*, 66–67.
35. Christiansen and Chater, "Now-or-Never Bottleneck," 1.
36. Halliday, *Spoken and Written Language*, 53.
37. Crystal, *English Tone of Voice*, 15.
38. Leech and Svartvik, *Communicative Grammar*, 22.
39. Descartes, *Meditations*, 27.
40. Descartes, *Oeuvres* VI, 32.
41. Descartes, VIII, 7.
42. Descartes, VII, 25.
43. Cottingham, *Descartes*, 66–73.
44. Wordsworth, qtd in Attridge, *Poetic Rhythm*, 2.
45. Chafe, *Discourse, Consciousness and Time*, 120.
46. Chafe, "Deployment of Consciousness," 32.
47. Peirce, "The Fixation of Belief."

48. Speaker 5, qtd in Chafe, "Deployment of Consciousness," 38.
49. Chafe, "Study of Consciousness."
50. Chafe, *Discourse, Consciousness and Time*, 121.
51. Chafe, 121.
52. James, qtd in Chafe, "Linguist's Perspective on William James," 622–623.
53. Vygotsky, *Thought and Language*, 150.
54. Chafe, "Linguist's Perspective on William James," 623.
55. Lacan, *The Four Fundamental Concepts*, 235.
56. Owen, interview by author, March 12, 2007.
57. Sullivan, interview by author, February 26, 2018.
58. Armantrout, interview by author, November 11, 2014.
59. Chafe, *Discourse, Consciousness and Time*, 53–54.
60. Baddeley, "Working Memory."
61. Chafe, *Discourse, Consciousness and Time*, 53.
62. Chafe, "Analysis of Discourse Flow," 4.
63. Chafe, *Discourse, Consciousness and Time*, 53–54.
64. Wordsworth and Coleridge, "Preface," 22.
65. Chafe, "Analysis of Discourse Flow," 3.

Chapter 11

Song

But there is still a huge lacuna here, as far as poetry-writing is concerned. For Marcella Polain,

> it's about hearing something and it's about the rhythm of that. Once I've got the rhythm of the first line, then I feel a propulsion into the poem. Or I know even if I don't feel the propulsion then, that I will be able to pick it up again and continue working on it. For me, it's about rhythm and I've got to get the rhythm right. I don't know what rhythm I'm looking for. I say or hear in my head the words, some words, and I build them until suddenly it feels right and then the poem has begun.[1]

Earlier, we heard Alison Croggon tell us that her lines are 'usually triggered by some kind of rhythm'.[2] Brook Emery indicated that 'with good poems, the texture of the words, the rhythm of the words and whatever images that come up, carry the thought'.[3] For Don Paterson, music is ' the very means by which the poem comes about . . . the engine of composition. It's not something that we add on'.[4] In his book *Poetic Rhythm*, Derek Attridge uses the same word as Paterson, 'engine', to describe the motor force within our poetry: 'The engine that drives this sonorous and meaningful activity is *rhythm*: the continuous motion that pushes spoken language forward, in more or less regular waves, as the musculature of the speech organs tightens and relaxes, as energy pulsates through the words we speak and hear, as the brain marshals multiple stimuli into ordered patterns'.[5]

Pursuing Attridge and others' thoughts on the matter will provide us with one further angle on the tantalising possibility of a 'worked over', but still more or less real-time compositional speaking, generating at least stretches of the poem. And far from contradicting the Chafean picture we have been developing – that our purchase on the world is focussed in a highly constrained, 'limited area of fully active consciousness surrounded by a penumbra of ideas in a semi-active state' – discussion of this matter will underline that the insistence of a rhythm can be a means of 'topic navigation' in its own right, a means of drawing what we impressionistically have in mind into conscious focus, even as we speak it.[6]

The key point in Attridge's discussion is that these 'waves' of energy are a speaker's everyday resources as well. To speak is to be rhythmic – albeit not quite as briskly rhythmic as a poem. As far as a stress-timed language like English goes, that rhythmic drive manifests most immediately in our tendency toward the alternation of stressed and unstressed syllables. Attridge comments that people will generally prefer 'bláck and spárkling éyes' to 'spárkling and bláck éyes' because 'the first phrase separates the stressed syllables by unstressed ones'.[7] For this same reason we say 'the únknown sóldier' with stress on the first syllable of the adjective, but 'This unknówn clarinéttist' with stress on the second.[8] It is to maintain a rhythm. The somewhat scandalous implication is that our everyday word choices are driven not just by meanings but also by rhythm. The ultimate origin of this tendency for rhythmic alternation in our conversational phrasing is muscular and has to do with the fact that, when engaged in activity, our muscles prefer to contract and relax in a regular rhythm.[9] Attridge mentions breathing, walking, running and chopping wood as analogous to speaking in this regard, reminding us how hard it is to do any of these thing in stops and starts. This metronomic preference drives aspects of syllabic stress, word choice and arrangement. It also provides a key driver for the quickenings and slowings in spoken English, and therefore in our poetry as well. For instance, we speed up when uttering a sequence of two unstressed syllables. As proof of this, consider John F. Leonard's remark that 'the phrase "músical cháirs" takes roughly the same amount of time to say as "músic cháirs"'.[10] It is because we are trying to space our stressed syllable to occur at roughly equal intervals. And we slow down when we come to a sequence of two stressed syllables, for the very same reason: a bláck dáy. The quickenings and slowings coursing through the lines of any Shakespearean sonnet are ultimately attributable to this same metronomic drive in our speaking.

Michael Halliday and Christian Matthiessen also note these tendencies: 'When you speak, naturally and spontaneously, without paying attention to the process of speaking, the strong syllables tend to occur at roughly even intervals'. They add, interestingly, that however approximate that rhythm might be, it is sufficient 'to provide a clear measure, a rhythmic progression with which the listener keeps in phase'.[11] This invocation of the listener's participation might bring to mind Deborah Tannen's comments on the rhythmic quality of conversation, cited earlier. Deborah Coates goes so far as to describe conversation – from this same rhythmic perspective – as a form of 'jamming', with 'solo' and 'ensemble' modes. She is analysing how the North American women she has recorded will often speak over the top of one another's words and/or simultaneously echo them when engaged in friendly group discourse.[12] As noted earlier, when we find ourselves starting to speak at the same time as another speaker it is because we are, in fact, in time with them.

Poetic rhythm, Attridge comments, 'is a heightening and an exploitation of the rhythm of a particular language. To be able to speak English, therefore, is to be familiar with the rhythms that English poetry uses'.[13] The founding of any poem's rhythms in its language's speech rhythms explains Vladimir Mayakovsy's otherwise outrageous assertion that in spite of the magnificent cadences of his Russian lines, 'I don't know a single one of the metres'.[14] It did not stop him writing in them.

Attridge's work explains how rhythm might drive the selection of words during poetic composition, on the grounds that it already does this simply when we speak, and in the process underlines that we can compose poetic rhythms at pace because we are already doing an albeit fainter version of this every day as we speak. But to see how such rhythmic pulsing informs what Chafe calls 'topic navigation', that is our storytelling and other expository practices, it is important to note that the more or less steady alternation of stressed and unstressed sounds discussed above is not the only consequence of the alternating, muscular pulse informing our speech. There is also metrication. Consider the 'gifted raconteur', whose live conversational monologue Andrew Pawley and Frances Hodgetts Syder recorded in the 1970s (timings for pauses are given in fractions of a second):

(1) Y'know I had four uncles. (.4)
(2) They all volunteered to go away. (1.6)
(3) and ah – (.2) that w's one Christmas (.4)
(4) th't I'll always remember, (.7)
(5) because ah my four uncles came round,
(6) they were all in uniform. (1.1)
(7) An' ah – (.2) they're going t'have Christmas dinner with us. (.3)
(8) An' what was more important
(9) they were gonna provide it. (.3)
(10) An that was really something. (.9)
(11) Well y'know we had a fantastic time. (1.1)
(12) There were all kinds of relations there.
(13) I dunno where they all come from,
(14) I didn't know 'alf o' th'm. (.9)
(15) An' ah – (.2) the kids sat on the floor, (1.5)

(16)   and ol'Uncle Bert he – (.2) ah o'course he w's the life and soul of the party (.2)
(17)   Uncle Bert 'ad a black bottle, (1.5)
(18)   an ah – (.2) 'e'd tell a few stories,
(19)   an' 'e'd take a sip out of the black bottle,
(20)   'n' the more sips he took outa that bottle, (1.0)
(21)   the worse the stories got. (1.6)[15]

Pawley and Syder remark that G, as they call him, 'speaks at a measured pace in short rhythmic chunks, usually in clauses of four to eight words, giving an effect almost like a recitation of blank verse'.[16] In other words, G is a kind of organic poet, an effect achieved by contouring one's utterance to the shape of the intonation unit. Successful political leaders often achieve a comparable effect, by segmenting their speech into similarly sized units, southern Baptist preachers too – as much research has attested.[17] One can certainly speak verse, with all the mesmerising power that implies.

What is more, these are scalar phenomena, present to varying degrees in all conversation. Note, to this end, Deborah Tannen's strategy of breaking transcripts of recorded speech into lines 'to reflect the rhythmic chunking that is created in speaking by intonation and prosody'.[18] Ethnographer Dennis Tedlock likewise uses the lineation conventions 'found in our drama and poetry' in his transcriptions of Native American narratives.[19] For his part, Tedlock insists that such oral narratives, however conversational, are 'better understood (and translated) as dramatic poetry than as an oral equivalent of written prose'.[20] We have also seen a number of linguistic transcripts segmented into lines – albeit with no conscious reference to poetry.

Reflecting on such materials, one can see the sense in Halliday and Mathiessen's suggestion that, 'The "line", in verse, evolved as the metrical analogue of the tone group [intonation unit]: one line of verse corresponded to one tone group of natural speech'.[21] Egbert Bakker makes a similar claim: the prime way speech becomes metrical is through a formalising of our natural tendency to produce it in short bursts. Bakker comments that the 'coincidence of intonation with metrical units is a universal characteristic of performed poetry in oral traditions' and underlines that the Homeric hexameter typically comprises two such units.[22] But Bakker also points to how the line might emerge as the more integral unit: 'The rhythmical, prosodic features of intonation units may become regularised to the point that they become metrical. So meter emerges from discourse . . . but at some point it becomes so rigid as to constitute a structure in itself, regulating the flow of speech'. Bakker describes this as a 'shift from meter as nascent and emergent to meter as a structure in its own right'.[23] A sense of formality seems to arise in the process, further distinguishing poetic from conversational rhythms.

In chapter 8, we noted the way the repetitiveness that is part and parcel of everyday conversation will, once placed within the forcefield of the poem, take on an appearance of formality and artifice. Attridge suggests that poetic rhythm can serve to effect an air of 'impersonality' as well, and sees this as functioning in productive tension with the way 'rhythm can often work effectively as an imitation of the spoken voice'.[24] The two go hand-in-hand: 'The rhythmic forms of poetry – especially metrical poetry – furnish utterances with a public quality, even when they seem most personal and intimate'.[25] Australasian readers, familiar with the idiom, might feel a certain formality of diction and content in the jocular style of storytellers like G ('An' what was more important/they were gonna provide it') as well. Yet far from damming up the composer's suppleness of emotion and intellect, this impersonal and public quality seems to have the very opposite effect. For the marshalling of these speech rhythms through line-breaks, particularly when the number of stresses in the line becomes regular enough to function as a perceptible meter, not only amplifies that rhythm's clarity and force, it seems to induce in the speaker a much greater letting go. As Bakker remarks, 'The usual account of speech as deriving from consciousness is insufficient here, for the singer's consciousness not only produces the speech but is also propelled forward by the rhythmical movement of the language'.[26] Just prior to this passage we find Bakker describing metrical verse as 'the rhetorical enhancement and manipulation of the basic properties of ordinary speech'.[27] Now rhetoric is interestingly defined by Bakker as that which serves, in any given case, 'to accommodate the discourse to the listener's consciousness and to stimulate the participation of the audience in the flow of the discourse'.[28] The implication of this cluster of ideas is that one of the key members of the audience who is being stimulated to participate in a poetic discourse's rhetorical flow is the very poet uttering! The poet participates in the verse's rhetorical flow by allowing the selecting power of the rhythm to cast up potential items for voicing.

The productive, speaking power inherent in metre serves for Bakker to rationalise the reference across so many distinct performance traditions to the idea of a power, 'neither opposed to the speaker's consciousness nor identical to it', driving the verse.[29] Note, as evidence of these effects, the way our 'gifted raconteur', G, by cleaving so closely to the intonation unit as his compositional frame, achieves so much more fluency than the conversational speakers cited in previous chapters. Yet he, too, is extemporising his description of Uncle Bert's drunken storytelling, clause by clause. G's gift is the gift of rhythm itself, generating the extraordinary capacity to speak poetry in real-time which we have tracked through this book, and might now want to claim as a key means of 'topic navigation' for contemporary poets as well, poets using the drive of the line and rhythm's own innate selecting power to draw them through their topic, which is to say, to draw them through 'a conceptual unit that is too large to be accommodated within the limited capacity of fully active consciousness'.[30]

But I have to acknowledge, even as I cite Bakker's illuminating discussion of the compelling 'rhetoric' of metrical patterning, a restriction on its relevance to my archive. The issue, as noted back in chapter 1, is that the poets we interviewed mainly write in free verse. Of course, free verse works with metrication too, with brilliant nuance when it works well.[31] But its rhythms are clearly less driving than Homer's hexameter or, for that matter, the rough ballad meter effectively coursing through G's intonation units. The poet who, in Bakker's terms, is at once composer and audience member stimulated to participate in his own performance, is simply not 'propelled forward by the rhythmical movement of the language' in as driving a manner, when it comes to free verse.[32]

Bakker writes of the 'dislocation of consciousness' by metre.[33] The phenomenon seems somewhat attenuated among the poets interviewed. Here, for instance, is where Polain stood on the question of whether she ever felt as if someone else was doing the writing. 'I know I'm heading in that direction but no, I've never felt that and I don't understand when people say that. I just don't get it'.[34] Recall too, Aileen Kelly's comments on poetry-writing and acting. She also referred to waiting: 'There are times when what I'm doing is sitting very quietly and waiting for something to happen. . . . There are times when working on a poem is more like meditation: blanking my mind and waiting for something to come up'.[35]

NOTES

1. Magee, "Marcella Polain Interview," 41.
2. Croggon, interview by author, April 24, 2007.
3. Emery, interview by author, October 25, 2014.
4. Paterson, interview by Kevin Brophy, July 2, 2013.
5. Attridge, *Poetic Rhythm*, 2.
6. Chafe, "Analysis of Discourse Flow," 3; Chafe, "Study of Consciousness," n.p.
7. Attridge, *Poetic Rhythm*, 39.
8. Attridge, 39.
9. Attridge, 3–4.
10. Leonard, "Rhythm, Form and Meter," 571.
11. Halliday and Matthiessen, *Functional Grammar*, 13.
12. Coates, "Construction of a Collaborative Floor," 55.
13. Attridge, *Poetic Rhythm*, 4
14. Mayakovsky, *How are Verses to be Made*, 145.
15. G, qtd in Pawley and Syder, "One-Clause-at-a-Time," 181–182 (modified by author). Pawley and Syder's transcription conventions are given at 166, fn3.

16. Pawley and Syder, "One-Clause-at-a-Time," 182.
17. Tannen, *Talking Voices*, 166–185.
18. Tannen, "Talking Voice," 635.
19. Tedlock, "Translation of Style," 46.
20. Tedlock, "Learning to Listen," 114.
21. Halliday and Matthiessen, *Functional Grammar*, 16.
22. Bakker, *Poetry in Speech*, 50.
23. Bakker, 184.
24. Attridge, *Poetic Rhythm*, 12.
25. Attridge, 12.
26. Bakker, *Poetry in Speech*, 138.
27. Bakker, 129.
28. Bakker, 146.
29. Bakker, 138.
30. Bakker, 3.
31. Carper and Attridge, *Meter and Meaning*, 137–138.
32. Baker, *Poetry in Speech*, 138.
33. Bakker, 136.
34. Magee, "Marcella Polain Interview," 42.
35. Kelly, interview by author, April 30, 2007.

Part IV

SUDDENNESS AND ART

Chapter 12

The Split in the Archive

I return to the split in our archive which occasioned this inquiry. Over the years 2013–2015, we asked a large group of poets if they saw any link between their practice of composition and the aspects of real-time, face-to-face speaking highlighted in W.H. Auden's comment that '[w]hen we genuinely speak we do not have the words ready to do our bidding, we have to find them. And we do not know exactly what we are going to say until we have said it, and we say and hear something new that has never been said or heard before'.[1] The question divided our interviewees and one of the driving factors behind this study has been the attempt to work out why. Why were two-thirds of the poets positively disposed to the idea that Auden's words might in some way illuminate the realities of poetic composition? Why were the remaining poets so dismissive of it?

We are ready at this point to table some conclusions. I focus firstly on the poets who favoured the quotation. It is significant that Rae Armantrout, Brook Emery and Don Paterson each commented on the poems they most like to read, as their first response to Auden's words. What characterised such poems for Armantrout was that 'you can see that the writer is thinking about what he or she just said, and responding to it'.[2] Emery's initial response, having quoted Eliot and Forster saying something quite similar to Auden, was that his preferred poem is the one that seems to perform its ideas in the very act of coming to them. The poem Paterson likes will embody 'epiphany'.[3] It was only after having made these aesthetic aims clear that these three poets proceeded, in their respective interviews, to reflect on their own compositional practices. The effect was to flag a strong element of goal-directedness to those practices of generating poetry along the lines Auden suggests, perhaps as a way of obviating associations with stereotypical images of inspired poets. Whether that was the driver or not, the strategic relevance of such a compositional practice is clear, once these overarching aesthetic aims are established. For surely one of the best ways to achieve a 'spontaneous, almost improvised' (Williams) texture is actually to improvise.[4]

The strategic value of a practice based around a real-time speaking for the page becomes even more acute once we take on board the links established over recent chapters between the sub-sentential bursts in which we actually speak and poetic lineation. To break any of the verbatim interview transcripts cited in chapters 8 or 9 into lines based on the speaker's intonation units will, as noted there, considerably diminish the sense of chaos, because the internal logic – and the rhythm – of the speaker's in-the-moment utterance will then reveal itself. For actually, we improvise something like lines, or half-lines, every single time we speak. What will also be apparent, if you cut those prose transcripts into the intonation units in which they were actually generated, will be the fact that any such speaker is drawing upon their albeit hazy consciousness of a larger cluster of ideas and evaluations, to convey whatever topic they are, in that staggered fashion, attempting to communicate. That is to say, something like the lineation (plus caesural pausing) of a poem, and also something like the hazy unity of its topics, are there in the foreground and background of most any real-time narration. In the Homeric and South Slavic cases, we saw evidence that improvising via rather more formalised versions of such conversational mechanisms before a live audience has been and remains a genuine cultural practice. Actually, that kind of 'rapid composing in performance' constitutes the 'predominant form of verbal art in the history of the human species'.[5] As for the written offshoot, my own conclusion is that the textual, historical, psychological and linguistic research described over the course of this book corroborates the idea that one might indeed think up free verse in the manner of speaking it, all the while transcribing what emerges. At least for stretches.

But it is equally significant that the overwhelming majority of the poets who linked Auden's comments on speech to their own compositional practice also reported that they work in other, typically more accretive modes. They swap between them. In sum, the matter is a technical one, to do with the means to achieving an outcome, given the cognitive apparatus evolution has bequeathed us, the rhythmic pulse driving its operations, and the kinds of artforms we have developed to work with these inheritances.

That might make poetry writing sound easy. Yeats – or one of his voices – put it this way:

I said, 'A line will take us hours maybe;
Yet if it does not seem a moment's thought,
Our stitching and our unstitching has been naught.'[6]

There are worlds of nuance in that 'maybe'. After all, poetry is not something you can simply buy with more time. On the other hand, nothing in these pages should be allowed to minimise Yeats's reference to the hours taken on one line. A large component of the opposition to the Auden quotation seems attributable to its failure to reference such pains. But here I reiterate the caveat stated earlier in this book: to label what one does at such times 'work' is to obfuscate something much more like repeated, frustrated action with no necessary recompense at all. Yeats puts it in terms of 'stitching and unstitching', hardly a valorisable activity – until it suddenly is.

The linguistic considerations in recent chapters might allow us to add another dimension here, too. The prose sentence is an innately revised entity and our relative freedom in coming up with yet another one surely has something to do with the fact that sentences do not ultimately have to reflect the reality of how we actually do think or speak within the crystallising pressure of the moment. As for the line of poetry, 'if it does not seem a moment's thought'. Approached from this angle, it would seem that the poets rejecting Auden's words were not ultimately taking issue with the idea that the right words might come with suddenness. It is rather that they were underscoring the rarity – the unbankable nature – of the phenomenon. Perhaps they also had in mind that commitment whereby a poet returns again and again to a composition, custodian of all the past selves through whom the work has arrived to this point; somehow that poet does not despair, maintaining enough hope that the rest will come and an overall shape for the work be found, trusting to their better selves to somehow be there at the exact right time when it will. So one works with one's own traditions, instance after instance, in spite of odds. Or just shatters the whole thing at some point and finds it that way. There is something in the unlikelihood of any poem ever turning out right that Auden's reference to 'genuinely speaking', and related concepts like psychologist Mihaly Csziksentmihalyi's well-known 'flow', seems simply to trivialise.[7] Somehow the thing has to work, even though this is generally speaking impossible.

The conclusion seems clear. Writing in a manner redolent of the risky, real-time uncertainty of actual face-to-face speaking is one technical means, among others, for achieving the finish to which almost all of the poets we interviewed subscribe. Others get there slowly, more accretively. That Armantrout and Emery mention their employment of additional practices underlines the technical function that 'rapid composing in performance' has for them.[8] The same could be claimed of many of the poets. And why should multiple practices not combine in the repertoire of one and the same poet, to be called upon when needed? We saw in chapter 4 how multiple techniques might make up the compositional history of one and the same now canonical poem. Actually, that is probably the norm, when it comes to writing poetry.

But that is another way of saying that no one producing this type of verbal art has the comfort of a tried practice to rely on.

POETS' OBJECTIONS TO THE IDEA OF ORIGINALITY

The argument I have just rehearsed would be a first answer to the question tabled in chapter 1, as to why the poets we interviewed had such divided responses to Auden's claims about the creative powers of real-time speaking. The more considered version would admit that something remains substantially unexplored in the thesis I have just advanced. The fact is that much of the ire that Auden's words aroused actually centred on the last part of the quotation, with its reference to the unpremeditated, genuine speaker producing 'something new that has never been said or heard before'.[9] While the notion of a speech-like spontaneity in composition split the field, with two-thirds on one side, a third on the other, this component of the quotation was unifying. Almost all opposed it.

It is instructive that the only poet, among the 14 whom I interviewed over the years 2013–2015, who offered explicit support for Auden's reference to conversation producing 'something new that has never been said or heard before', nonetheless characterised the idea as 'improbable'.

> I tell my students that it is possible. We have 5,000 years of written literature, and maybe 800 years of something recognisable as English, but it is still possible, on very little investment, to say something that's never been said before. It is still possible to put certain words together in a pattern that has – to our knowledge – never occurred before. I find that deeply moving: that it is still possible to create something new within language. I find it improbable and moving.[10]

G. C. Waldrep's qualification, 'to our knowledge', underlines the difficulty of making such a claim at this conjuncture. He knew he was going out on a limb.

The almost total repudiation of the idea of poetic originality, by the very poets to whom that supposed faculty is attributed, is intriguing. Kenneth Goldsmith may have been wearing his heart on his sleeve here, in relation to his proclaimed discipline of 'uncreative writing'. But note that Rae Armantrout had an issue with the idea too: 'I think the ending [to Auden's statement] has a bit of hubris to it'. So did C. K. Williams, as we saw earlier. These are both poets who have been celebrated for their unique voices. C. D. Wright has likewise been celebrated for it: recall Joel Brouwer's description of her as a poet who 'belongs to a school of exactly one'.[11] But Wright, too, had little time for Auden's reference to 'something new that has never been said or heard before':

I am not a huge booster for originality. When I do encounter an original, I know it. Maybe I have met three. Not necessarily artists. We are just trying to put an extra fine point on it – what we think we see, what we honestly perceive – as we possibly can. Aiming high without a snowball's chance in hell of hitting the mark.[12]

These poets' general dissatisfaction with the idea that their work might equate to what 'has never been said or heard before' suggests that we have still not elucidated the composition of poetic thought. Why did the latter part of the Auden quotation call forth such specific disfavour? If they are not engaging in acts of origination, just what is it that poets do, to find an utterance others will regard as original? And how can we avoid the feeling – I share it with Waldrep – that 'something new' does emerge from their language all the same?

Poetic originality has been the underlying concern of this book, and will be the explicit topic of its final chapter. But we will follow Wright's lead in rejecting the concept of 'originality' itself, as too freighted in unhistorical connotations, for all Walter Benjamin's attempts to restore the concept of origin (*ursprung*) to philosophy, by defining it in terms of 'that which emerges from the process of becoming and disappearance . . . an eddy in the stream of becoming'.[13] Benjamin's act of redefinition does, nonetheless, usefully remind us of how any poetic event seems to point back to, or at least reverberate with, the deep histories leading us to that point, at very same time that it propels us forward, to the indeterminate possibilities for how to act next.

'You simply are more awake. That's a very important word for me. Alert and awake. That's why I write' (Owen).[14]

Our way in to the poets' general repudiation of the idea that 'something new, that has never been said or heard before' might be found in their work, will be through a final consideration on suddenness. One way of reading the linguistic work cited over the last few chapters would be to acknowledge that each successive burst of speech we utter is, in its own way, an act of innovation and discovery. But speech is also often banal. The reason, surely, is that one of the key means speakers have for negotiating the dysfluency that always threatens to result from the pressure of composing one's discourse on the spot is to avail themselves of pre-fabricated phrasing. Another way of reading Parry and Lord's massive corpus of improvised, South Slav epics is to see it as the world's first evidence of this, which required huge sets of mechanically recorded data to bring to light. The fact is that speaking in formulas is just as much a part of everyday conversation as finding one's words in the moment. Or rather, the words we find, moment-by-moment, generally are just that: formulas, strung together rather loosely. Poets are no exception.

NOTES

1. Auden, "Words and the Word," 105.
2. Armantrout, interview by author, November 11, 2014.
3. Paterson, interview by Kevin Brophy, July 2, 2013.
4. Magee, "Interview with C. K. Williams," 92.
5. Lord, *Singer of Tales*, 17; Antović and Cánovas, "Not Dictated by Metrics," 21.
6. Yeats, "Adam's Curse," 88.
7. Csikszentmihalyi, *Flow*.
8. Lord, *Singer of Tales*, 17.
9. Auden, "Words and the Word," 105.
10. Waldrep, interview by author, July 9, 2013.
11. Brouwer, "Counting the Dead."
12. Wright, "An Interview."
13. Benjamin, *Origin of German Tragic Drama*, 44.
14. Owen, interview by author, March 12, 2007.

Chapter 13

'Great Goblets of Magnolialight'

Transcriptions of verbatim speech provide a vivid insight into the function of pre-fabricated phrasing, by showing just how difficult it can be to string words together in the moment. Andrew Pawley and Frances Hodgetts Syder recorded 'F, a draughtsman in his mid-20s', in New Zealand in the 1970s. In the following, F is 'discussing evangelical Christianity with several hostel mates'.[1] It rapidly becomes apparent that F 'does not have the words ready to do his bidding, but has to find them' (Auden) there and then, something almost painful to recreate in one's head as one reads the transcript.[2] Each dash in the lines that follow stands for a detectable pause:

(1) Yeah – I think – y'know, –
(2) Ah – I've found – in um – y'know, – um – not in religion at the beginning of this year, y'know, –
(3) ah – ah – the experiences I had on – ah – on Queen's Birthday weekend, y'know. –
(4) The peace that I found. –
(5) Simply being able to throw my –
(6) or – not – not to throw myself
(7) just to – sort of – just to – y'know – ah just hold on to another person – y'know,
(8) let – just – just – y'know ah[3]

Pawley and Syder give each clause in the transcript a separate line. This is not entirely straightforward, considering the lack of consensus among linguists as to just what a clause is.[4] Breaking F's discourse into clauses does, however, clarify its movement somewhat. But even when given in clausal chunks, the chaos is still notable. Witness the 31 dashes. F is clearly struggling to convey his experience of the divine.

Pawley and Syder note that the act of transcribing such a text,

> leads readily to three unsurprising conclusions about the planning of spontaneous speech: (i) it is not easy to think and talk at the same time; (ii) speech itself bears some observable marks of the planning process; (iii) speakers often embark on constructions without having formulated their full lexical content. . . . [F's discourse] reminds us that it is no mean feat to keep talking fluently and coherently even for ten seconds.[5]

Pawley and Syder proceed to address themselves to the 'puzzle' of how we ever manage to speak with fluency, given the heavy cognitive burden that real-time speech production involves. They offer two solutions.

We pre-empted the first of these solutions in chapter 11, having foreshadowed it back in chapter 7, in relation to Homer. It is that speakers will often parcel what they have to say into a succession of short 'clauses which show little structural integration with earlier or later constructions'.[6] Pawley and Syder's chief example of this strategy is G, the 'gifted raconteur', whose storytelling served, in chapter 11, to demonstrate how readily conversation can take on metrical qualities, when one speaks in this staggered fashion.[7]

(17) Uncle Bert 'ad a black bottle, (1.5)
(18) an ah – (.2) 'e'd tell a few stories,
(19) an' 'e'd take a sip out of the black bottle,
(20) 'n' the more sips he took outa that bottle, (1.0)
(21) the worse the stories got. (1.6)[8]

It transpires from Pawley's later work that speaking in short, syntactically discrete, clausal blocks affords fluency to a range of high-pace, real-time discourses including the auctioning of houses and livestock, live radio commentary on sporting matches and oral epic verse.[9] The agents of such genres manage, with practice, to coral their statements into the two to three second chunks that characterize the window of conscious attention, and in this way to speak, and in a sense even to sing, a fluent language, live.

Pawley and Syder's second solution to the 'puzzle' of how we ever manage to speak with fluency is related to the fact that the words that such professionally fluent speakers utter tend to be heavily formulaic. This is the solution with most bearing on the question of how contemporary poetic diction comes to sound so full of potential and new, and at the same time so deep in its response to past usage–all the things we gesture at with the term 'originality'. Yet it is unlikely to seem so promising from the outset. For the second way speakers minimize the dysfluencies that listeners so rapidly find irritating and indeed exhausting is to rely upon their stores of 'memorized complete clauses and sentences'.[10] The simple fact is that F's discourse would sound even more chaotic, were it not for the prefabricated elements smattered through it: 'at the beginning of this year'; 'on Queen's Birthday weekend'; 'The peace that I found'; 'Simply being able to'. Note the absence of mid-phrase pauses in these four clearly formulaic utterances, and the stark contrast they present in this regard to strings like 'let – just – just – y'know ah'.[11] Taking that comparison on board, we might say that what F is really doing in the excerpt is lurching from pre-fabricated expression to pre-fabricated expression, and experiencing a great deal of difficulty at the joins.

Pawley and Syder proceed to argue that the completely fixed expressions in English like *simply being able to* are vastly outnumbered by the store of only partially fixed ones. G's expression 'We had a fantastic time', will sound as ossified as the four phrases cited from F, above.[12] A few seconds' reflection reveals that it is only partially so. One can equally well hear a speaker say 'I had a fantastic time'; 'They are having a fantastic time'; 'We will have a fantastic time', and so forth. Pawley and Syder refer to such partially fixed expressions as 'lexicalized sentence stems'. They define them as expressions which 'contain a nucleus of fixed lexical items . . . with one or more variable elements'.[13] An example they offer is: 'I'm sorry to keep you waiting', which can also be formulated as 'I'm so sorry to have kept you waiting', 'Mr X is sorry to keep you waiting all this time', and so on. Pawley and Syder comment that such 'lexicalized sentence-stems' are repeatedly on our lips.[14] (Or should that be 'in'? Keats: 'And all the dead whose names are in our lips'.)[15] They need to be, because speakers frequently want to utter longer strings, more akin to those one finds in prose, than the relatively short and discrete segments characteristic of sporting commentators, colloquial storytellers, livestock auctioneers and Homeric poets.

G himself provides an instance of this expanded speaking, in his use of a *the more . . . the worse . . .* construction over clauses 20 to 21 of the excerpt above: "'n' *the more* sips he took outa that bottle, (1.0)/*the worse* the stories got. (1.6)'.[16] When they encompass multi-clausal relations in this manner, such 'lexicalised sentence stems' facilitate fluency in real-time speaking by affording conversationalists a literally formulaic sense of where their utterance is heading over the words immediately to follow.[17] In fact, they amount to a partial exception to the 'one-clause-at-a-time' constraint Pawley and Syder otherwise adumbrate. For even though we do not seem able in any instance to encode the exact words we want to say more than one clause (Chafe would say, 'one intonation unit') at a time, it would seem that this cognitive constraint 'does not apply to the planning of syntactic frames, only to their lexical content. It appears that grammatical frames in which two or more clauses are joined can be planned independently of their lexical realizations'.[18]

One might think of this idea in terms of the way a common academic phrase like *On the one hand* sets up a 'construction frame' for an *On the other hand* contrast shortly thereafter.[19] It may be that the contents of the second term of that contrast are only 'semi-actively' present in our minds, as we advance into our articulation of the first term. But we know a contrastive frame is in place and have had enough experience of contouring familiar ideas into the distinct shape it offers, so that we can advance into our discourse with reasonable faith in our capacity to get the words to land right. We can see something of that order in the following transcript, which is from a University of Michigan philosophy seminar on the unity of consciousness, recorded in the year 2000.

> And, just to give us a, just to remind you the various kinds of theory that we've been looking at here, both for the unity of consciousness and personal identity, have some similar themes, um, similar sorts of theories have been proposed, so, some people have thought that we a- what explains who you are, what makes you the particular individual that you are at a particular time is that you have, a distinctive immaterial soul . . .[20]

The lecturer is clearly grappling with the difficulty of finding the right words to generalize about the theories under discussion at the start of this utterance. But note how their diction seems to relax at the point at which they alight upon the correlative construction (*'what* + VERB . . ., *is that* + VERB. . .'). The fact that such an overarching 'lexicalised sentence stem' has come to mind seems to be what allows the lecturer the freedom to try out a first formulation (*'what explains* who you are') and then to repair it with a more precise one (*'what makes* you the particular individual that you are at a particular time'). A certain breathing space is available for such reformulations, because the broad outline of the second part of the correlation (*'is that'*), if not the exact words ('you have, a distinctive immaterial soul'), is already at hand– and not just for the speaker, but in key ways for the listener as well, trying to follow along. When people say they are 'used to giving lectures', much of what they mean is that they are familiar, and comfortable, with taking these sorts of compositional risks, live before an audience. In sum, what Pawley and Syder call 'lexicalised sentence stems' do much, though of course not all, of the work of laying out our propositions for us.

But for all the gains that pre-fabricated phrasing provides, it does come at a price. I do not mean that speaking in this formulaic manner condemns a speaker to sounding mechanical. As we have seen a number of contemporary Homerists argue, there are all sorts of ways in which a discourse predominantly composed of formulaic elements can still ripple with life, including the unexpected that is so much a part of life. The disadvantage of speaking formulaically is rather, Pawley and Syder point out, that it is so easy to get the formulas wrong, particular the partially fixed ones. As foreigners to a language find again and again, there does not seem to be any good reason why one should not say 'the talk holds water' or 'the novel holds water'. After all, 'the theory holds water'.[21] What is more, even after one has learnt that *the theory holds water* is acceptably 'nativelike', there are further 'rules' to learn, each as apparently arbitrary as the next: 'It turns out you can say *the theory doesn't/didn't hold water*, but it is not quite idiomatic to say *the theory isn't holding much water any more*, or *the theory will hold some water tomorrow*'.[22]

Our consideration on poetic diction will emerge at this juncture. The point will be that by placing such severe restrictions on what can be said in a natural way, these omnipresent, fixed and partially fixed expressions hint at the much greater potential of the language housing them. For the phrases poets use are not the opposite of what is formulaic and every day in language, but rather the extension of such usages, more or less readily inferable from them. In that regard, there is nothing new about speaking poetically at all.

The Butterfly's Assumption Gown
In Chrysoprase Apartments hung
This Afternoon put on –[23]

IT'S FORTY PAST FIVE

To see how formulaic speech indexes all that is strange, poetic and yet recognisably part of the language, it will be worth sketching a little more of the context of Pawley and Syder's intervention.

It transpires that there is something of a history to the idea that we tend to use far less of a language than is available to us. Towards the end of the 1950s, Noam Chomsky launched the generationally compelling principle that language use centres upon speakers' creative processing of vocabulary through an innate set of grammatical rules. In a famous attack upon B.F. Skinner's *Verbal Behavior*, Chomsky established that without some such generative principle, we have little way to account for creativity, in his specific sense of the word, that is little way to account for the fact that even a child will have the ability to 'construct and understand utterances which are quite new, and are, at the same time, acceptable sentences in his [*sic*] language'.[24] As Alison Wray concedes, we need some way to account for the individual's capacity to generate new strings of language from established patterns, if we are to make sense of our ability not only to produce, but even just to understand, such novel moments in poetic texts as 'when, for instance, word classes are changed (e.g. *he sang his didn't he danced his did*), or unaccustomed morphological relations are created (e.g. *and you and I, light-tender-holdly, ached together in bliss-me body*)'.[25] Yet, while the Chomskyan revolution proceeded apace through the 1960s, contrary voices had already in the early years of that decade started to emerge.

In a 1961 article, Dwight Bolinger queried whether a sentence as commonplace as 'I went home' is really generated anew from its component parts each time.[26] For it might be that the entire phrase *I went home* comes to mind and tongue as 'the result of repetition, countless speakers before us having said it and transmitted it to us in toto. Is grammar something where speakers produce (i.e. originate) constructions, or where they "reach" for them, from a pre-established inventory, when the occasion presents itself?'[27] Further challengers to absolute distinctions between vocabulary and syntax included Chafe, who in the late 1960s pointed to the difficulty idiomatic language posed to Chomsky's position.[28] The diffusion of cheap mechanical recording devices from the 1950s on was meanwhile making developments like Pawley and Syder's 300,000 word corpus of New Zealand and Australian speakers possible, with the clear evidence it provided that formulaic phrasing is a key element of fluent speech. Paul Hopper added his own force to such arguments in the course of his 1987 attack on the notion that language-use relies upon 'an abstract, mentally represented rule system which is somehow implemented when we speak'.[29] Close reading of conversational transcripts shows that language in use is 'a kind of pastiche, pasted together in an improvised way out of ready-made elements'.[30] Often, Hopper added, with echoes of Bolinger, it is not even clear where 'to draw the line between a formulaic and a non-formulaic expression'.[31] Actually, this kind of 'gradience' between prefabricated and improvised expressions is also evident in the Homeric epics, as the latest work in that field is starting to show.[32] But it was the growth of computing power, Wray observes, that has done most to sway linguists to the idea that wholly and partially fixed expressions radically contour the linguistic space that we as speakers and writers inhabit. Wray mentions a 1998 study that found the phrase *a large number* was five times more common than *a great number* in a 2.7 million word corpus of academic prose.[33] The statistic reinforces the likelihood that a string like *a large number* comes to the scholarly writer as a single, oft-repeated unit.

Michael Hoey's 2004 work *Lexical Priming: A New Theory of Words and Language* continued this trajectory, with a powerful demonstration that we work with genre- and context-specific, formulaic blocks to compose our writing, and by extension our speech, avoiding vast swathes of possible expressions in the process. Basing his analysis on a corpus of 95 million words of news and features from the *Guardian* newspaper, Hoey shows that the second of the following two sentences is far, far less likely to occur in such a context, even though it appears to be as 'grammatically' correct as the first:

(1) In winter Hammerfest is a thirty-hour ride by bus from Oslo, though why anyone would want to go there in winter is a question worth considering.

(2) Through winter, rides between Oslo and Hammerfest use thirty hours up in a bus, though why travelers would select to ride there then might be pondered.[34]

Hoey proceeds to demonstrate that *in winter*, the first phrase in sentence (1), appears 507 times in his 95 million word corpus, whereas *through winter*, its 'equivalent' in sentence (2), appears only 7 times. Likewise, the *by bus* phrase in sentence (1) appears 116 times in that corpus, while the *rides between* phrase in sentence (2) occurs only once, and *in a bus*, also in (2), only 16 times. Similarly, the *would want* in sentence (1) occurs 573 times, while (2)'s *would select* is found only 21 times. On the other hand, the phrase *use x hours up*, from sentence (2) ('use thirty hours up in a bus'), is not attested to at all.[35] It is worth adding that similar comparisons apply to numerous other elements of these two sentences. Hoey assays the pair from different angles through each successive chapter of *Lexical Priming* and the conclusion in each case is clear: the idea that the first of the sentences above 'is natural; the second is clumsy' is not a simple judgement of taste, but a statistical fact.[36]

Hoey adds that according to the dominant ways we have thought about language over the last 200 years, 'there is no reason to regard the naturalness or clumsiness of the sentences as being of any importance'.[37] He argues that, to the contrary, 'naturalness' is a selective factor in every sound we utter, and with that a determinative force upon grammar itself, the very existence of which it might even be said to undermine.[38] Hoey sees recent work on corpora like his as 'reversing the traditional relationship between grammar as systematic and lexis as loosely organized, amounting to an argument for lexis as systematic and grammar as more loosely organized'.[39] The fact is that only a restricted number of the many possible ways to say something ever tend to get said, the ones that strike us as 'natural'. There are rhythmic drivers here, to be sure, in that we display a clear bias when speaking a strongly stress-timed language like English for the stressed syllables to come at regular intervals, in accordance with the muscular preferences referred to in chapter 11: these kinds of considerations clearly exert a selective pressure on which phrases become fixed.[40] But the phenomenon is otherwise profoundly arbitrary. And it is pervasive, extending, by Hoey's account, well beyond the idioms and 'lexicalised sentence stems' Pawley and Syder investigated, to the point where all of our vocabulary would seem to have something fixed or partially fixed about its patterns of usage.

We are closing in on what Samuel Taylor Coleridge referred to as 'the true nature of poetic diction'.[41] For to entertain this ever-mounting linguistic evidence is to realize that most of the infinite number of generable strings in any given language are foreign. They cannot actually be said without sounding unnatural. Yet they can be said, as Hoey's capacity to produce for the comparison above a second, odd-speaking but intelligible version of the first sentence of Bill Bryson's 1991 travel book, *Neither Here, Nor There*, demonstrates. Pawley and Syder provide further evidence of this same point. Claiming that 'one of the main attractions' of the Chomskyan tradition has been its 'focus on the creative power of syntactic rules', they argue that it is nonetheless the case that 'native speakers do not exercise the creative potential of syntactic rules to anything like their full extent'.[42] Yet one might. Actually, we hear such non-native uses every day–for instance, among second language speakers. It is, Pawley and Syder write, a 'characteristic error of the language learner' to assume, in relation to any partially fixed expression, 'that an element in the expression may be varied according to a phrase structure or transformational rule of some generality' when the expression is in fact 'transformationally 'defective'. There are only so many ways to generate those strings without starting to sound childish, foreign or strange.[43] Pawley and Syder give the following as examples of such erroneous but nonetheless sayable and what is more intelligible reaches of the English language: '*You are pulling my legs* (in the sense of deceiving me). *John has a thigh-ache*, and *I intend to teach that rascal some good lessons he will never forget*'.[44] Expressions for telling the time are no less arbitrarily restricted. It's 5.40 pm. Why not:

(a) It's six less twenty.
(b) It's two thirds past five.
(c) It's forty past five.
(d) It exceeds five by forty.
(e) It's a third to six.
(f) It's ten minutes after half-past five.[45]

I find something zany in these demonstrations of Pawley and Syder's and, in fact, the pair remark in a footnote that native speakers often generate non-nativelike strings for humorous purposes. What is more, it seems clear that speakers can produce such humorous strings at pace. One 'gets on a roll'. It strikes me that there are philosophic resonances to this list as well. Witness the curious bending of time in *It's forty past five*. I think Wittgenstein. (Or should that be, I think of Wittgenstein?) The dishabituation of time is also a subversive theme. 1789 brought about a whole new calendar, while the 1830 overthrow of the Bourbons began with bullets fired at public clocks, as the revolutionary Walter Benjamin reminds us.[46] But this is as much as to suggest that there is something deeply poetic in Pawley and Syder's statement that 'only a small proportion of the total set of grammatical sentences are nativelike in form'.[47] (Should that be 'is nativelike'?)

Our capacity to generate and understand what can't quite be 'naturally' said is surely there in these lines from Medbh McGuckian's 2016 poem, 'White Cortina Outside Stardust Ballroom':

>   . . . the sky slowly
> sipped away to willow ashes.
>
> It seemed to have, I would like to say,
> hands, though they were not seen,
> those breathless ghosts of mine.
> All cherries had taken their farewell
> of their perfect cherry colour.
> I could feel everyone praying for me
>
> like a little forest bird,
> the otherest.[48]

And if the highly formulaic language of Homeric epic poets is to be thought of as a 'special language' within the body of the larger language that hosted it, as Albert Lord suggests, might we not conclude that the potential language which McGuckian taps into here is itself host to the much smaller body of expressions we actually tend to utter?[49] It is the host, to native and foreign alike.

The *otherest*.

Five forty, but also *It's a third to six*. I note the strange patina to the latter. It feels fresh, as well as odd, and yet not entirely new. Actually, for all its oddness, it seems to bring the deeply Germanic roots of our number words to the fore.

As such, there is a curious parallel between such expressions and the figure Samuel Taylor Coleridge provided to accompany his argument about 'the true nature of poetic diction', in his 1817 *Biographia Literaria: or, Biographical Sketches of My Literary Life and Opinions*.[50] Coleridge has just asserted that poetic diction should satisfy two criteria, both to do with the type of reading experience it should generate. The first, a criterion of iterability, is founded on the claim that it is 'not the poem which we have *read*', but only 'that to which we *return*, with the greatest pleasure' which 'possesses the genuine power and claims the name of *essential poetry*'. The second, a criterion of irreplaceability, holds that any aspects of a poet's phrasing that can 'be translated into other words of the same language, without diminution of their significance, either in sense or association, or in any worthy feeling' are to that extent 'vicious in their diction'.[51] I will return to this second criterion shortly. But what I have most in mind in turning to Coleridge at this point is the striking analogy that he reports resorting to during youthful discussions on the topic:

> I was wont boldly to affirm that it would be scarcely more difficult to push a stone out from the pyramids with the bare hand, than to alter a word, or the position of a word, in Milton or Shakespeare (in their most important works at least) without making the author say something else, or something worse, than he does say.[52]

I cite this admittedly youthful analogy–for all its blindness to the instability of canonical textual traditions (is that definitive set of words those of the folio, or the quarto?)[53]–because we are only so far here from the idea of words that feel 'nativelike', or natural. The words in Milton and Shakespeare's 'most important works' feel as naturally given, and as irreplaceable, as blocks of stone. Yet, at the same time, we seem to be straying into the enigmatic and the foreign–the stones of the pyramids, no less.

> ... the sky slowly
> sipped away to willow ashes.

My point is that linguistics is pushing us in a similar direction. It shows that any given language will tend to privilege a small set of regularly repeated phrasings, implying a vast field of sayable but typically unsaid variants upon those phrases in the process, a store of foreigner thought native to the language itself.

If that analysis is at all apt, it might explain the resistance to concepts of originality among the poets we interviewed, poets whose work nonetheless seems so consistently to platform it. It is language itself that casts up this diversity–particularly when you are forging clauses and larger coherences at the coalface of what you feel but cannot yet understand, particularly when in the sway of a rhythm, and under the epochal imperative to find the hitherto unsaid in what is about to be said.

But inasmuch as this is the case, poetic speech would seem to buck some of the trends Pawley and Syder associate with extemporaneous speaking. They hold that even though a speaker will usually proceed with ease in conversation, especially once some clause-chaining and/or pre-fabricated phrasing sets in, that speaker will rapidly become aware of the 'skill and work' required by the mere act of stringing phrases together 'when he [*sic*] is required to express his thoughts on an unfamiliar subject, or to deliver an unrehearsed monologue to a silent audience'.[54] Compare Rae Armantrout's comment on the uncertainty of her process, as cited in the first chapter of this book: 'I do not know where I am going. I don't even know if a poem will happen. I just hope'.[55] I also quoted Kevin Young: 'There is a way in which, even in the poem, you are wrestling with that silence, that inability to speak, or the difficulty of doing so'.[56] Maxine Chernoff told me, 'I am writing into the tension of things changing all the time'.[57] All of these situations seem likely, by Pawley and Syder's analysis, to induce maximum dysfluency. But we have also seen references, through these pages, to the rhythmic flow of the line driving the selection of words, as when Alison Croggon told me that, 'The lines float up. . . . They're usually triggered by some kind of rhythm', and also expressions of surprise at what emerged: 'There are times . . . when I look back at a poem and think, did I really write that?'[58] In the more or less Parryan terms of Pawley and Syder's argument, one would expect a public discourse that departs so constitutively from everyday topics and phrasings to be far less fluently produced than Croggon's comments on rhythmic flow and sudden arrival suggest. After all, fixed and partially fixed expressions are apparently there to save on processing time, and so facilitate fluency. But, as noted earlier, the pair also refer to the way 'native speakers sometimes deliberately make an unusual substitution, expansion or transformation to a lexicalised phrase in order to add an element of freshness, humor, surprise etc. to their talk. Oscar Wilde is one wit who exploited this procedure to considerable effect'.[59] The idea emerges from Ronald Carter's corpus-based researches on creativity in everyday conversations as well.[60] There is no indication that such acts of wit require considerable pausing to be achieved. As for poetic utterance, is there not a ready resource for those rhythmic drives to choose from, in all the things the language might–but we by convention do not–say, each and every time we speak? In short, is it not simply a matter of trusting to habit, while taking a leap?

PELEIADIC ACHILLEUS

The resort to what is familiar to convey the new is a key consequence of our time-pressured plight as speakers. This is so much the case that Parry's insights into the pre-composed nature of so much Homeric diction, and the live production demands necessitating that, can even be seen as pre-empting the theories of nativelike/formulaic speaking rehearsed above. It is certainly striking to find a mirror image of Parry's table of the *hupodra idōn prosephē* (looking darkly then said) construction, as cited in chapter 5, in linguist Joan

Table 13.1

SUBJECT	[DRIVE]	me you { him } her the producer[1]	mad { crazy } up the wall

[1] Bybee, *Language, Usage and Cognition*, 27.

Bybee's 2010 illustration (table 13.1, above) of the *drive crazy* 'resultative construction' on the lips of many a speaker of contemporary English.

Thus Bybee formalises the bevvy of expressions like 'It drives me crazy', 'It drove the producer mad', 'This room drives me up the wall'.[61] Contemporary developments in the study of such constructions bring us substantially closer 'toward describing Homeric language as we would any natural language', Chiara Bozzone notes.[62] For their part, Cristóbal Pagán Cánovas and Mihailo Antović state that 'it seems that what speakers carry around in their heads is a mental corpus . . . or *constructicon*, a collection of constructions analogous to the singer's repertoire of formulas, along with the knowledge of how to recombine and reuse these constructional / formulaic patterns'.[63] For Cánovas and Antović, the fact that 'the pressure for a fast negotiation of meaning is much stronger in oral composition in performance than in everyday language', and that 'idiomaticity is enhanced' as a consequence, does not undermine the relevance of Parry and Lord's work to the study of how everyday speaking proceeds. To the contrary, the 'verbal and thematic patterns, constructions and frames, are exposed potentially even more clearly than they are in everyday speech' in the Homeric and Balkan epics.[64] So when we read Parry, insisting upon the multi-authored nature of Homeric verse–' It is not possible . . . that one man by himself could work out more than the smallest part of the series of formulas of the type Πηληιάδεω Ἀχιλῆος [*Pēlēiadeō Achilēos*]'–what we find is a clearer articulation of the forces each and every one of us labours under, whatever the language we speak.[65] No single individual could possibly have invented each and every one of the formulaic expressions they speak. A population of time-pressed past users sings through our utterances too.

Medbh McGuckian's description of her practice of composing poems provides a rich image of this state of affairs:

> I prefer for actual poem making my biro my notebook my preliminary sketch of words and phrases on preferably a single page then to transfer that logically on to a larger notebook and fish for a catchy title then work towards that. People in the house relax me and they know my family that I am busy and they do not

disturb me or ask questions. Not late at night mostly early evening rarely morning. A dictionary is helpful as I am not looking words up on the phone as Virginia [Woolf] would. Yes quiet silence subdued no music hardly the central heating. No tea during this time it feels sacred like a Mass or ritual. Open for ghosts and memory delighting in the quest the restraint the oddity of English in Ireland the total remoteness of the language and yet it is all there is.[66]

McGuckian describes herself working with 'a preliminary sketch of words and phrases' and a dictionary. I write that her description of this provides a rich image for our plight as language users. In part, this is because of the resonance of her final words, which surely applies to the metropoles as well: 'the total remoteness of the language and yet it is all there is'. But the key point here is that any speaker must possess some such 'dictionary' as well, in the form of what we have seen Cánovas and Antović refer to as a 'a mental corpus . . . or *constructicon*, a collection of constructions' that users 'carry around in their heads'.[67] No one can invent all of this by themselves.

Poets, just like any of us, reach for what is formulaic and given.

But what McGuckian produces strains the bounds of any normative dictionary, or even of any construction grammar.

> You, who were the spaces between words in the act of reading,
> A colour sewn on to colour, break the blue.[68]

Or take a line from C. D. Wright, the line that provides the title for this very chapter:

> Chlorophyll world. July. Great goblets of magnolialight.[69]

Who talks like this? And yet something feels profoundly spoken about it. Note, too, the title of the book in which this line of Wright's is found, *Deepstep Come Shining*. The phrase sounds strangely dialectical, English, and yet not of any English that we know. How might one translate it back into English, without loss? '[I]t would be scarcely more difficult to push a stone out from the pyramids' (Coleridge).

Drawing on the clues in Pawley and Syder's work, and then in the work of their colleagues, I have claimed that the potential language a poet taps into is host to that much smaller range of expressions we actually utter, when speaking in an acceptably 'nativelike' manner. From such a perspective, contemporary poetic diction is not the opposite to the habitual expressions enshrined in dictionaries, construction grammars, or in the kinds of 'mental corpus' now being labelled *constructicons*, but rather is implied by all such nativelike usages. It is the 'possibility' in which they 'dwell'.[70]

But that was just a first approximation. What the works cited to this point cannot help us with is the fact that not all unconventional utterances are treated alike.

EMAIL ME A RECEIPT

Compare 'She kissed him unconscious' and 'She filled the water into the cup', both unusual phrasings.[71] Why does the one feel fresh, and the other come across as awkward? Likewise, compare 'Four days after the military coup, they had disappeared her husband' with 'He vanished the rabbit'.[72] Why does the employment of the verb *disappear* in the first of these phrases feels so grimly apt, to the point that the usage has now taken on journalistic currency, while the seemingly similar use of *vanish* in the latter feels at best cute, but more likely awkward, and even somehow wrong?

In asking 'How is it that native speakers know to avoid certain expressions while nonetheless using language in creative ways?', Adele Goldberg points to an issue that has so far eluded us.[73] In addition to our contrast between the nativelike and the non-nativelike, there is a further distinction to be made. Pursuing it will get us closer to what our poetry aims at, so as to achieve those curiously fresh but also long-historied expressions, which we gesture at through terms like 'originality', and which sit so strangely with the idea of national literary traditions, given how odd the poetry of a G. C. Waldrep, a C. D. Wright or a Brook Emery actually is. At the same time, it will take us straight to the fact that innovative usages come about regardless of whether people with the title 'poet' are on the scene or not. As we shall see, those new usages are winnowed into language by mechanisms that place a premium on what cannot otherwise be said. This would be a further reason for poets to resile from any claim to exercise 'originality'. Language is poetic in its own right. And fast to change.

To open the further distinction that Goldberg alerts us to, consider the phrase that provides the title to her 2019 book, *Explain Me This: Creativity, Competition, and the Partial Productivity of Constructions,* a work which continues and expands the trends initiated in Bollinger, Chafe, Pawley and Syder, Hopper, Wray, Hoey and their colleagues' work, not to mention Parry's, back before all of them. Goldberg is interested in the phrase *Explain me this* because it constitutes one of those utterances 'that are perfectly understandable, but which nonetheless tend to be avoided by native speakers of English. If asked, speakers will agree that there is something mildly 'off' about them, even though they may have difficulty articulating exactly why'.[74] It transpires that the English double-object construction (e.g. *Tell me this*; *I asked him the question; Give me that watch*) is confined (largely) to 'Germanic (sounding) verbs'. 'Latinate (sounding)' verbs like *request, transfer* and *explain*, on the other hand, have a strong tendency to use a prepositional phrase to indicate the party affected by their action: *Can you request permission from him?; I transferred the money to the bank; Explain this to me*. The equally Latinate verb, *guarantee*, constitutes an exception to these trends (*Can you guarantee me this loan?*), while *purchase* is a partial one. Native speakers somehow master such abstruse tendencies, which in this case are actually quite recent–the fact that Latinate verbs can be found taking a double-object in writings from as late as the 18th century underlines how arbitrary and historically-given the 'rules' of the matter are.[75]

We have, of course, seen a number of examples of a similar arbitrariness in our discussion of partially-fixed expressions, above. What that earlier analysis did not address, however, was how it is that some unconventional deployments of the double-object result in an *Explain me this* effect, whereas others, for instance, *Text me your number*, succeed to the point of entering into wider circulation. The fact that the word *text* is from the Latinate wing of the language, with its dispreference for the double-object construction, underlines that it is not at all obvious what served to distinguish this expression, when first coined (the OED dates it back to 1998), from 'mildy 'off'' usages like *Explain me this*.[76] To put resistance to the latter down to sheer racism gets at something, but it leaves unclear why *Text me your number* attracted no such prejudice. Nor does there seem to have been any precedent in their respective constructions to justify the appearance of 'Blog him out of jail' or 'I coughed a moth out of my mouth' within the web-based corpuses Goldberg works with, though both sound natural enough, in fact fine.[77] What, to put the matter back in the terms of Goldberg's title, explains this 'partial productivity of constructions'?

'Construction' is Goldberg's word for the prefabricated template expressions we have seen Pawley and Syder refer to as 'lexicalised sentence stems', though 'construction' has much wider diffusion among contemporary linguists, and greater remit, as we are starting to see. A construction, as Joan Bybee puts it, comprises 'a form/meaning pairing that has sequential structure and may include positions that are fixed as well as positions that are open'.[78] Such a notion of 'construction' effectively restates Saussure's concept of the arbitrariness of the sign, with its relevance to what others call grammar or syntax underlined, as Thomas Hoffman and Graeme Trousdale note.[79] The term allows thinkers like Goldberg and Bybee to draw parallels between highly specific expressions like Pawley and Syder's *The theory holds water*, with its more or less arbitrary (or, at least, historically given) restrictions on what can fill the various slots in the template, and seemingly more grammatical entities like the double-object clause, which, as we have just seen, comes freighted with a range of effectively arbitrary restrictions as well. The rise over the last 30 years of construction grammars, which ignore distinctions like vocabulary and grammar to focus instead on the kinds of templates we are considering, has gone hand in hand with studies of grammaticalization. The term refers to 'the process by which a lexical item or sequence of items becomes a grammatical morpheme' (Bybee), the point being that inflections and other such seemingly fixed markers of syntactic function do not arise from some sort of logical fiat, as the binding rules of the language, but rather emerge through the same historical processes of routinization that cause regularly repeated chunks like *holds water* to settle into template expressions with open slots.[80] For instance, our 'weak verb' past tense ending in *-ed* seems to have come about from the repeated compounding, back in proto-Germanic, of present tense verbs with the then equivalent of our word *did* (perhaps *$ded\bar{o}$ or *$ded\bar{e}$), to give expressions along the lines of *walk-did, laugh-did* or *groan-did*. A reduction of sounds occurred in the process, as generally happens with very common usages (e.g. *I will not* -> *I won't; I don't know* -> *I dunno*), and in this way the second word in the compound fused into its now recognizable form as a weak verb inflection, giving us our current forms *walked, laughed, groaned* and so forth.[81] These shifts in thinking about the relation between grammar and vocabulary have been accompanied by the increasing realization that traditional grammatical categories like noun, verb and adjective simply do not survive the attempt to identify core properties across languages. As Anna Siewerska remarks, 'The analysis of the various constructions referred to in the literature as PASSIVE leads to the conclusion that there is not even one single property which all these constructions have in common'.[82] 'It is even difficult', Goldberg comments, 'to come up with criteria that hold of all members of a grammatical category *within* a language'.[83] At the level of the specific language, what we find is 'not a monolithic system, but a massive collection of heterogenous *constructions*', each the product of 'local storage and real time processing', as a multitude of speakers engage in the same basic task of 'reusing words and constructions that you've used in prior utterances to describe some other experience, not the one you are describing right now' (Croft).[84]

This brings us back to Goldberg's question as to 'the partial productivity of constructions', though now we have followed her and her colleagues' extension of the term 'construction' to exclude any sense of innate grammatical rules or processes other than historically compacted habit itself, there seems even less for the analyst to go on. How do we explain native speakers' capacity to find that third, innovative space, in between the nativelike and the recognizably wrong? Why is the one innovation–'Hey man, bust me some fries'–fine, and another–'She considered to say something'–the cause for quizzical looks, teasing and in the worst cases outright racism?[85] How are such distinctions among unconventional usages made, given that all we have to go on in any case is prior usage itself?

An initial plank in Goldberg's response to the puzzle of how speakers distinguish between what is felicitous and what awkward in novel uses of familiar constructions is provided by the concept of 'coverage'.[86] Coverage is a measure for predicting the acceptability of any new use of a given construction and it involves a number of factors to do with how open the construction has been to distinct uses in the past, and how similar the new item is to those attested cases. Yet even though coverage has real pertinence to the issues under discussion, Goldberg argues that a construction's past behaviours are not, in themselves, sufficient to show why *Explain me this* feels wrong, and expressions like *Can we vulture your table?* fresh.[87] To hone in on these two examples, both are poorly covered, in terms of the types of words their respective constructions have hitherto allowed. In the case of *Explain me this*, corpus study reveals, as we have seen, that the double object construction has a genuine dispreference for 'Latinate (sounding)' verbs like *request, transfer* and *explain,* which almost always indicate recipients via a prepositional phrase instead (*Explain this to me*).[88] But *Can we vulture your table?* is also poorly covered by prior instances of the construction in question (the 'transitive-causative construction'). The usage is counter-intuitive enough to for it to be counted as a case of 'coercion', which is to say, a situation where context modifies meaning, though we might, even more specifically, label it 'coercion by override', Jenny Audring and Geert Booij's term for situations where the overarching meaning of a construction forces a whole new meaning upon a word.[89] *Vulture* is, after all, a noun–or at least it has been to this point–and here it is being made to act as a verb. And yet, of the two, it is this very expression, *Can we vulture your table?*, that feels fine, and even edgy, not to mention redolent with prior uses of the word 'vulture', the sensuality of which, that is, the feel of the word on the tongue, is brought out in the process. You could imagine it finding its way into a poem.

Conversely, we find cases where all of the various criteria Goldberg marshals under the concept of coverage ('type frequency', 'variability', 'similarity of the coinage to attested types'–the features I alluded to above) seem satisfied, and the coinage still feels wrong, as, for instance, when a second language speaker uses 'cooker' to refer to someone who cooks.[90] That same speaker might proceed to refer to a 'spier' like James Bond. Clearly, neither usage amounts to a felicitous instance of the highly frequent and highly variable *–er* agentive noun construction, for all the similarity *cooker* and *spier* bear to felicitous forms like *plumber, teacher, dancer.*[91]

Goldberg's solution to the conundrums rehearsed to this point is strikingly simple, and it throws all the cards on the table in the process.

It is based on the fact that all known languages have a strong tendency to eliminate true synonymy. Words that appear to be synonyms will in fact tend to differ in key ways: 'they may differ, for example, in terms of formality (*dog* vs *pooch*), perspective (*ceiling* vs *roof*) or attitude (*skinny* vs *slim*)'.[92] As for usages that truly do seem synonymous, one will over time tend to prevail. Darwinian metaphors seem appropriate here. Repeated expressions compete for a 'distributional niche', and the stronger drive out the weaker.[93] Goldberg uses statistics to back up these claims: a 2009 study of the then 520 million word Corpus of Contemporary American English (COCA) found that in 99 percent of cases *explain* took a prepositional phrase (*Explain it to me*), rather than a double-object.[94] *Tell* on the other hand was found 99 percent of the time with a double-object (*Tell me the story*).[95] Pointing to her readers' intuitive sense that *elephant* is more common than *pachyderm*, Goldberg argues that we are very much adept at registering such linguistic frequencies, in our own right.[96] They form part and parcel of the constructicon, or 'mental corpus', that each of us 'carry around'.[97] Indeed, it is our awareness of such statistical factors that motors the 'Darwinian' dynamics just described.

As for Goldberg's solution to the puzzle exercising us to this point, the reason innovations like *email me a receipt*, *influencer*, and *They disappeared her husband* are found acceptable, to the point of spreading through the language (while *Explain me this*, *cooker* and *She considered to say something* are not), is because there is no competing way to say it. As Goldberg and her colleague, Clarice Robenalt, explain, 'When speakers already have a conventional way to express a particular meaning, they judge novel reformations of that meaning to be less acceptable. However, when no competitor exists, speakers display a willingness to extend a verb to a construction in which it does not normally appear'.[98] *Explain me this* feels wrong because it is pre-empted by *Explain this to me*. But one can *vulture* a table.

On the other hand, Goldberg argues, the fact that fluent second-language speakers still find it difficult, even after many years in a language, to avoid infelicitous phrases points to a deficiency in their capacity to register patterns of usage in the language in question. The reason their capacity is reduced, Goldberg believes, is that those speakers are simultaneously occupied in inhibiting competition from the highly routinized ways to say the same thing in their own tongues: *explícame esto*, *объясни мне это*, *jelaskan ini padauk*. Second language speakers are simply not as good at avoiding innovations in the specific cases where one is expected to, where competitor forms already exist and are common, the very thing that keeps native speakers sounding nativelike, even as the language changes. They are not as good, in Goldberg's terms, at 'statistical pre-emption'.[99] But the key thing that concerns us here is Goldberg's startling thesis as to why the innovations that work, do work. As we have just seen, coinages like *They disappeared her husband* arise and flourish in the language–whether as singular, happy moments or ongoing usages–because there is no competing way to convey that meaning, or at least to say it so succinctly. Likewise, *Text me the photo*, *Can we vulture your table?* and *She kissed him unconscious.* But unlike *She considered to say something.*

Goldberg never announces it as such, but to see that she is effectively offering a theory of poetic diction here, one only has to turn back to the line of Wright's providing the title of this chapter and ask if there is any obvious and competing way to get at the things she evokes with that strange, old-new word, *magnolialight*?

Chlorophyll world. July. Great goblets of magnolialight.[100]

Of course this is more or less what Coleridge told us, in insisting that any aspects of a poet's phrasing that can 'be translated into other words of the same language, without diminution of their significance, either in sense or association, or in any worthy feeling' are to that extent 'vicious in their diction'.[101] But what Coleridge does not seem to have realized is that this criterion applies to all forms of linguistic innovation, not just poetry (and it operates among speakers of all classes, one might add, *pace* Coleridge's more Tory moments).[102] For what Goldberg's explication of the *Explain me this* phenomenon points to is the existence, within everyday language, of an inbuilt mechanism for generating, and what is more for ensuring, poetic innovation.

Amplify this point with the idea, central to construction grammars like Goldberg's, that there are no universal rules of grammar, nor even a stable distinction between grammar and vocabulary, just 'a massive collection of heterogenous *constructions*', as disparate as that *–ed* past tense construction, the *–gate* construction (*Pizzagate, Sguidgygate, Dick-Cheney-shot-a-guy-in-the-face-gate* . . .), that agentive noun construction (*worker, doer, writer*, but not *editer*), the X *out* construction (meaning 'to go into an unusual mental state': *bliss out, wig out, stress out, freak out.* . .).[103] As we saw over the first half of this chapter, acceptable usage of any such construction is dependent on the fundamentally arbitrary traditions of inclusion and exclusion history has bequeathed us. But what Goldberg's theory adds to the picture, in radical contrast to all such historical factors, is that you can use a construction in almost any way you like and still be recognized as speaking a well-formed version of it, on one simple proviso: what you say conveys something we did not previously have the words for.

The point can be extended beyond language as well, to encompass innovation in all manner of behaviour ('cinematography, choreography, of course, but also pictorial, musical, sculptural 'writing'. One might also speak of athletic writing, and with even greater certainty of military or political writing'), provided there is no competing way to 'say' the same thing in that medium, and change is something the gatekeepers allow.[104] They may not. The language people speak is pervasive and consequently much harder to control.[105] What is also hard to control is the example it provides.

There is certainly a history, but there is, at the same time, a stark lack of foundation to the new.

One wonders, therefore, how it arises, in any individual case. How can one intend to say–other than in the most general sense of wishing to have said something of that order–what we currently have no way of actually saying, an utterance that may well render past 'rules' irrelevant in the process?

and then again, on the wall of the floor
with fingers that can't stop scraping

flying at conversation
beyond perception

INTENSIFYING

For Coleridge the word *intend* would not do. Or rather, he wished we could go back to its earlier meanings. As late as the seventeenth century *intend* meant 'to stretch out, extend, expand, increase'. 'As when a Bow is successively intended and Remitted' runs the illustrative quotation in the OED. So one intended in 1678.[106] The reason Coleridge wants those older meaning of the word at this point in the *Biographia Literaria* is that he is discussing 'the will'. It is the will, by Coleridge's lights, which brings poetic language into being.

We are in chapter 7. This is the somewhat buried chapter where Coleridge first formulates his theory of poetic composition, a formulation much more direct and challenging than the opaquely-theological gestures of chapter 13, that locus classicus of contemporary citation, which takes us to the primary and secondary imaginations, the 'repetition in the finite mind of the eternal act of creation in the infinite I Am' and so forth.[107] In chapter 7, Coleridge dilates upon the 'general law of association' determining that the mind will move along habituated grooves–a factor only glimpsed in chapter 13, though it is in fact integral to what Coleridge means by 'imagination' there.[108] To gloss Coleridge's 'general law of association' in our terms, you might note that the language of our thoughts is also the language we speak and as such is in a constant state of exchange with a community of other speakers, with the upshot that its associations are more likely than not to be shared. A speaker starts to say 'On the one . . '. and you assume the word 'hand' will follow. You might be in a conversation with that person, or you might even be hearing yourself, as you speak to another, and come out with the same old phrases. The associations move along their habituated grooves. Coleridge likens their power to the current of a river; also to gravity.[109]

As for the poetic act, 'the will' that brings it into being operates upon such forces of habit, but it can hardly be said to master them. Working against the tendencies of the 'law of association' is more like working against gravity, which one can only do by working *with* gravity. In fact, it is what we do at every step, and much more dramatically when we leap:

> Let us consider what we do when we leap. We first resist the gravitating power by an act purely voluntary, and then by another act, voluntary in part, we yield to it in order to light on the spot which we had previously proposed to ourselves. Now let a man [*sic*] watch his mind while he is composing; or, to take a still more common case, while he is trying to recollect a name; and he will find the process completely analogous.[110]

One wishes to recall a name, through an act of will launches one's mind upon that project, and then 'by another act, voluntary in part', one yields to the various names the mind suggests in response to that effort. So one comes up with *magnolialight*. The *otherest*. There are parallels to James's 'it thinks' here ('thought goes on . . . If we could say in English 'it thinks', as we say 'it rains' or 'it blows', we should be stating the fact most simply'). But as well as theorising thinking this way, Coleridge elucidates a strategy for generating the new from it.[111] It is by forcing one's mind to think otherwise and seeing what associations come back when one does.

The process is almost athletic. 'As when a Bow is successively intended and Remitted' (OED). For just as the 'true practical law of association' is that 'whatever makes certain parts of a total impression more vivid or distinct than the rest will force the mind to recall these in preference to others equally linked', so 'the will itself, by confining and *intensifying* the attention may arbitrarily give vividness or distinctness to any object whatsoever' (my italics).[112] Coleridge is talking about images here, but the idea applies to words just as well. You train your mind on some such habitual usage, impel it to focus the matter otherwise, and see what expressions it alights upon when you do.

The word 'intensifying' is itself a case in point. In a footnote on it, Coleridge writes that he came up with the word, 'though I confess it sound uncouth to my own ear', because *intend* had, as pointed out above, lost its earlier connotations.[113] Already by the time of Coleridge's writing it had moved too close to its now primary OED meaning of '[t]o have in the mind as a fixed purpose; to purpose, design' for it to do service for the force Coleridge believed one directs into one's attentional apparatus at such times, and the unpredictability as to what precise words will return.[114] One presumes that Coleridge focused as much as he could on what the language wanted a word for, launched his mind for analogies into that space and yielded to it, with the consequences that this particular, novel usage of the *–ify* construction–on the model of *clarify* (first attested circa 1398), *beautify* (1425) and *transmogrify* (1656)–came to mind, in an act of will-driven imagining we might think of as 'not wholly different in kind from remembering' (Chafe).[115] What Coleridge found through that leap lacked a competitor and so could win its way into the OED, where the poet is now listed as its coiner.[116]

He intensified his attention to what he lacked a word for, drew it back like a bow.

The more addiction beset him, the more categories like 'the will' featured in Coleridge's discourse, Will Christie remarks.[117]

The problem with theorising suddenness as Coleridge does here, in this reference to how one might use the will to 'light on the spot which we had previously proposed to ourselves', is, as I hinted above, to do with how one might propose any such spot to oneself, without having a word for it in the first place. I am not referring to cases of phenomena that have a sensory presentation, so called concrete objects, which we can think about while lacking words for them, but rather things we cannot even sense, like tomorrow.[118] Wittgenstein challenges us to 'say and mean a sentence, for example "it will probably rain tomorrow". Now think the same thought again, mean what you just meant, but without saying anything (either aloud or to yourself)'.[119] Prior to having a word, or some such name, for it, it is very hard–impossible?–to propose the idea of tomorrow to oneself.

Perhaps one calls to mind some cluster of already existing signifiers, in the vicinity, paints what's missing through them, leaps that way?

We were in Gundabooka, on Ngemba country, visiting the poet and novelist Paul Collis's people. They are Barkindji, people of the Barka, the great inland river that runs from between Bourke and Breewarina in the North down some 1,500 kilometres away into what's known on the map as Wellington, South Australia. Barka means 'darling'. The irony is that the colonists thought they were naming it the Darling River in 1829 after Ralph Darling, governor of New South Wales. The dirt is red at Gundabooka, the heat is vivid and you know that the Barkindji have gathered here for millennia. I was trying to work on the final lines of what eventually became the poem below–most of it written in Manhattan, after losing my senses in a Marina Abramović installation.[120] Something in that New York work had set me off, a memory of a phone call, a phone call of a memory, something insisted.

There have been continual depredations on Paul's land since the settlers came: human, environmental. This is not the place to write of them. It is healing country.

What I had on the road trip out to Gundabooka was a poem that hadn't quite got through. I had already replaced the promissory-note ending cited above, my first draft's final line, 'beyond perception', with

it is what in the telephone
will always feel dead

and unburied the voice

but it wasn't quite there. I was staring into the red dirt, as intense as the sun itself, the unbearable history of what we have done to these people, trying to call to mind all the experiences of sensory deprivation I could, a cluster of things none of which spoke the words I needed. *You can't hear.* I wrote it down.

Getting a Call in Darkness

I stepped hands out, into my
flying thoughts of inside a bullet

lying first against the wall's patience
then head to the floor deaf and blind

a telephone call from the wall
on the floor spinning

I want to say to you before you died
and then again, while crying

on the floor of that squander
and then again, on the wall of the floor

with fingers that can't stop scraping
flying at conversation

it is what in the telephone
will always feel dead

and unburied the voice
you can't hear

    I am trying in this New York far outback New South Wales vignette to provide a figure for the currents one tries to tap into.
    I cannot guarantee it, but I suspect the poets' steely refusal to any claim to originate the new in language involved something of the following as well. Part of the process of every poem I've written to date, including those

minutes in Manhattan when I rushed out with those 'flying thoughts of inside a bullet' lines–or at least some of them–has involved trying what will happen if I speak for the page in the wrong way. It is not as simple as that because it requires emotion and confusion as well. Or not, and most of the time it does not work anyway. But when we speak on a topic in a way others do not but the language makes available, when we are at the right emotional pitch for the words to find a sensuality there, associations coursing through us as they always are, the act of trying phrases awry, even prior to knowing what one really wants to say there, can at times be enough to bring new concepts and sensibilities about–provided no competitor formulation exists when one does. I am referring to the decision to intensify one's faculties to that degree of acuteness and plasticity, leaping foreignly, without any clear idea of what needs to be said but that it has to be different to the way we usually speak. There is something to say that cannot be said but is real I live it. What you alight upon through that kind of reckless intending in all the old sense of the word may suddenly have ideas in its own right. Not what we but what the language has to say, if only we knew how to take its call.

NOTES

1. Pawley and Syder, 'One-Clause-at-a-Time," 169.
2. Auden, "Words and the Word," 105.
3. F, qtd in Pawley and Syder, 'One-Clause-at-a-Time," 169.
4. Pawley and Syder, 174–177.
5. Pawley and Syder, 169–170.
6. Pawley and Syder, "Two Puzzles," 202.
7. Pawley and Syder, "One-Clause-at-a-Time," 182.
8. G, qtd in Pawley and Syder, "One-Clause-at-a-Time," 181–182 (modified by author).
9. Pawley, "Developments" 15–16; Pawley, "How to Talk Cricket," 348; Pawley, "Developments," 5–6.
10. Pawley and Syder, "Two Puzzles," 205.
11. Pawley and Syder, 169.
12. G, qtd in Pawley and Syder "One-Clause-at-a-Time," 182.
13. Pawley and Syder, "Two Puzzles," 205.
14. Pawley and Syder, 210.
15. Keats, "Fall of Hyperion," 444 (1.45).
16. G, qtd in Pawley and Syder, "One-Clause-at-a-Time," 181–182 (my italics).
17. Pawley and Syder, "Two Puzzles," 210.
18. Pawley and Syder, "One-Clause-at-a-Time," 164.
19. Pawley and Syder, 196.
20. SEM475JU084, in Simpson, Rita C. et al., eds., *Michigan Corpus of Academic Spoken English* (MICASE). Recorded February 21, 2000; MICASE

transcription conventions are given in Simpson, Lee and Leicher, *MICASE Manual*, 10–16.
21. Pawley, "Developments," 29.
22. Pawley, 30.
23. Dickinson, "1329," 513.
24. Chomsky, "Review," 5.
25. Wray, *Formulaic Language*, 12.
26. Bolinger, "Syntactic Blends," 381.
27. Bolinger, 381.
28. Chafe, "Idiomaticity."
29. Hopper, "Emergent Grammar," 140.
30. Hopper, 145.
31. Hopper, 146.
32. Bozzone, *Constructions*.
33. Wray, *Formulaic Language*, 7.
34. Bryson, qtd in Hoey *Lexical Priming*, 5. Sentence (1) is the first sentence of Bill Bryson's 1991 travel book, *Neither Here, Nor There*. Sentence (2) was constructed by Hoey for the experiment.
35. Hoey, *Lexical Priming*, 6–7.
36. Hoey, 6.
37. Hoey, 9.
38. Hoey, 6.
39. Hoey, 9.
40. Attridge, *Poetic Rhythm*, 39.
41. Coleridge, *Biographia Literaria*, 1.
42. Pawley and Syder, "Two Puzzles," 193.
43. Pawley and Syder, 215.
44. Pawley and Syder, 215.
45. Pawley and Syder, 197–198.
46. Benjamin, "Theses on the Philosophy of History," 253.
47. Pawley and Syder, "Two Puzzles," 193.
48. McGuckian, "White Cortina," 30–31.
49. Lord, *The Singer of Tales*, 22.
50. Coleridge, *Biographia Literaria*, 1.
51. Coleridge, 11.
52. Coleridge, 12.
53. Eggert, *Securing the Past*, 135–156.
54. Pawley and Syder, "Two Puzzles," 199–200.
55. Armantrout, interview by author, November 11, 2014.
56. Young, interview by author, November 20, 2014.
57. Chernoff, interview by author, November 17, 2014.
58. Croggon, interview by author, April 24, 2007.
59. Pawley and Syder, "Two Puzzles," 224, fn19
60. Carter, *Language and Creativity*.
61. Bybee, 26, citing examples from the British National Corpus (BNC).

62. Bozzone, *Constructions*, 35
63. Cánovas and Antović, "Formulaic Creativity," 72.
64. Cánovas and Antović, 69.
65. Parry, "Oral Verse-Making I," 314.
66. McGuckian, interview by author, email of March, 6, 2015.
67. Cánovas and Antović, "Formulaic Creativity," 72.
68. McGuckian, "Breaking the Blue," 84.
69. Wright, *Deepstep Come Shining*, 193.
70. Dickinson, "466," 215.
71. Goldberg, *Explain me This*, 37; Robenalt and Goldberg, "Nonnative Speakers," 66.
72. Goldberg, *Explain me This*, 142; 3.
73. Goldberg, 3.
74. Goldberg, 1.
75. Goldberg, 41.
76. *Oxford English Dictionary*, s.v. "Text" ("Draft Additions, March 2004"); Goldberg, *Explain me This*, 1.
77. Goldberg, *Explain me This*, 62; 76.
78. Bybee, *Language, Usage and Cognition*, 9.
79. Hoffman and Trousdale, "Construction Grammar."
80. Bybee, *Language, Usage and Cognition*, 106.
81. Bybee, *Language Change*, 98.
82. Siewerska, qtd in Croft, *Ten Lectures*, 147.
83. Goldberg, *Explain me This*, 39.
84. Bybee and Hopper, "An Introduction," 2; Croft, *Ten Lectures*, 157.
85. Goldberg, *Explain me This*, 2; 3.
86. Goldberg, 97.
87. Goldberg, 2.
88. Goldberg, 41
89. Goldberg, 31; Audring and Booij, "Cooperation and Coercion," 628.
90. Goldberg, *Explain Me This*, 63; 97.
91. Goldberg, 74.
92. Goldberg, 23.
93. Goldberg, 26.
94. Goldberg, 86.
95. Goldberg, 41.
96. Goldberg, 17.
97. Cánovas and Antović, "Formulaic Creativity," 72.
98. Robenalt and Goldberg, "Nonnative Speakers," 69.
99. Goldberg, *Explain Me This*, 86
100. Wright, *Deepstep Come Shining*, 193.
101. Coleridge, *Biographia Literaria*, 11.
102. Coleridge, 197.
103. Bybee and Hopper "Introduction," 2; Jackendorf, qtd in Audring and Booij, "Cooperation and Coercion," 633.

104. Derrida, *Of Grammatology*, 9.
105. Lacan, "The Instance of the Letter," 414.
106. *Oxford English Dictionary*, s.v. "Intend."
107. Coleridge, *Biographia Literaria*, 167.
108. Coleridge, 73.
109. Coleridge, 72.
110. Coleridge, 71–72.
111. James, "Stream of Thought," 22.
112. Coleridge, *Biographia Literaria*, 73.
113. Coleridge, 73, fn1.
114. *Oxford English Dictionary*, s.v. "Intend."
115. *Oxford English Dictionary*, s.v. "Clarify"; "Beautify"; "Transmogrify"; Chafe, *Discourse, Consciousness and Time*, 33.
116. *Oxford English Dictionary*, s.v. "Intensify."
117. Christie, *Coleridge*, 163.
118. Slobin, "Thinking for Speaking."
119. Wittgenstein, *The Blue and Brown Books*, 42.
120. Abramović, *Generator*.

References

Abramović, Marina. *Generator*. New York: Sean Kelly Gallery, October 24–December 6, 2014. Installation.

Alderson-Day, Ben, and Charles Fernyhough. "Inner Speech: Development, Cognitive Functions, Phenomenology and Neurobiology." *Psychological Bulletin* 141, no. 5 (2015): 931–65.

Antović, Mihailo, and Cristóbal Pagán Cánovas. "Not Dictated by Metrics: Function Words in the Speech Introductions of South-Slavic Oral Epic." *Language and Communication* 58 (January 2018): 11–23.

Aristotle. *Ars Rhetorica*. Edited by W. D. Ross. Clarendon Press, 1959.

———. *Metaphysics*. Translated by W. D. Ross. Complete Works of Aristotle: The Revised Oxford Translation. Edited by Jonathan Barnes. 2 vols. Vol. 2, Princeton, NJ: Princeton University Press, 1984.

———. *Rhetoric*. Translated by W. Rhys Roberts. The Complete Works of Aristotle. Vol. 2.

Armantrout, Rae. *Versed*. Middletown, CT: Wesleyan University Press, 2009.

———. Interview by Author. November 11, 2014.

Attridge, Derek. *Poetic Rhythm: An Introduction*. Cambridge; New York: Cambridge University Press, 1995.

———. "Meaning in Movement: Phrasing and Repetition." In *Moving Words: Forms of English Poetry*, 31–49. Oxford: Oxford University Press, 2013.

———. Interview by author. March 12, 2018.

Auden, W. H. "Words and the Word." In *Secondary Worlds: The T. S. Eliot Memorial Lectures Delivered at Eliot College in the University of Kent at Canterbury, October 1967*, 103–26. London: Faber, 1968.

———. "The Living Thoughts of Kierkegaard." In *The Living Thoughts of Kierkegaard*, vii–xxx. New York: New York Review of Books, 1999.

Audring, Jenny and Booij, Geert. "Cooperation and Coercion." *Linguistics* 54, no. 4 (2016): 617–37.

Baddeley, Alan. "Working Memory: Looking Back and Looking Forward." *Nature Reviews: Neuroscience* 4, no. 10 (October 2003): 829–39.

Bakker, Egbert J. "Homeric Discourse and Enjambment: A Cognitive Approach." *Transactions of the America Philological Association* 120 (1990): 1–21.

———. *Poetry in Speech: Orality and Homeric Discourse.* Ithaca, NY: Cornell University Press, 1997.

———. "Mimesis as Performance: Rereading Auerbach's First Chapter." *Poetics Today* 20, no. 1 (Spring 1999): 11–26.

———. "How Oral Is Oral Composition?". In *Pointing at the Past: From Formula to Performance in Homeric Poetics.* Washington, DC: Center for Hellenic Studies, 2005.

———. "Rhapsodes, Bards, and Bricoleurs: Homerizing Literary Theory." *Classics@* 3 (2005). http://chs.harvard.edu/CHS/article/display/1311

———. "The Study of Homeric Discourse." In *A Companion to Ancient Epic*, edited by Ian Morris and Barry B. Powell, 284–304. Maiden, MA: Blackwell, 2005.

Baldessari, John. "I Will Not Make Any More Boring Art." 1971. Lithograph.

Bartlett, Frederic C. *Remembering: A Study in Experimental and Social Psychology.* Cambridge: Cambridge University Press, 1950.

Benjamin, Walter. "Theses on the Philosophy of History." Translated by Harry Zohn. In *Illuminations*, 245–55. London: Fontana, 1973.

———. *The Origin of German Tragic Drama.* Translated by John Osborne. London; New York: Verso, 2003.

Berkoff, Steven. *I Am Hamlet.* London: Faber, 1989.

Berry, Eleanor. "Modern American Poetry and Modern American Speech." In *The Linguistics of Literacy*, edited by Pamela Downing, Susan D. Lima and Michael Noonan, 47–67. Amsterdam; Philadelphia, PA: J. Benjamins Pub. Co., 1992.

Biber, Douglas, and Susan Conrad. *Register, Genre, and Style.* New York: Cambridge University Press, 2009.

Biber, Douglas and Camilla Vásquez. "Writing and Speaking." In *Handbook of Research on Writing, History, Society, School, Individual, Text*, edited by Charles Bazerman, 535–48. New York: Lawrence Erlbaum, 2008.

Bishop, Elizabeth. "Elizabeth Bishop, Interview with Elizabeth Spires." In *Women Writers at Work: The Paris Review Interviews Edited by George Plimpton*, edited by George Plimpton, 152–73. New York: Modern Library, 1998.

Boal, Augusto. *Games for Actors and Non-Actors.* Translated by Adrian Jackson. 2nd ed. Abingdon, UK: Routledge, 2002.

Boden, Margaret. "What is Creativity?" In *Dimensions of Creativity*, edited by Margaret Boden, 75–117. Cambridge, MA: MIT Press, 1994.

Bolinger, Dwight L. "Syntactic Blends and Other Matters." *Language* 37, no. 3 (1961): 366–81.

Bourdieu, Pierre. "The Field of Cultural Production, Or: The Economic World Reversed." In *The Field of Cultural Production: Essays on Art and Literature*, edited by Randal Johnson, 29–73. New York: Columbia University Press, 1993.

———. "The Production of Belief: Contribution to an Economy of Symbolic Goods." In Bourdieu, *Field of Cultural Production*, 74–111.

Bowra, C. M. *Homer*. London: Duckworth, 1972.
Bozzone, Chiara. "Constructions: A New Approach to Formularity, Discourse, and Syntax in Homer." PhD Diss., University of California, Los Angeles, 2014. https://escholarship.org/uc/item/6kg0q4cx.
Brouwer, Joel. "Counting the Dead." *New York Times*, June 22 2008, Sunday Book Review. http://www.nytimes.com/2008/06/22/books/review/Brouwer-t.html.
Bryson, Bill. *Neither Here nor There: Travels in Europe*. London: Secker & Warburg, 1991.
Bushell, Sally. "Textual Process and the Denial of Origins." *Textual Cultures: Texts, Contexts, Interpretation* 2, no. 2 (2007): 100–17.
Bybee, Joan L. *Language, Usage and Cognition*. Cambridge; New York: Cambridge University Press, 2010.
———. *Language Change*. Cambridge: Cambridge University Press, 2015.
Bybee, Joan L., and Clay Beckner. "Usage-Based Theory." In *The Oxford Handbook of Linguistic Analysis*, edited by Bernd Heine and Heiko Narrog. New York: Oxford University Press, 2009.
Bybee, Joan L., and Paul Hopper. "Introduction to Frequency and the Emergence of Linguistic Structure." In *Frequency and the Emergence of Linguistic Structure*, edited by Joan L. Bybee and Paul Hopper, 1–26. Amsterdam; Philadelphia, PA: John Benjamins Pub. Co., 2001.
Byron, George Gordon Byron. *A Variorum Edition, Cantos I-V*. Vol. 2 of *Byron's Don Juan*. Edited by T. G. Steffan and Willis Winslow Pratt. Austin, TX: University of Texas Press, 1957.
Cameron, Sharon. *Lyric Time: Dickinson and the Limits of Genre*. Baltimore, MD: Johns Hopkins University Press, 1979.
Cánovas, Cristóbal Pagán, and Mihailo Antović. "Formulaic Creativity: Oral Poetics and Cognitive Grammar." *Language and Communication* 47 (March 2016): 66–74.
Carper, Thomas, and Derek Attridge. *Meter and Meaning: An Introduction to Rhythm in Poetry*. London: Routledge, 2003.
Carter, Ronald. *Language and Creativity: The Art of Common Talk*. London: Routledge, 2004.
Carver, Raymond. "Cathedral." In *Cathedral: Stories*. 208–28. New York: Knopf, 1983.
Chafe, Wallace L. "Idiomaticity as an Anomaly in the Chomskyan Paradigm." *Foundations of Language* 4, no. 2 (1968): 109–27.
———. "The Deployment of Consciousness in the Production of a Narrative." In *The Pear Stories: Cognitive, Cultural, and Linguistic Aspects of Narrative Production*, edited by Wallace Chafe, 9–50. Norwood, NJ: Ablex Pub. Corp., 1980.
———, ed. *The Pear Stories: Cognitive, Cultural, and Linguistic Aspects of Narrative Production*. Norwood, NJ: Ablex Pub. Corp., 1980.
———. "Integration and Involvement in Speaking, Writing, and Oral Literature." In *Spoken and Written Language: Exploring Orality and Literacy*, edited by Deborah Tannen, 35–52. Norwood, NJ: Ablex Pub. Corp, 1982.

———. "Evidentiality in English Conversation and Academic Writing." In *Evidentiality: The Linguistic Coding of Epistemology*, edited by Wallace L. Chafe and Johanna Nichols, 261–72. Norwood, NJ: Ablex Pub. Corp., 1986.

———."Linking Intonation Units in Spoken English." In *Typological Studies in Language: Clause Combining in Grammar and Discourse*, edited by John Haiman and Sandra A. Thompson, 1–28. Amsterdam; Philadelphia, PA: J. Benjamins, 1988.

———. "Punctuation and the Prosody of Written Language." *Written Communication* 5, no. 4 (1988): 395–426.

———. *Discourse, Consciousness, and Time: The Flow and Displacement of Conscious Experience in Speaking and Writing*. Chicago: University of Chicago Press, 1994.

———. "A Linguist's Perspective on William James and the Stream of Thought." *Consciousness and Cognition* 9, no. 4 (December 2000): 618–28.

———. "The Analysis of Discourse Flow." In *The Handbook of Discourse Analysis*, edited by Deborah Schiffrin, Deborah Tannen and Heidi E. Hamilton, 671–87. Oxford: Blackwell, 2001.

———. "Consciousness and Language." In *Cognition and Pragmatics*, edited by Sandra Dominiek, Jan-Ola Östman and Jef Verschueren, 135–45. Amsterdam: John Benjamins Company, 2009.

———. "Linguistics and the Study of Consciousness." In *The Oxford Companion to Consciousness*, edited by Axel Cleeremans, Tim Bayne and Patrick Wilken. 409–11. Oxford University Press, 2009.

———. *Thought-Based Linguistics: How Languages Turn Thoughts into Sounds*. Cambridge: Cambridge University Press, 2018.

Chafe, Wallace L., and Jane Danielewicz. *Properties of Spoken and Written Language*. Berkeley, CA: University of California; Pittsburgh, PA: Carnegie Mellon University, 1987.

Chater, Nick. *The Mind Is Flat: The Illusion of Mental Depth and the Improvised Mind*. London: Allen Lane, 2018.

Chenoweth, N. Ann, and John R. Hayes. "Fluency in Writing: Generating Text in L1 and L2." *Written Communication* 18, no. 1 (2001): 80–98.

———. "The Inner Voice in Writing." *Written Communication* 20, no. 1 (2003): 99–118.

Chernoff, Maxine. *Without*. Emersons Green, Bristol, UK: Shearsman Books, 2012.

———. Interview by author. November 11, 2014.

Chomsky, Noam. "A Review of B. F. Skinner's Verbal Behaviour." *Language* 35, no. 1 (1959): 26–58.

Christiansen, Morten H., and Nick Chater. "The Now-or-Never Bottleneck: A Fundamental Constraint on Language." *Behavioural and Brain Sciences* 39 (2016): 1–72.

Christie, William. *Samuel Taylor Coleridge: A Literary Life*. Basingstoke, UK; New York: Palgrave Macmillan, 2007.

Clark, John Lee. "Melodies Unheard: Deaf Poets and Their Subversion of the 'Sound' Theory of Poetry." *Sign Language Studies* 7, no. 1 (2006): 4–10.

Coates, Deborah. "The Construction of a Collaborative Floor in Women's Friendly Talk." In *Conversation, Cognitive, Communicative and Social Perspectives*, edited by Talmy Givón, 55–91. Amsterdam: John Benjamin Publishing, 1997.

Coleridge, Samuel Taylor. *Biographia Literaria; or, Biographical Sketches of My Literary Life and Opinions.* London: Dent; New York: Dutton, 1962.

Cottingham, John. *Descartes.* New York: B. Blackwell, 1986.

Crispi, Luca, Sam Slote, and Dirk van Hulle. "Introduction." In *How Joyce Wrote Finnegans Wake: A Chapter-by-Chapter Genetic Guide*, edited by Luca Crispi and Sam Slote, 3–48. Madison, WI: University of Wisconsin Press, 2007.

Croggon, Alison. Interview by author. April 24, 2007.

Croft, William. *Ten Lectures on Construction Grammar and Typology.* Leiden: Brill, 2020.

Crystal, David. *The English Tone of Voice: Essays in Intonation, Prosody and Paralanguage.* London: Edward Arnold, 1975.

Csikszentmihalyi, Mihaly. *Flow: The Psychology of Optimal Experience.* New York: Harper Collins, 1991.

Cumming, Naomi. *The Sonic Self: Musical Subjectivity and Signification.* Bloomington, IN: Indiana University Press, 2000.

Damasio, Antonio R. *Descartes' Error: Emotion, Reason, and the Human Brain.* London: Penguin, 2005.

De Biasi, Pierre-Marc. "What Is a Literary Draft? Toward a Functional Typology of Genetic Documentation." Translated by Ingrid Wasenaar. *Yale French Studies*, no. 89 (1996): 26–53.

De Man, Paul. *Romanticism and Contemporary Criticism: The Gauss Seminar and Other Papers.* Edited by E. S. Burt, Kevin Newmark and Andrzej Warminski. Baltimore, MD: Johns Hopkins University Press, 1993.

Derrida, Jacques. *Of Grammatology.* Translated by Gayatri Spivak. Baltimore: Johns Hopkins University Press, 1976.

———. "Two Words for Joyce." In *Post-Structuralist Joyce: Essays from the French*, edited by Derek Attridge and Daniel Ferrer, 145–60. Cambridge: Cambridge University Press, 1984.

Descartes, René. *Oeuvres de Descartes.* Edited by Charles Adam and Paul Tannery. 12 vols. Paris: Léopold Cerf, 1897–1913.

———. *Meditations, Objections, and Replies.* Edited and Translated by Roger Ariew and Donald A. Cress. Indianapolis, IN: Hackett Pub., 2006.

Dickinson, Emily. "466." *The Poems of Emily Dickinson.* Edited by R. W. Franklin, 215. Cambridge, MA: Belknap Press of Harvard University Press, 1998.

———. "576." In *The Poems of Emily Dickinson.* 260.

———. "1329." In *The Poems of Emily Dickinson.* 513.

Durkin, Philip. *The Oxford Guide to Etymology.* Oxford; New York: Oxford University Press, 2011.

Eggert, Paul. *Securing the Past: Conservation in Art, Architecture, and Literature.* Cambridge; New York: Cambridge University Press, 2009.

Eliot, T. S. "The Three Voices in Poetry." In *Essays on Poetry and Poets*, 89–102. London; Boston: Faber and Faber, 1957.

———. "The Waste Land." In *Collected Poems 1909-1962*, 61–86. London: Faber, 1963.

Eliot, T. S., and Valerie Eliot. *The Waste Land: A Facsimile and Transcript of the Original Drafts Including the Annotations of Ezra Pound.* San Diego, CA: Harcourt Brace, 1994.

Emery, Brooke. Interview by author, October 25, 2014.

Evans, Vyvyan. *The Crucible of Language : How Language and Mind Create Meaning.* Cambridge, UK: Cambridge University Press, 2015.

Fehrman, Carl Abraham Daniel. *Poetic Creation: Inspiration or Craft.* Translated by Karin Petherick. Minneapolis, MN: University of Minnesota Press, 1980.

Fernyhough, Charles. *The Voices Within: The History and Science of How We Talk to Ourselves.* New York: Basic Books, 2016.

Finnegan, Ruth H. *Oral Poetry: Its Nature, Significance, and Social Context.* Cambridge; New York: Cambridge University Press, 1977.

———. "Speech, Language and Literacy: A Case Study from West Africa." In *Literacy and Orality: Studies in the Technology of Communication*, 106–36. Calendar Press, 2014.

Foley, John Miles. *Homer's Traditional Art.* University Park, PA: Pennsylvania State University Press, 1999.

———. *How to Read an Oral Poem.* Urbana, IL: University of Illinois Press, 2002.

———. "Epic as Genre." In *The Cambridge Companion to Homer*, edited by Robert Fowler, 171–87. Cambridge: Cambridge University Press, 2004.

———. "Oral Tradition and Its Implications." In *A Companion to Ancient Epic*, edited by Ian Morris and Barry B. Powell, 146–73. Malden, MA: Blackwell Pub., 2005.

———. "Oral Dictated." In *The Homer Encyclopaedia*, edited by Margalit Finkelberg, 602–603. Chichester, West Sussex; Malden, MA: Wiley-Blackwell, 2011.

———. *Oral Tradition and the Internet: Pathways of the Mind.* Urbana, IL: University of Illinois Press, 2012.

Forster, E. M. *Aspects of the Novel.* Harmondsworth, Middlesex; Ringwood, VIC: Penguin, 1962.

Freud, Sigmund. *The Psychopathology of Everyday Life.* Translated by James Strachey. Penguin Freud Library. 15 vols. Vol. 5, Harmondsworth, UK: Penguin, 1975.

Froese, Tom. "Interactively Guided Introspection Is Getting Science Closer to an Effective Consciousness Meter." *Consciousness and Cognition* 22, no. 2 (June 2013): 672–76.

García, John F. "Milman Parry and A. L. Kroeber: Americanist Anthropology and the Oral Homer." *Oral Tradition* 16, no. 1 (2001): 58–84.

Gaskin, Claire. Interview by author. January 20, 2007.

Goldberg, Adele E. *Explain Me This: Creativity, Competition, and the Partial Productivity of Constructions.* Princeton, NJ: Princeton University Press, 2019.

Goldsmith, Kenneth. *Day.* Great Barrington, MA: The Figures, 2003.

———. *The Weather.* Los Angeles, CA: Make Now Press, 2005.

———. *Uncreative Writing: Managing Language in the Digital Age.* New York: Columbia University Press, 2011.

———. Interview by author. July 6, 2013.

Halliday, Michael A. K. *Spoken and Written Language.* Warun Ponds, VIC: Deakin University Press, 1985.

———."Spoken and Written Modes of Meaning." In *Comprehending Oral and Written Language*, edited by Rosalind Horowitz and S. Jay Samuels, 55–82. San Diego, CA: Academic Press, 1987.

———. "'They'd Been Going To've Been Paying Me All This Time': On the Complementarity of Speaking and Writing." In *Complementarities in Language*, 127–68. Beijing: The Commercial Press, 2008.

Halliday, Michael A. K., and Christian M. I. M. Matthiessen. *Halliday's Introduction to Functional Grammar.* 4th ed. Abingdon, UK: Routledge, 2014.

Hamacher, Werner. "95 Theses on Philology." Translated by Catharine Diehl and Jason Groves. In *Minima Philologica*. 1–106. New York: Fordham University Press, 2015.

Hass, Robert. "Lowell's Graveyard." In *Twentieth Century Pleasures: Prose on Poetry*, 3–25. New York: Ecco Press, 1984.

Haubold, Johannes. "Homer after Parry: Tradition, Reception and the Timeless Text." In *Homer in the Twentieth Century: Between World Literature and the Western Canon*, edited by Barbara Graziosi and Emily Greenwood, 27–46. Oxford; New York: Oxford University Press, 2007.

Hayman, David. "Introduction." In *A First-Draft Version of Finnegans Wake*, 3–44. Austin, TX: University of Texas Press, 1963.

Hegel, Georg Wilhelm Friedrich. *Hegel's Philosophy of Right.* Translated by T. M. Knox. London: Oxford University Pres, 1967.

Heidegger, Martin. "The Thinker as Poet." Translated by Albert Hofstadter. In *Poetry, Language, Thought*, 1–14. New York: Harper & Row, 1971.

Herbert, W. N., and Matthew Hollis. *Strong Words: Modern Poets on Modern Poetry.* Tarset, UK: Bloodaxe, 2000.

Hirst, Damien. "The Physical Impossibility of Death in the Mind of Someone Living." Tiger shark, glass, steel, 5% formaldehyde solution, 1991. Sculpture.

Hoey, Michael. *Lexical Priming: A New Theory of Words and Language.* London; New York: Routledge/AHRB, 2005.

———. Interview by Paul Magee, March 6, 2018.

Hoffman, Thomas and Graeme Trousdale. "Construction Grammar: Introduction." In *The Oxford Handbook of Construction Grammar*, edited by Thomas Hoffmann and Graeme Trousdale. Oxford: Oxford University Press, 2013.

Homer. *The Odyssey with an English Translation by A. T. Murray, Ph.D.* Cambridge, MA; Harvard University Press: 1919. [*Cited in the text as Od.*]

———. *Iliadis Libros I-XII.* In Homeri Opera, edited by David B. Munro and Thomas W. Allen. 3rd ed. 5 vols. Vol. 1. Oxford: Oxford University Press, 1920. [*Cited in the text as Il.*]

———. *Iliadis Libros XIII-XXIV.* In Homeri Opera, edited by David B. Munro and Thomas W. Allen. 3rd ed. 5 vols. Vol. 2. Oxford: Oxford University Press, 1920. [*Cited in the text as Il.*]

Hoover, Paul. Interview by author. November 14, 2014.
Hopper, Paul. "Emergent Grammar." *Proceedings of the Thirteenth Annual Meeting of the Berkeley Linguistics Society* 13 (1987): 139–57.
Hughes, Ted. *Poetry in the Making: An Anthology of Poems and Programmes from Listening and Writing.* London: Faber, 1967.
Hurlburt, Russell, T., Christopher Heavey, and Jason M. Kelsey. "Towards a Phenomenology of Inner Speaking." *Consciousness and Cognition* 22, no. 4 (December 2013): 1477–94.
Iser, Wolfgang. *The Implied Reader: Patterns of Communication in Prose Fiction from Bunyan to Beckett.* Baltimore, MD: John Hopkins University Press, 1974.
Jack, Anthony. "Introspection: The Tipping Point." *Consciousness and Cognition* 22, no. 2 (June 2013): 670–71.
James, William. "The Stream of Thought." In *The Writings of William James*, edited by John McDermott, 21–73. New York: Modern Library Edition, 1968.
Jarrell, Randall. "Recent Poetry." In *In Kipling, Auden & Co.: Essays and Reviews, 1935-1964*, 221–41. Manchester: Carcanet New Press Ltd, 1980.
———. "The Year in Poetry." In *Kipling, Auden & Co.: Essays and Reviews, 1935-1964*, 242–47. Manchester, UK: Carcanet New Press Ltd, 1980.
———. "The Woman at the Washington Zoo." In *In No Other Book: Selected Essays*, edited by Brad Leithauser, 89–97. New York: HarperCollins Publishers, 1999.
Jarrety, Michel. "The Poetics and Practice of Theory." In *Reading Paul Valéry: Universe in Mind*, edited by Paul Gifford and Brian Stimpson, 105–20. Cambridge, UK; New York,: Cambridge University Press, 1998.
Joyce, James. *A First-Draft Version of Finnegans Wake.* Edited by David Hayman. Austin, TX: University of Texas Press, 1963.
———. *Finnegans Wake.* Edited by Erik Bindervoet, Finn Fordham and Robert Jan-Henkes. Oxford: Oxford University Press, 2012.
Kant, Immanuel "An Answer to the Question: What Is Enlightenment." In *Practical Philosophy*, edited by Mary J. Gregor, 11–12. Cambridge: Cambridge University Press, 1997.
Kant, Immanuel. *Critique of the Power of Judgment.* Translated by Paul Guyer and Eric Matthews. Edited by Paul Guyer. Cambridge, U.K.: Cambridge University Press, 2000.
Kaufer, David S., John R. Hayes, and Linda Flower. "Composing Written Sentences." *Research in the Teaching of English*, 20, no.2 (1986): 121–40.
Keats, John. "The Fall of Hyperion, a Dream." In *The Poetical Works of John Keats*, edited by H. Buxton Forman, 443–57. London: Oxford University Press, 1915.
———. *Selected Poems and Letters of John Keats.* Edited by Robert Gittings. London: Heinemann, 1966.
Kellog, Ronald T. "Working Memory Components in Written Sentence Production." *American Journal of Psychology* 117, no. 3 (Autumn 2004): 341–61.
Kellog, Ronald T., Thierry Olive, and Annie Piolat. "Verbal, Visual, and Spatial Working Memory in Written Language Production." *Acta Psychologica* 124, no. 3 (March 2007): 382–97.
Kelly, Aileen. Interview by author. April 30, 2007.

Kenner, Hugh. "The Urban Apocalypse." In *Eliot in His Time: Essays on the Occasion of the Fiftieth Anniversary of the Waste Land*, edited by A. Walton Litz, 24–49. Princeton, NJ: Princeton University Press, 1973.

Kirshenblatt-Gimblett, Barbara. "Barbara Kirshenblatt-Gimblett on Edible Art." *Artforum International* 28 (1989): 20–23.

Kleist, Heinrich von. "Feelings before Friedrich's Seascape." In *An Abyss Deep Enough: Letters of Heinrich Von Kleist, with a Selection of Essays and Anecdotes*, edited and Translated by Philip B. Miller, 231–32. New York: Dutton, 1982.

———. "On the Gradual Production of Thoughts whilst Speaking." In *Selected Writings*, Translated by David Constantine, 405–409. Indianapolis: Hackett Pub., 2004.

———. "Reflection: A Paradox." Translated by David Constantine. In *Selected Writings*, 411.

Kocot, Noelle. Interview by author. July 13, 2013.

Kuhn, Thomas S. *The Structure of Scientific Revolutions*. 2nd ed. Chicago: University Of Chicago Press, 1970.

Labov, William. "The Logic of Nonstandard English." *Georgetown Monographs on Language and Linguistics* 22 (1969): 1–31.

Lacan, Jacques. *The Four Fundamental Concepts of Psychoanalysis*. Seminar of Jacques Lacan. Translated by Alan Sheridan. London: Hogarth Press, 1977.

———. "The Instance of the Letter in the Unconscious, or Reason since Freud." In *Écrtis: The First Complete Edition in English*, Translated by Bruce Fink in collaboration with Héloïse Fink and Russell Grigg, 412–41. New York: W. W. Norton & Co., 2006.

———. *The Seminar of Jacques Lacan Book XVIII: The Other Side of Psychoanalysis*. Translated by Russell Grigg. New York: Norton, 2007.

Lattimore, Richmond, trans., *The Odyssey of Homer*. Translated by Richmond Lattimore. New York: Harper & Row, 1967.

Lattimore, Richmond, and Richard P. Martin, trans., *The Iliad of Homer*. Chicago; London: University of Chicago Press, 2011.

Latour, Bruno, and Steve Woolgar. *Laboratory Life: The Social Construction of Scientific Facts*. Beverly Hills, CA: Sage Publications, 1979.

Leader, Zachary. *Revision and Romantic Authorship*. Oxford; New York: Clarendon Press; Oxford University Press, 1996.

Leech, Geoffrey N., and Jan Svartvik. *A Communicative Grammar of English*. 3rd ed. London: Longman, 2002.

Leonard, John F. "Rhythm, Form and Metre." In *Seven Centuries of Poetry in English*, edited by John F. Leonard, 567–86. Melbourne, Vic.: Oxford, 2003.

Levine, David N., Ronald Calvanio, and Alice Popovics. "Language in the Absence of Inner Speech." *Neuropscyhologia* 20, no. 4 (1982): 391–409.

Lord, Albert Bates. "Homer, Parry and Huso." In *The Making of Homeric Verse: The Collected Papers of Milman Parry*, edited by Adam Parry, 465–78. Oxford: Clarendon Press, 1971.

———. *The Singer Resumes the Tale*. Edited by Mary Louise Lord. Ithaca, NY: Cornell University Press, 1995.

———. *The Singer of Tales*. 2nd ed. Edited by Stephen A. Mitchell and Gregory Nagy. Cambridge, MA: Harvard University Press, 2000.

Lotman, Yuri. *Analysis of the Poetic Text*. Edited and translated by D. Barton Johnson. Ann Arbor, MI: Ardis, 1976.

MacSweeney, Mairéad, Bencie Woll, Ruth Campbell, Philip K. McGuire, Anthony S. David, Steven C. R. Williams, John Suckling, Gemma A. Calvert, Michael J. Brammer. "Neural Systems Underlying British Sign Language and Audio-Visual English Processing in Native Users." *Brain: A Journal of Neurology* 125, pt. 7 (July 2002): 1583–93.

Magee, Paul. "Marcella Polain Interview." *Blue Dog: Australian Poetry* 8, no.15 (August 2009): 36–44.

———. "Swimming in Minus." In *Stone Postcard*, edited by John Leonard, 31. Elwood, VIC: John Leonard Press, 2014.

———. "The Meaning of It—The Music of It: An Interview with C. K. Williams." *Salmagundi Magazine* 190–191 (Spring-Summer 2016): 86–105.

———. "Writing as Discovery: Investigating a Hidden Component of Scholarly Method." *Interdisciplinary Literary Studies* 21, no. 3 (2019): 297–319.

Magee, Paul and Forrest Gander. "Paul Magee interviews Forrest Gander." *Cordite Poetry Review* 47 (August 2014). http://cordite.org.au/interviews/magee-gander/

Manning, Peter J. "Don Juan and the Revisionary Self." In *Romantic Revisions*, edited by Robert Brinkley and Keith Hanley, 210–26. Cambridge: Cambridge University Press, 1992.

Martz, Louis L. "Origins of Form in Four Quartets." In *Words in Time: New Essays on Eliot's Four Quartets*, edited by Edward Lobb, 189–204. London: Athlone, 1993.

Marx, Karl. "Speech at the Anniversary of the People's Paper." In *Selected Works by Karl Marx and Frederick Engels in Three Volumes* 500–502. Moscow: Progress Press, 1970.

———. "Der achtzehnte Brumaire des Louis Bonaparte." In *Werke, Artikel, Entwürfe Juli 1851 bis Dezember 1852*, edited by Inst. für Marxismus-Leninismus. Gesamtausgabe (Mega), 96–188. Berlin: Dietz Verlag, 1985.

Mayakovsky, Vladimir. "How Are Verses to Be Made?" Translated by Alex Miller. In *Maxim Gorky, Vladimir Mayakovsky, Alexei Tolstoy and Konstantin Fedin on the Art and Craft of Writing*, 123–61. Moscow: Progress Publishers, 1972.

McGann, Jerome. "Romanticism and its Ideologies." *Studies in Romanticism* 21, no.4 (Winter 1982): 573–99.

McGuckian, Medbh. "Breaking the Blue." In *Marconi's Cottage*, 84. Oldcastle, Co. Meath: Gallery, 1991.

———. Interview by author. Email correspondence. February 19, 21, 26, March 3, 6, 2015.

———."White Cortina outside Stardust Ballroom." In *Blaris Moor*, 30–31. Winston-Salem, NC: Wake Forest University Press, 2016.

McKimmie, Mal. Interview by author. January 18, 2007.

Mendelson, Edward. *Later Auden*. New York: Farrar, Strauss and Giroux, 1999.

Minchin, Elizabeth. *Homer and the Resources of Memory: Some Applications of Cognitive Theory to the Iliad and the Odyssey.* New York; Oxford: Oxford University Press, 2001.

Mitchell, Stephen A. and Gregory Nagy. "Introduction to the Second Edition." In *The Singer of Tales*, vii–xxx. Cambridge, MA: Harvard University Press, 2000.

Moran, Richard. "Artifice and Persuasion: The Work of Metaphor in the Rhetoric." In *Essays on Aristotle's Rhetoric*, edited by Amélie Rorty, 385–98. Berkeley and Los Angeles, CA: University of California Press, 1996.

Myers, Peter. *The Sound of Finnegans Wake.* London: The Macmillan Press, 1992.

Nagy, Gregory. *Homeric Questions.* Austin, TX: University of Texas Press, 1996.

———. "Albert Lord." In *The Homer Dictionary*, edited by Margalit Finkelberg, 487–88. Chichester, West Sussex; Malden, MA: Wiley-Blackwell, 2011.

Neave, Lucy. "What Constitutes Discovery? An Analysis of Published Interviews with Fiction Writers and Biomedical Scientists." *New Writing: The International Journal for the Practice and Theory of Creative Writing* 18, no. 2 (June 2020): 1–13.

Ni Chuilleanáin, Eiléan. Interview by Kevin Brophy. June 17, 2013.

Nisbett, Richard E. and Timothy Decamp Wilson. "Telling More Than We Can Know: Verbal Reports on Mental Processes." *Psychological Review* 84, no. 3 (1977): 231–59.

Ong, Walter J. *Orality and Literacy: The Technologizing of the Word.* London; New York: Routledge, 1988.

Owen, Jan. Interview by author. March 12, 2007.

Parry, Adam. "Introduction." In *The Making of Homeric Verse: The Collected Papers of Milman Parry*, edited by Adam Parry, ix–lxii. Oxford: Clarendon Press, 1971.

Parry, Milman. "Studies in the Epic Technique of Oral Verse-Making. I. Homer and Homeric Style." In *The Making of Homeric Verse: The Collected Papers of Milman Parry*, edited by Adam Parry, 266–324. Oxford: Clarendon Press, 1971.

———. "Studies in the Epic Technique of Oral Verse-Making II: The Homeric Language as the Language of an Oral Poetry." In *The Making of Homeric Verse*, 325–64.

———. "A Comparative Study of Diction as One of the Elements of Style in Early Greek Poetry (MA)." In *The Making of Homeric Verse*, 421–36.

———. "On Typical Scenes in Homer." In *The Making of Homeric Verse*, 404–407.

———. "The Distinctive Character of Enjambment in Homeric Verse." In *The Making of Homeric Verse*, 251–65.

———. "The Traditional Epithet in Homer." In *The Making of Homeric Verse*, 1–190.

Paterson, Don. Interview by Kevin Brophy. July 13, 2013.

Pawley, Andrew. "How to Talk Cricket: On Linguistic Competence in a Subject Matter." In *Currents in Pacific Linguistics: Papers on Austronesian Languages and Ethnolinguistics in Honour of George W. Grace*, edited by Robert Blust, 339–68. Canberra: Linguistic Circle of Canberra, 1991.

———. "Developments in the Study of Formulaic Language since 1970: A Personal View." In *Phraseology and Culture*, edited by Paul Skandera, 3–48. Berlin: Walter de Gruyter, 2007.

Pawley, Andrew, and Frances Hodgetts Syder. "Two Puzzles for Linguistic Theory." In *Language and Communication*, edited by Jack C. Richards and Richard W. Schmidt, 191–225. London; New York: Longman, 1983.

———. "The-One-Clause-at-a-Time-Hypothesis." In *Perspectives on Fluency*, edited by Heidi Riggenbach, 163–99. Ann Arbor, MI: University of Michigan Press, 2000.

Peirce, Charles S. "The Fixation of Belief." In *Philosophical Writings of Peirce*, edited by Justus Buchler, 5–22. New York: Dover, 1955.

———. "The Essentials of Pragmatism." In *Philosophical Writings of Peirce*, 251–68.

Petitmengin, Claire, Anne Remillieux, Beatrice Cahour and Shirley Carter-Thomas. "A Gap in Nisbett and Wilson's Findings? A First Person Access to Our Cognitive Process." *Consciousness and Cognition* 22, no. 2 (June 2013): 654–99.

Pinsky, Robert. *The Situation of Poetry: Contemporary Poetry and Its Traditions*. Princeton, NJ: Princeton University Press, 1976.

Plato. *Ion*. In *Statesman. Philebus. Ion*. Translated by Harold North Fowler, W. R. M. Lamb. Loeb Classical Library 164. Cambridge, MA: Harvard University Press, 1925.

———. *Phaedrus*. Translated by Alexander Nehamas and Paul Woodruff. Edited by Alexander Nehamas and Paul Woodruff. Indianapolis, IN: Hackett, 1995.

Poe, Edgar Allan. "The Philosophy of Composition." In *Selected Writings of Edgar Allan Poe: Poems, Tales, Essays and Reviews*, 480–92. Harmondsworth: Penguin, 1967.

Polain, Marcella. "When Bees See Blue." In *Therapy Like Fish: New and Selected Poems*, 132–33. Elwood, VIC: John Leonard Press, 2008.

Pound, Ezra. "A Retrospect." In *Literary Essays*, edited by T. S. Eliot, 3–13. London: Faber and Faber, 1954.

Rainey, Lawrence S. "Introduction." In *The Annotated Waste Land with Eliot's Contemporary Prose*, 1–54. New Haven, CT: Yale University Press, 2006.

Quinn, Marc. "Self." Blood (artist's), liquid silicone, stainless steel, glass, perspex and refrigeration equipment, 2006. Sculpture.

Rancière, Jacques. "The Aesthetic Revolution and Its Outcomes: Emplotments of Autonomy and Heteronomy." *New Left Review*, no. 14 (2002): 133–51.

———. "Politics and Aesthetics: An Interview with Peter Hallward." Translated by Forbes Morlock. *Angelaki: The Journal of the Theoretical Humanities* 8, no. 2 (2003): 191–211.

Robenalt, Clarice, and Adele E. Goldberg. "Nonnative Speakers Do Not Take Competing Alternative Expressions into Account the Way Native Speakers Do." *Language Learning, A Journal of Research in Language Studies* 66, no. 1 (2016): 60–93.

Sawyer, R. Keith. *Explaining Creativity: The Science of Human Innovation*. Oxford; New York: Oxford University Press, 2006.

Schank, Roger C., and Robert P. Abelson. *Scripts, Plans, Goals, and Understanding: An Inquiry into Human Knowledge Structures*. Hillsdale, NJ; New York: L. Erlbaum Associates, 1977.

Schechner, Richard. "Magnitudes of Performance." In *By Means of Performance: Intercultural Studies of Theatre and Ritual*, edited by Richard Schechner and Willa Appel, 19–49. Cambridge; New York: Cambridge University Press, 1990.

Schiffrin, Deborah. *Discourse Markers*. Cambridge; New York: Cambridge University Press, 1987.

Shelley, Percy Bysshe. "A Defence of Poetry." In *The Selected Poetry and Prose of Shelley*, edited by Bruce Woodcock, 635–60. Hertfordshire: Wordsworth Editions, 2002.

Shillingsburg, Peter. "Text as Matter, Concept and Action." *Studies in Bibliography* 44 (1991): 31–82.

Simpson, Rita C., Sarah. L. Briggs, J. Ovens, and John. M. Swales, eds. *The Michigan Corpus of Academic Spoken English* (MICASE). Ann Arbor, MI: The Regents of the University of Michigan, 2002.

Simpson, Rita C., David Y. W. Lee, and Sheryl Leicher. *MICASE Manual*. Ann Arbor, MI: English Language Institute, University of Michigan, 2002.

Slobin, Dan. "From 'Thought and Language' to 'Thinking for Speaking'." In *Rethinking Linguistic Relativity*, edited by John J. Gumperz and Stephen C. Levinson, 70–96. Cambridge: Cambridge University Press, 1996.

Slowiaczek, Maria L. and Clifton, Charles Jr. "Subvocalization and Reading for Meaning." *Journal of Verbal Learning and Verbal Behaviour* 19, no. 5 (1980): 573–82.

Spinoza, Benedictus de. "Tractatus Politicus." In *The Political Works: The Tractatus Theologico-Politicus in Part, and the Tracatatus Politicus in Full*, edited by A. G. Wernham. Oxford: Clarendon Press, 1958.

Steffan, T. G. *The Making of a Masterpiece*. Byron's Don Juan, edited by T. G. Steffan and Willis Winslow Pratt. 4 vols. Vol. 1, Austin, TX: University of Texas Press, 1957.

Stillinger, Jack. *Multiple Authorship and the Myth of Solitary Genius*. New York: Oxford University Press, 1991.

———. "Keats's Extempore Effusions and the Question of Intentionality." In *Romantic Revisions*, edited by Robert Brinkley and Keith Hanley, 307–20. Cambridge: Cambridge University Press, 2006.

Sullivan, Hannah. *The Work of Revision*. Cambridge, MA: Harvard University Press, 2013.

———. *Three Poems*. London: Faber and Faber, 2018.

———. Interview by author, February 26, 2018.

Sylvester, David, and Francis Bacon. *Interviews with Francis Bacon, 1962-1979*. London: Thames And Hudson, 1987.

Tannen, Deborah. "'Oh Talking Voice That Is So Sweet': The Poetic Nature of Conversation." *Conversation* 65, no. 3 (Fall 1999): 631–55.

———. *Talking Voices: Repetition, Dialogue, and Imagery in Conversational Discourse*. 2nd ed. Cambridge: Cambridge University Press, 2007.

Taplin, Oliver. *Homeric Soundings: The Shaping of the Iliad*. Oxford, UK; New York: Clarendon Press; Oxford University Press, 1992.

Tedlock, Dennis. "Learning to Listen." In *The Spoken Word and the Work of Interpretation*, 107–23. Philadelphia, PA: University Of Pennsylvania Press, 1983.

———. "On the Translation of Style in Oral Narrative." In *The Spoken Word*, 31–61.

———. "The Spoken Word and the Work of Interpretation in American Indian Religion." In *The Spoken Word*, 233–46.

Tee, Mark Ve-Yin. *Coleridge, Revision and Romanticism: After the Revolution, 1793-1818*. Continuum Literary Studies Series. London; New York: Continuum, 2009.

Van Orden, Guy. "A Rows Is a Rose: Spelling, Sound and Reading." *Memory and Cognition* 15, no. 3 (1987): 181–98.

Van Orden, Guy, and Heidi Kloos. "The Question of Phonology and Silent Reading." In *The Science of Reading: A Handbook*, edited by Margaret J. Snowling and Charles Hume. Oxford: Blackwell, 2005.

Vendler, Helen. *Poets Thinking: Pope, Whitman, Dickinson, Yeats*. Cambridge, MA: Harvard University Press, 2004.

Vertov, Dziga. "'Kinoks-Revolution'—Selections." Translated by Val Telberg. In *Film Makers on Film Making: Statements on Their Art by Thirty Directors*, edited by Harry M. Geduld, 79–105. Bloomington, IN; London: Indiana University Press, 1967.

Virgil. *Books I-VI*. In The Aeneid of Virgil, edited by R. D. Williams. 2 Vols. Vol.1, London, New York: Macmillan; St. Martin's Press, 1972.

Vygotsky, L. S. *Thought and Language*. Massachusetts Institute of Technology; Wiley, 1962.

Waldrep, G. C. Interview by author. July 9, 2013.

Webb, Jen and Ian Wedde. "Slipperiness of Being, A Conversation Between Jen Webb and Ian Wedde." *Axon: Creative Explorations* 3, no.2 (October 2013). http://axonjournal.com.au/issue-5/slipperiness-being

Wittgenstein, Ludwig. *Philosophical Investigations*. Translated by G. E. M. Anscombe. Oxford: B. Blackwell, 1953.

———. *Preliminary Studies for the "Philosophical Investigations": Generally Known as the Blue and Brown Books*. New York: Harper, 1965.

Wordsworth, William. *The Prelude*. Edited by J. C. Maxwell. Harmondsworth: Penguin, 1971.

Wordsworth, William, and Samuel Taylor Coleridge. "Preface." In *Lyrical Ballads 1805*, edited by Derek Roper, 18–48. London: Collins, 1968.

Wray, Alison. *Formulaic Language and the Lexicon*. Cambridge; New York: Cambridge University Press, 2002.

Wright, C. D. "Deepstep Come Shining." In *Like Something Flying Backwards: New and Selected Poems*. Highgreen, Northumberland: Bloodaxe, 2007.

———. "An Interview with C. D. Wright by Paul Magee." *American Poetry Review* 44, no. 6 (November/December 2015). https://aprweb.org/poems/an-interview-with-c-d-wright-by-paul-magee

———. "Tree of Obscurity." *ShallCross*. Port Townsend, WA: Copper Canyon Press, 2016. Kindle.

Wu, Duncan. *30 Great Myths About the Romantics*. Chichester, West Sussex: Wiley-Blackwell, 2015.

Yao, Bo, Pascal Belin, and Christoph Scheepers. "Silent Reading of Direct Versus Indirect Speech Activates Voice-Selective Areas in the Auditory Cortex." *Journal of Cognitive Neuroscience* 23, no. 10 (October 2011): 3146–52.

Yeats, William Butler. "Adam's Curse." In *Collected Poems of W.B. Yeats*, 88–90. London: Macmillan, 1950.

Young, Kevin. Interview by author. July 20, 2014.

Index

Page references for figures are italicized.

Abramović, Marina, 222
academic speech. *See* speaking academically
academic writing. *See* writing academically
acting, 50, 91–92, 172–73
adjectives, 7, 159
afterthought, 119–20, 134, 139–40
and: continuative, 1, 4, 117, 119, 122–25, 134–36, 139–40, 146, 148–51; co-ordinating, 119, 122–23, 134, 146; *d'/de* in Homer, 119–20, 123–25, 134–35; tendencies in literary usage of, 122–23, 134, 136, 139
anti-romanticism. *See* romanticism
Aristotle, 35–37
Armantrout, Rae, 26–27, 31, 50, 101, 104–6, 168, 180, 195, 197–98, 211
Attridge, Derek, 133–35, 166–67, 170, 185–89
Auden, W.H., 10, 15–17, 19–28, 31, 33, 45–46, 53, 96–97, 135–36, 195–99, 201
audience, 92–95, 101–6, 110, 112–16, 141, 186–87, 189–90

Bacon, Francis, 6–7
Baddeley, Alan, 181
Bakker, Egbert J., 116–27, 134–38, 188–90
Baldessari, John, 89
Barkindji people, 222–23
Bartlett, Frederick, 111, 181
Benjamin, Walter, 10, 199, 208–9
Berry, Eleanor, 138–43
Biber, Douglas and Vásquez, Camilla, 142, 151, 160
Bishop, Elizabeth, 27
Bolinger, Dwight, 206
Bourdieu, Pierre, 39, 44
Bozzone, Chiara, 206, 212
Brophy, Kevin, 15, 17, 59, 93
Brouwer, Joel, 18, 69
Bryson, Bill, 207–8
Bybee, Joan, 211–12, *212*, 215
Byron, George Gordon, 37, 52–53

caesura, 8, 134, 175, 196
Cameron, Sharon, 34–35, 37
Cánovas, Cristóbal Pagán and Antović, Mihailo, 212–13

Carter, Ronald, 211
Carver, Raymond, 98
Chafe, Wallace, 3, 12, 43, 97, 117–18, 120–22, 139–40, 143, 157–61, 170, 174–81, 203
Chafe, Wallace and Danielewicz, Jane, 148, 159–61
Chernoff, Maxine, 15, 25, 94–95, 104, 168, 211
Chomsky, Noam, 205–6, 208
Christie, Will, 222
Clanchy, Michael T., 126
clauses, 139, 142–43, 146, 151, 176, 201–4
Coates, Deborah, 186–87
cognitive script. See memory
Coleridge, Samuel Taylor, 11, 51–52, 208–10, 213, 219–22
Collis, Paul, 222
composition of literary poetry: accretive modes, 16–17, 19–22, 26–27, 52, 54, 62, 196–97; and attentiveness, 26, 91–95, 137, 165, 171–72, 179–80, 195; critique of 'work' metaphor for, 40, 51, 197; and emotion, 63, 91, 94, 96–97, 137, 180, 196–97, 211; as intermittent/epiphanic, 15–16, 23, 26–27, 45, 50, 55, 57–63, 96, 99, 136, 190, 195; as a marshalling of multiple selves, 33–35, 95–96, 99–106, 197; as more immediate than prose, 162, 165–66, 169–70, 175–76; as occurring in multiple modes, 23, 26–27, 96–97, 99–101, 196–97; as performance, 22–24, 50, 59–60, 91–95, 100, 102, 189–90, 197; as potentially speech-like, 8, 11, 45, 57–58, 135–43, 148–62, 176–81, 185–90, 195–97, 210–11; and visualization, 56–57, 94–95, 156. See also acting; 'idea' for a poem; intending; intensifying; lines; memory; revision; rhythm; suddenness; thinking by speaking; writing
composition of oral poetry. See oral poetry; oral theory
composition of speech. See speaking
conferences. See speaking academically
consciousness, 189–90; active and semi-active, 139–40, 177–81; relation to intonation unit, 125, 174–81, 202, 204; as a window of three seconds, 5, 8, 96, 117–18, 120, 123, 158–59, 174–81
constructions, 212–19, *212*; as the basis of language, 69, 210–11, 215–16. See also formulaic language; grammar; poetic diction
corpus linguistics, 3, 206, 211, 218
creativity, 205–6, 208
Croggon, Alison, 165–66, 173, 211
Croiset, Maurice, 116, 118–19, 139
Crystal, David, 175
Csikszentmihalyi, Mihalyi, 197

Damasio, Antonio, 62
De Biasi, Pierre-Marc, 58
De Man, Paul, 49
Derrida, Jacques, 9–10
Descartes, René, 97, 171, 176–77, 179
Dickinson, Emily, 34–37, 137, 205
dictation. See speaking for the page; writing
drafts. See manuscripts; revision
Durkin, Phillip, 83, 115

Eliot, T.S., 24, 53–56, 60–63, 89, 138–43, 146
Emery, Brook, 24–27, 50, 103, 168, 185, 195, 197, 214

'false starts', 147–48
Fehrman, Carl, 51, 58–59, 62
fillers (*um, ah, y'know*), 4, 143, 146, 148–50, 158
Finnegan, Ruth, 78–79, 117
Foley, John Miles, 80, 82–83, 113–16
Fónagy, Ivan, 88–90

formulaic language: difficult to get right, 205, 214–19; as key to native fluency, 202–19. *See also* constructions; poetic diction
formulas: in Balkan verse, 75–77, 82–83, 115; in everyday language, 69, 115–16; functions of, 68, 71–72, 80–81, 113–16; in Homeric verse, 68–73, 81, 113–15, 206, 210–12. *See also* formula systems; Homer; oral poetry; oral theory
formula systems, 68–69, *69*
Forster, E.M., 24
Freud, Sigmund, 6, 35
Frost, Robert, 136, 138–43

Gander, Forest, 104–5, 168–69
Gaskin, Claire, 19, 169, 172–73
genuineness, 21, 23, 46
Goldberg, Adele, 214, 216–19
Goldsmith, Kenneth, 16, 96–98, 168
Grammar, 205; as arbitrarily restricted, 208–9, 214–19; in Chomskyan theory, 205–6; Homeric, 116–26, 134–35, 137–38; no universal rules of, 206–8, 215–16, 219. *See also* constructions; formulaic language; sentences; speaking; writing

Halliday, Michael A.K., 146–47, 151–53, 159, 175
Halliday, Michael A.K. and Mathiessen, Christian, 3, 138, 186
Hass, Robert, 137
Haubold, Johannes, 78
hedges (*like, sort of*), 143, 150
Hegel, Georg W. F., 96
Heidegger, Martin, 62
Hoey, Michael, 166–67, 169–70, 206–8
Homer, 78; as an Audenesque/Kleistean figure, 81–82, 109–10, 117–18, 120, 123–25, 135; *The Iliad*, 67–68, 70, 72–73, 80, 112–14, 118–20, 123–27, 135; an individual, or a collective?, 67, 71–73, 95–96; liveliness of, 36, 109–10, 120, 125, 127; *The Odyssey*, 67–68, 70, 72–73, 77, 80–81, 114, 126–27, 135; recent work on, 81–82, 109–27, 211–13; as similar to a conversational transcript, 110, 118–24, 126–27, 137, 211; transmission of, 45–46, 67–68, 71–79, 126–27, 136–38, 161–62. *See also* formulas; oral poetry; oral theory; originality; poetic thinking
Hoover, Paul, 25, 104, 168–69
Hopper, Paul, 206
Horace, 8, 31, 35
Hughes, Ted, 172–73
Hurlburt, Russell, 43, 171

'the idea for a poem', 16, 20–21, 25–26, 165, 173, 179
imagination. *See* memory
inner speech, 147–49, 171; among the speech and hearing impaired, 149, 154, 156–57; as the means of writing, 149–50, 153–62, 165, 169, 178–80; relation to reading, 153–55; relation to speaking, 7–8, 147–48, 171–72, 220. *See also* reading; speaking for the page; suddenness; thinking by speaking; writing
intending, 7, 178, 220–24
intensifying, 221–22
interviews, 146–53; as necessarily revised, 16–17, 145–47, 149, 152–53
intonation units, 196, 203; defined, 117, 120–21; examples of, 117–24, 145–46; expansion of when writing, 120, 158–59, 175–76, 180; other terms for, 117, 175, 181; relation to clauses, 139, 176; relation to thinking and consciousness, 122, 125, 145–46, 176–79. *See also* consciousness; knowledge; line; memory; rhythm; semi-active consciousness; sentences; speaking; writing
introspective observation, 38–39, 43–45

Iser, Wolfgang, 37

Jack, Anthony, 43
James, William, 62, 177–78, 181, 221
Jarrell, Randal, 18, 35
Joyce, James, 53–54, 62

Kant, Immanuel, 3, 6, 8, 89
Keats, John, 49–52, 203
Kelly, Aileen, 168, 172–73, 190
Kleist, Heinrich von, 1–8, 45, 117, 174, 176, 179
knowledge, 2–3, 5–6, 110–13, 175–81
Kocot, Noelle, 15, 103, 105–6, 168–69

Lacan, Jacques, 6, 179
Leader, Zachary, 49, 52
lecturing. *See* speaking academically
Leech, Geoffrey, and Svartvik, Jan, 145, 175
Leonard, John F., 186
lexicalized sentence stems, 69, 203–4
Lichtenberg, Georg Christoph, 135
lines: relation to intonation units, 145, 166, 170, 188, 196; as units of poetic composition, 165–66, 169, 172–73, 179–80; vs sentences, 165–71, 173
liveliness, 26, 31–37, 40, 109–10, 120, 125, 127
Lord, Albert Bates, 73–83, 87–88, 90–96, 102, 110, 112–14, 161–62
Lotman, Yuri, 88–89
Lowell, Robert, 137

manuscripts, 49, 51–52, 54–56, 58–63
Marx, Karl, 6
Mayakovsky, Vladimir, 187
McGuckian, Medbh, 56–57, 59–60, 168–69, 209–10, 212–13, 221
McKimmie, Mal, 19
Međedović, Avdo, 77–78, 82–83, 89–90, 92, 161
memory, 97, 110–13, 170, 175, 179–81, 220–24
metaphor, 35–37, 169

meter. *See* rhythm
Minchin, Elizabeth, 79, 110–14
moment, 24–28, 61
Moore, Marianne, 168–69
Moran, Richard, 36
multiformity, 76

Nagy, Gregory, 75, 90, 127
Neave, Lucy, 166
Ngemba Country, 222
Ngunnawal Country, 11
Ni Chuilleanáin, Eiléan, 59–60, 94, 168–69
Nietzsche, Friedrich, 37, 146–47
Nisbett, Richard E. and Wilson, Timothy Decamp, 38–39, 43–44
non-verbal thought, 222
Novalis, 135

'one-clause-at-a-time hypothesis', 3–5, 117, 135, 158, 176, 201–5
Ong, Walter J., 114, 116–17, 139
oral-formulaic theory. *See* oral theory
oral poetry: as rapidly composed in performance, 45–46, 64, 71–78, 87–88, 90–91, 96, 109–27, 135–38, 196; relation of to the unusual and unexpected, 78, 80–83, 87–90, 109–10, 112–13, 204–5; as 'spoken' like a language, 46, 58, 88, 109–27, 202, 212; transmission of, 67–68, 71–79, 82–83; as vast in relation to written poetry, 80, 91, 196. *See also* formulas; formula systems; Homer; oral theory; rhythm; themes
oral theory: criticisms of Parry-Lord model of, 78–79, 81–82, 87–88, 90, 102, 110, 112–14; recent developments in, 81–82, 109–27, 206, 212; texts and cultures applied to, 73–75, 78–80, 113; useful for theorizing literary composition?, 80–82, 87–96, 102, 109–10, 116, 127, 162, 196, 211–13. *See also*

Homer; oral poetry; originality; poetic thinking
originality: critiques of the concept of, 16, 21, 75–76, 198–99, 210, 214; as possible, 23, 198–99; relation to oral poetry, 75–76, 78, 80–81, 87–89, 112–13; 'required' of literary poetry, 81, 87–89, 199
Owen, Jan, 179–80, 199

painting, 6, 8, 32, 98
paragraphs, 167
parataxis, 80, 116–18, 125–26, 202
Parry, Milman, 67–74, 78–82, 87, 95–96, 101, 109–10, 112–14, 118, 136–37, 199, 211–12, 214
partially-fixed expressions. *See* constructions; formulaic language
Paterson, Don, 7, 15–16, 25, 60, 93–95, 100, 103, 168–69, 185, 195
Pawley, Andrew and Syder, Frances Hodgetts, 3–5, 7, 117, 176, 187–88, 201–4, 206–7, 210–11, 213, 215
Peirce, Charles Saunders, 162
perceptual moment. *See* consciousness
performance. *See* audience; composing of literary poetry; oral poetry
Petitmengin, Claire, 43–44
philosophers, 58, 155
Pinsky, Robert, 49–50, 102
Plato, 33, 79
poetic diction: close relation to formulaic language, 6–7, 11, 199, 202, 204–5, 208–24; as eschewing synonymy, 69–70, 209–10, 213–14, 219; as indice to past and potential language, 199, 202, 209, 211, 217, 219; as innate to language, 186–90, 214, 217–20. *See also* formulaic language; originality; poetic thinking
poetic thinking: analogised to leaping, 221–22, 224; in non-literary contexts, 219; as simultaneous with utterance, 15–16, 24–26, 28, 31–32, 45–46, 51, 64, 72, 79, 81–82, 87–88, 90, 96–97, 100, 109–27, 134–38, 148, 165–66, 169–73, 179–81, 185–90, 196, 211, 214, 224; as a textual illusion, 8–9, 26–27, 32–37, 40, 51, 57–58, 137. *See also* acting; composition of literary poetry; 'the idea for a poem'; memory; oral poetry; poetic diction; semi-active consciousness; suddenness
Poets: image of as heroic and/or unique, 18, 37, 51, 137, 198; interview research with, 10, 17–19, 28n10; rejecting the concept of originality, 16, 21, 198–99, 214, 223–24; reliability of their self-reports?, 33, 38–39, 43–45; as split in response to Auden quotation, 15–19, 22, 45, 195–99; varied in their speech patterns, 149–53. *See also* interviews; originality; philosophers; reviews; workshopping
Polain, Marcella, 91–95, 99–100, 168–69, 185, 190
Pope, Alexander, 137
Pound, Ezra, 53–55, 61, 63, 105
pre-fabricated phrasing. *See* constructions; formulaic language
primitivism, 116–17, 146–47
prose: illusory immediacy of, 9, 32–33, 57–58, 157. *See also* writing; writing academically
prosody, 36, 154–55, 185–89

Rainey, Lawrence, 54
Rancière, Jacques, 89
reading: illusions about composition fostered by, 32–37, 57–58, 137, 157; medieval practices of, 126–27; silent reading, 153–55, 159
repetition: conversational functions of, 140–41, 189; in literary verse, 141–43; in oral poetry, 67, 69–78, 82–83, 123; and rhythm, 140–41, 186, 189. *See also* formulas; formula systems; sameness; themes

reviews, 105–6
revision, 100, 157, 196–97; anti-revisionism, 51–53; associated with rationality, 58–63; different modes of, 53–55, 58–63, 92, 99, 223; as innate to composition of literary poetry, 16, 19–23, 33–35, 45, 51–52, 62, 94; as innate to first draft prose, 157–62, 166–70, 197
rhythm: as compositionally generative, 24, 165, 173, 180, 189–90, 210–11; selective pressure of on word-choice, 71, 186, 207; in spoken language, 186–90, 202–3
Romanticism: anti-Romanticism, 9, 49–53, 181; as our aesthetic epoch, 58, 89; Romantic compositional theory, 50–52, 181

sameness: cultural determinants of, 82–83. *See also* repetition
Schank, Roger C. and Abelson, Robert A., 111–12
semi-active consciousness, 5; defined, 139, 177; and poetic composition, 176–81. *See also* consciousness; intonation unit; knowledge; memory; suddenness; thinking by speaking; topics
sentence-final intonation, 121–22, 139–40
sentences: in Homer, 118–20; in speaking, 1–5, 121–22, 135, 137, 139–40, 166; in writing, 133, 137, 166–71, 173
Shelley, Percy Bysshe, 51, 58–60
Shillingsburg, Peter, 36
silent reading. *See* reading
Slowiaczek, Maria L. and Clifton Jr, Charles, 149, 154
speaking: difficulty of composing speech, 5–7, 117–18, 123, 139, 150, 158–60, 199, 201–5, 210–11; no single spoken style, 153, 160; popular obliviousness as to grammatical form of, 4–5, 10, 118, 138–43, 145–47; typical grammatical features of, 116–26, 134–35, 138–43, 146–48, 150–55; when 'on a roll', 161, 170, 187–88, 208, 210–11; as window on thinking, 4, 117, 124–26, 134–35, 147–48, 160, 173. *See also* formulaic language; inner speech; oral poetry; rhythm; speaking academically; suddenness; thinking by speaking
speaking academically, 3–4, 6, 7, 10, 118, 139, 159–60, 204
speaking for the page, 149–62, 224
Spinoza, 40
Stillinger, Jack, 49–51
story patterns, 73
subvocalization. *See* inner speech; reading
suddenness: appearance of valued in poems, 24, 26, 31–37, 40, 148; defined, 6–8; in inner speech, 7–8, 149; not *ex nihilo*, 6–7; when speaking, 6, 21, 46, 56, 61, 109–10, 118, 125–26, 148, 158, 173–81; when writing poetry, 8–10, 22–26, 51–52, 56, 58, 92, 149, 165, 169–73, 176–81, 189–90. *See also* acting; composition of literary poetry; inner speech; intending; intensifying; knowledge; lines; oral poetry; poetic diction; poetic thinking; revision; speaking for the page; thinking by speaking
Sullivan, Hannah, 51, 53, 55–56, 166–70, 173
synonymy. *See* poetic diction
syntax. *See* grammar

Tannen, Deborah, 140–41, 186, 188
technological change, 3, 53, 55–56, 147, 167, 206
Tedlock, Dennis, 79, 188

themes, 73, 77, 110–13. *See also* oral poetry; oral theory
thinking by speaking: aloud, 1–8, 15, 19, 117, 123–26, 173, 177–78; in one's head, 7, 147–48, 165, 171–73, 220, 222, 224. *See also* inner speech; intending; intensifying; oral poetry; poetic thinking; speaking; suddenness
topics, 139, 173, 176–81, 185–90. *See also* semi-active consciousness

Ugljanin, Salih, 76–77, 80

Valéry, Paul, 59–60
Vendler, Helen, 137
Vlahovljak, Mumim, 77, 82–83
Vygotsky, Lev, 147–49, 179

Waldrep, G.C., 22–25, 92–95, 103, 105, 168–69, 198, 214
Webb, Jen, 17, 31
Wedde, Ian, 31–32, 35, 168
Williams, C.K., 21–22, 32–33, 37, 44, 96–98, 101–2, 104–5, 168–69, 196, 198
Williams, William Carlos, 138–43
Wittgenstein, Ludwig, 83, 208, 222

Wordsworth, William, 19, 52–54, 133–36, 176–81
'worked-over' nature of writing. *See* revision; writing
workshopping, 103
Wray, Alison, 205–6
Wright, C.D., 16–18, 20–21, 50, 69–70, 98–100, 104, 106, 167–69, 198–99, 213–14, 219, 221
Writing: ancient and medieval practices of, 126–27; as grammatically distinct from speaking, 10, 17, 118–20, 122–25, 138–43, 145–54, 157–61; post-structuralist metaphor of, 9–10; writing as dictation to self, 148–62, 224. *See also* composition of literary poetry; inner speech; lines; manuscripts; revision; sentences; speaking for the page
Writing academically, 149, 151–53, 159–60, 166–70, 178–79
Wu, Duncan, 51–52

Yeats, William Butler, 19, 137, 196–97
Young, Kevin, 15, 102–3, 211

Zogić, Đemo, 82–83

About the Author

Paul Magee studied in Melbourne, Moscow, San Salvador and Sydney. He is author of the prose ethnography, *From Here to Tierra del Fuego* (University of Illinois Press, 2000), and was the convener of the UNAUSTRALIA conference in 2006, which featured keynote addresses from the Australian Parliament House. Paul has published extensively on the relationship between poetry and knowledge. His first book of poems, *Cube Root of Book* (John Leonard Press: 2006), was shortlisted for the Adelaide Festival Award for Innovation in Literature. His second, *Stone Postcard* (John Leonard Press: 2014), was named in *Australian Book Review* as one of the books of the year for 2014. Paul is an associate professor of poetry at the University of Canberra.

www.ingramcontent.com/pod-product-compliance
Lightning Source LLC
Chambersburg PA
CBHW020114010526
44115CB00008B/824